THE LIBERIAN CIVIL WAR

THE LIBERIAN CIVIL WAR

MARK HUBAND

FRANK CASS
LONDON • PORTLAND, OR

First Published in 1998 in Great Britain by
FRANK CASS PUBLISHERS
Newbury House, 900 Eastern Avenue
London, IG2 7HH

and in the United States of America by
FRANK CASS PUBLISHERS
c/o ISBS, 5804 N.E. Hassalo Street
Portland, Oregon 97213-3644

Website http://www.frankcass.com

Copyright © 1998 Mark Huband

British Library Cataloguing in Publication Data:

Huband, Mark
    The Liberian Civil War
    1. Liberia – History – Civil War, 1989–
    I. Title
    966.6'2'03

ISBN 0-7146-4785-3 (cloth)
ISBN 0-7146-4340-8 (paper)

Library of Congress Cataloging-in-Publication Data:

Huband, Mark
    The Liberian Civil War / Mark Huband.
        p.   cm.
    ISBN 0-7146-4785-3 (cloth). – ISBN 0-7146-4340-8 (pbk)
    1. Liberia–History–Civil War, 1989– I. Title.
    DT636.5.H83 1988
    966.6203–dc21   97-40370
                                                        CIP

Typeset by Vitaset, Paddock Wood, Kent
Printed in Great Britain by
Bookcraft (Bath) Ltd, Midsomer Norton, Somerset

For my parents,
David and Ann Huband, with love,
and
Michael Holman,
who sent me on my way

Contents

All the photographs appearing in this
book are the work of Patrick Robert
of Sygma photographic agency,
Paris, France, except where indicated.
They were taken between 1990–96.

Acknowledgements

I would like to thank the following for their encouragement, which helped bring this book to completion: Stephen Smith, Philip Cavendish, Gillon Aitken and, in particular, Katie Duckworth for their advice on the text; Bill Berkeley, Marie Jane Camejo, Bob Caputo and Michael Maren for their kind hospitality during research visits to the United States; Scott Stearns for the invaluable research material he so generously provided; Edith Odemo, for her tireless and unforgettable help in Nairobi; Catherine Bond for her timely encouragement; Robert Easton, Jacqueline Lewis and Andrew Humphrys at Frank Cass & Co., to whom I shall always be immensely grateful for their enthusiasm and sensitivity to this story; finally, my wife, Marceline, and my children, Olivier and Zara, who conceded gracefully when I gave them no choice but to allow me to complete this book.

Foreword by Stephen Smith

If the world of the media ran smoothly, if it were not so shamefully hollow, the civil war in Liberia should have been the Vietnam of an entire generation of journalists. It should have been their open wound, their unanswered question. But that is not what it became. There are a thousand reasons to explain why this is so. But, unless one considers journalists to be nothing more than news clerks delivering up their 'neutral' accounts like bureaucrats during office hours, none of these reasons is satisfactory. Perhaps it is because Liberia is a small country where nothing much is at stake? But then again, since the GIs left, not a great deal has been heard about Vietnam either. Perhaps it is because the great powers, with the United States at their head, were not engaged in Liberia? It is clearly the case that the great powers were hardly preoccupied with the conflict, and that they did not send troops to the historic Grain Coast. But is that to say that they should not have done so? Since the Liberian war started, there have been Sierra Leone, Somalia, the genocide of the Tutsis in Rwanda, the war in Congo-Zaire and the massacre of Hutu refugees ... the United States and the United Nations were obliged, ultimately, to become involved. They did so under the worst conditions, and with disastrous results. But where more than in Liberia was the United States present and implicated? From the creation of the country in 1847, the United States was the 'Big Brother' of a pitiful *alter ego*, the powerful guardian of a land which received its former slaves. On the beaches of Monrovia, American aid was handed out, with no accounting, as if to settle a debt with the past. The aid increased ten-fold during the grotesque, decade-long rule of Samuel Doe, whose bloody 1980 coup was interpreted, wrongly, as the historic revenge of the natives against the Americo-Liberians. This aid, a further effort to make amends, meant that America ultimately financed the slaughter of its rejected children.

Although this book takes all this evidence into account, its purpose is not to make out a case against the United States. Its aim is much wider. Beyond exposing America's politics of abandonment, it is a book about the tragedy of Liberia's mistaken identity. Liberians really believed themselves to be Americans; perhaps distant cousins, but perfectly assimilable and assimilated. Then, just forty-five days after the fall of the Berlin Wall, as the Cold War was finishing, Charles Taylor launched his cross-border raid and unleashed a civil war which, in the new geopolitical context, would turn the Liberians into 'monsters' in blue jeans and checked shirts. The world, with America at its head, left its humanity behind. It no longer saw in the Liberians an *alter ego* in difficulty; nor did it want to see itself in their image. From the moment the global rivalry with the Soviet Union's 'evil empire' ceased, the Liberians became nothing more than 'savages', nothing more than the 'trousered niggers' of a barely repressed Western racism. What could be done for them? Faced with the return of 'ancient demons', confronted by atavistic tribalism and unspeakable cruelty, how could the world have saved Liberia?

It is one of this book's great merits that it hides nothing of the extreme cruelty, the ethnic hatred, the drug abuse and the witchcraft that characterised Liberia's bloody carnival. But what is a carnival if it is not a world turned upside down? Masks were worn to hide faces that were already barely recognisable, faces already wracked with pain and anxiety. The violence was wanton precisely because it was expiatory. The tribes, which had been loosely designated (like the 'Mandingo', Muslim traders), served as the demarcation lines to identify the enemy, such being necessary in order to have a war. The drugs and the black magic confounded rationality, feeding the despair. But, while being very tough, because it is necessary to be explicit where illustration can obscure the truth, Mark Huband is looking for his own identity in the face of these people, looking for something he can himself relate to in the tortured soul of the 'madman'. He carries the reader with him, back to the places which are revived in his memory as he writes: 'streets roamed by murderers who had lost contact with the outside world, killers who had become the horror which perhaps lies inside us all – a brooding savagery, suppressed only by the absence of a stage upon which it can burst out'. Remember Bosnia or, stepping further back, the homeland of Hegel, Goethe and Mozart, which was able to become Nazi.

Liberia has a history which must be taken into consideration. Here, uniquely on the African continent, black people who came from elsewhere – the 'Americo-Liberians' or 'Congos' who were set down on the coast – colonised the indigenous blacks of that land who, from the beginning of the nineteenth century, were first reduced to slavery, then restricted to inferior positions and, throughout, forced away from the coast to live in the country's interior. That Liberia had not experienced its 'decolonisation' – albeit a failed one – until 1980, with a coup led by Master Sergeant Samuel Doe, leaves one to think that its accession to the rest of the continent's move to national sovereignty was not so much the result of an intrinsic maturity, of a popular will, but a consequence of the self-interested claims of a local elite in the face of the colonialist. To put it bluntly: the educated Africans wanted to take the place of their masters, the white colonialists. If they succeeded it was less through strength than through the weakness, bad conscience, shame and remorse of the white man. In Liberia, in place of the white man, colonial injustice, if not apartheid, between blacks also existed.

What followed was less dramatic. In the context of the Cold War, the United States turned Liberia into the African country closest to an American colony: with Firestone, the largest rubber plantation in the world; with Robertsfield airport, modified for stop-overs by American military forces; with US military installations and a sophisticated intelligence relay station; with the Voice of America's transmitting station for the entire African continent ... on the Grain Coast, America was at home and, in return, Liberia considered itself to be the fifty-first star upon its glorious flag. As proof, the Liberian flag and the Liberian currency barely reflected the country itself, both being 'borrowed'. On the trap of Americanisation, there are some excellent pages among those that follow. But Mark Huband also shows the ease with which a tyrant is created – the criminal negligence, the gentle caressing by a spineless guardian of a useful satrap or 'ally', as they were called during the Cold War. On this basis, Samuel Doe is equal to Zaire's Mobutu. On doing the calculation, taking into account the length of their respective rules and the size of their countries, one can deduce that if Mobutu had received as much foreign aid as Doe, he would have accumulated $30 billion, and not 'merely' the $5 or $10 billion with which he is now posthumously credited. It almost goes without saying that, if it had learned some lessons from Liberia, the West would have been able to make some economies.

A further and no less important strength of this book, which is as much a factual account and first-person reportage as a highly detailed investigation – with a wealth of previously unpublished information – and an analysis in the best sense of the word, is that it takes Africa seriously, viewing it from the political angle and not simply as a stage upon which events are reduced to theatre. The rebel chief, Charles Taylor, benefited from active Libyan support, as well as that of Burkina Faso. He knew how to extract favours from the Ivory Coast. He exploited the frustrations of Liberian exiles. It is for these reasons above all that he is in power today. Since the end of the Cold War regional power politics has not ceased to assert itself on the continent. Henceforth, external influences will be replaced by decisions made in the capitals of countries ranging from Eritrea to South Africa via Ethiopia, Uganda, Rwanda and Congo-Zaire. The fate of Africa is no longer decided in Washington, London or Paris, but increasingly in Asmara, Addis Ababa, Lagos, Kampala and Luanda. On reading this book, this will be understood.

Liberia was not the Vietnam of an entire generation of curious, courageous, anguished journalists. It did not lure more than a handful of reporters and photographers – and I fear that the world remembers nothing of their work, beyond the morbid exoticism of a 'savage' war, the passing thrill of their words and images of horror, momentarily recalled from the comfort of an armchair. The bloody carnival has been captured on glossy paper; the slow putting to death of Samuel Doe is nothing more than a video clip. Then we moved on to something else, and didn't raise our heads until Somalia's 'biblical famine', and the 'third genocide of the century' in Rwanda. The collective amnesia is organised, rhythmic and ritualised. The flood of daily news, this surfeit which leaves the world *informe* – the ancient Greek word for *appalling* – and its inhabitants *informed*, burying the critical sense of the lay person, the *krinein*, the Greek verb meaning to *distinguish*.

Mark Huband has made this distinction. He has written a history as well as an exhaustive investigation. He was particularly well placed, having been the first journalist to meet Charles Taylor in the Liberian forest, among the few who spent months in Monrovia under siege, and the only one to have sought explanations for what took place beyond Liberia itself, in neighbouring countries and in the United States. Above all, he made Liberia *his* affair, his personal Vietnam, his defeat, but also his hope of revitalisation.

This is a unique book. A mix of all the journalistic genres, which, close to the author's heart, is a story told from the gut, one which will broaden people's horizons, which will tell the reader a real story. Thanks to this work, what has taken place in Liberia, and what it means for tomorrow, will not be forgotten.

Stephen Smith is the Africa editor of the French daily newspaper *Libération*.

Introduction

DUPORT ROAD is a neat example of town planning. Pleasant villas lie set back from the roadside. At the end of its mile length there is a turning circle. The road is all tarmac, and the turning circle too. But where once the lawn in the centre of the turning circle was cut regularly by the well-to-do residents, the very slight breeze which sometimes blows through there now ruffles long thin grass, among which lie human skulls.

The skulls are from the war. They peer up from the rapidly growing grass. In the shade of the trees which mark the end of the road there is a hut. Inside the hut lives a man who knows how the skulls got there. I went to see this man with Stanton Peabody, the editor of *The Daily Observer*, once Liberia's most authoritative newspaper; it is now closed and its two-room office burned to the ground. Stanton's home is near Duport Road. During the early part of the civil war in 1990, when my stay in Liberia extended from weeks to months, he went into hiding in an apartment in the city centre opposite the one I lived in. It was a long time before he went back to Duport Road. But in the spring of 1991, when we thought the war was over, we drove back to his house and, on the way, went to see the man in his hut, who told us how he had watched through a crack in the planks of his wooden home as people were brought there and shot in the grass at the centre of the turning circle.

It was a very peaceful day. The skulls were dry. The sun was hot that early afternoon. The man nodded from his verandah and muttered continuously as we said goodbye and drove back down Duport Road to Stanton's house. Stanton told me as we drove away that the man was mad. That was why he had been left alone while the people were brought there to be shot. But it was the war which had turned him mad. Perhaps he had been a little mad before the war, but now he had become insane. I turned as we drove away, to see him rocking slightly on the chair in the shade of his verandah. Then he disappeared from view as we drove to Stanton's house.

Stanton's lodger had looked after the house until fighting had broken out in the area. I had been there once during the war, not knowing that this was his house. One rainy morning I had hidden among the huts as bullets flew overhead. Stanton took me there because he wanted to see if his lodger had returned. He knew she had a story to tell.

Even now she does not want her name to be given, though her story is one she wants to tell. As we ate rice and mashed leaves with a few strands of chicken, she told me how she had fled her home in the early months of the war and gone with thousands of others to the University of Liberia campus at Fendel, outside Monrovia. The rebel army, the National Patriotic Front of Liberia (NPFL), led by Charles Taylor, had confined everybody there to huts and campus buildings, and were exacting revenge on their real and imagined enemies. One morning her husband was taken away for questioning by the teenage gunmen. By nightfall he was not back. The next day he did not come back. Nor the next. Several days later Charles Taylor himself visited the campus. She wanted to approach him. She knew why her husband had disappeared. She did not know what had happened to him. But she knew what might have happened to him, because he was Nigerian. At that time Nigeria was considering sending a peacekeeping force to Liberia, in a bid to end the slaughter. Charles Taylor thought this would end his chances of seizing power, so he began to execute Nigerians discovered in his territory, in order to discourage the Nigerian initiative.

'I thought Charles Taylor might listen to me. I just wanted to know where my husband was,' she told me quietly. 'I really thought Charles Taylor might listen to me, because Charles Taylor is my second cousin. But he didn't see me standing there, and I didn't see my husband again.'

In December 1989, five years after fleeing Liberia, Charles Taylor returned to the country to launch a conflict which has left Africa's oldest republic in ruins. Acts of appalling violence and mass executions at sites throughout the country have been committed by all sides. As destructive has been the fear, which has prevailed from the first moment the armies of youngsters began overturning traditional authority, annihilating the small educated class and quickly evolving into a generation of teenage psychopaths, whose rule of terror in the territory they controlled has left Liberia a wilderness.

But the war did not start like that. It started with hope. By 1989 the nine-year presidency of Samuel Kanyon Doe had become a showpiece of brutality. As with the war, his rule was not supposed to have been like that. When Doe seized power in 1980, the expectations were as high as those which were later to greet the war launched to overthrow him. Liberia's recent history has been characterised by tragic disappointments, summed up in the title of a harrowing account of the Doe regime's human rights' abuses, *A Promise Betrayed*, by the American writer Bill Berkeley.[1]

Samuel Doe's 1980 coup ended the rule of Liberia's Americo-Liberians. After 133 years, the handful of extended families descended from freed slaves dispatched to West Africa from the plantations of the American south, saw their grip on power end with a bloody coup in the early hours of 12 April. They were usurped by low-ranking soldiers from the majority population of native Liberians, whose families had inhabited the territory that became Liberia when the freed slaves arrived.

Samuel Doe, then a master-sergeant, was the highest ranking of the troops who led the coup, and consequently assumed the position of president at the head of the Peoples' Redemption Council (PRC) government. President William Tolbert, his Americo-Liberian predecessor, was bayoneted to death in the private apartments of the presidential Executive Mansion. The coup-makers then arrested senior members of the government. After a bout of euphoric drinking, the new leaders of Liberia brought 13 of Tolbert's ministers to the golden beach which stretches the length of Monrovia on the Atlantic side. Telegraph poles had been planted in the sand. The ministers, most of them ageing old men, were stripped to their underwear and tied to the poles. Pleading for their lives, they were shot, while an enormous crowd looked on and television cameras rolled.

It is difficult to assess the long-term significance of the fact that Doe's rule was bathed in blood from the day it started. It is clear that the rule of the Americo-Liberians was characterised by prejudice, snobbery, and a kind of racial discrimination which set the 'Americos' apart from the Africans, despite both communities being black. More than a century of discrimination, which in the 1920s had led the League of Nations to accuse the Liberian élite of practising slavery, fired the resentment which brought Samuel Doe to power. There was certainly euphoria after his coup. But it is wrong to suggest that Doe's response to the Americo-Liberian hegemony was the natural response of all Liberians. Long before Doe appeared on the scene opposition to Americo-Liberian rule and the dominance of the True Whig Party had been vocal. Amos Sawyer, a university professor, had defied the discriminators by attempting to stand as mayor of Monrovia. Gabriel Bacchus Matthews had agitated for political freedoms. Others voiced the growing discontent, which erupted into riots in 1979 when the government raised the price of rice in a manner

---

1. Bill Berkeley, *A Promise Betrayed* (New York, Lawyers Committee for Human Rights, 1986).

which would have personally enriched the president, who had monopoly control over this staple commodity. That year President Tolbert recognised the tensions by legalising opposition political parties, but within six months he had jailed all their leaders.

Samuel Doe was the inevitable result of both the long-term discontent and the rising of tension immediately before the 1980 coup. But the opposition to Tolbert did have a more thoughtful basis than that evoked by those with whom Doe surrounded himself. Nevertheless, popular support for the coup was assured, and Doe initially fostered a climate of renewal by appointing civilians to ministerial positions and avoiding overt tribalism in nominations to government posts. But from the very first day it all started to go wrong, as Doe became prey to the ambitions of his fellow coup-makers, all of whom saw the rich pickings to be had now they were in government. Quickly, the PRC came to rule over a country which attracted bounty-hunters, both foreign and Liberian, keen to exploit the inexperience of the new government, bribe their way into contracts, use lax banking laws to launder earnings from the international narcotics trade and siphon-off funds granted the new regime in foreign aid.

At the centre of an increasingly complicated web sat Samuel Doe. He symbolised the contradictory forces at work in Liberia. Privately, he would tell his confidantes that he wanted to be as rich as Felix Houphouet-Boigny, the wealthy president of the neighbouring Ivory Coast. Publicly, he would promote the apparently modest aspiration of wanting to educate himself, and employed a university professor to teach him how to read and write, neither of which he could do when he became president. Doe came to symbolise what has been described in Liberia as the gulf between lofty ideals and base reality.

The base reality of Liberia has been unearthed by the war which erupted several years after Samuel Doe lost the last ragged semblance of his credibility, but during which time he clung on to power. Since 1989 that process has been painfully pursued to the point where there is now nothing left to speak of as Liberia.

Charles Taylor presented himself as a non-smoking, non-drinking Baptist when the war started. He attempted to project an image of goodness, solidity and family values, in contrast to Doe. Taylor's formative years had been spent in the United States, where his entire education had taken place. On taking command of the NPFL, however, he needed to claim native Liberian lineage in order to assure himself of native Liberian support. To achieve this he combined his Americanisation with reminders that his mother was from the native Gola tribe from north-west Liberia, while his father, an Americo-Liberian Monrovia judge, from whom he had inherited his distinctly Americo-Liberian surname, allowed him to stand shoulder to shoulder with the regime Doe had overthrown. He was, he generally claimed, all things to all men.

Taylor's subsequent failure to fight a short, effective war has left the question of Liberia's identity in greater confusion than ever before. Central to Doe's failure as the redeemer he purported to be, is the fact that he betrayed the expectations of the native Liberians. He no more redeemed them than had the Americo-Liberians. And the instability he fostered set Liberia adrift on the course upon which it is still sailing. Having failed to found a native Liberian identity that in any way replaced the long-lived institutional framework of Americo-Liberian rule, bound up as it was in freemasonry, fundamentalist Christianity and apartheid, Doe looked for inspiration to the country which came to be portrayed as the model for all Liberians, not just the Americo-Liberians, to follow – the United States.

In language, attire, aspirations and self-image, a superficial American influence pervaded every aspect of Liberian society, though with varia-tions between the rural and urban areas. Doe adopted a foreign policy intended to please the United States, his view of other African states reflecting American cold-war attitudes, and he did much to assist the United States, in the small way that a small country is able. In return, he received $500 million in foreign aid and was portrayed by the Reagan administration as a friend of the US. His brutality was either ignored or excused on the other side of the Atlantic Ocean.

For nine years this relationship was cemented. But then came the time when Liberia required something more, as its own existence came to be at stake, and then its people came to realise that their Big Brother no longer really cared about them. This realisation evolved into the understanding that it never really had. The United States' refusal to take any decisive steps to end the conflict in Liberia, leaving aside the question of whether such steps would have been wise or effective, can essentially be interpreted as the US response to Liberia's aspiration towards being a Little America. The two countries really have nothing in common, and never have done. But the leaders of both had long found it convenient to assert that historical ties signified a profound connection and common understanding, underpinned by a sort of loyalty.

Liberia's response to American inaction, when it realised no help would be forthcoming and that this civil war would be allowed to fight itself out, however long it took, was to unearth its own roots. Charles Taylor can no longer portray himself as possessing the residual influence of an American education. Nobody cares any longer where he did his Master's Degree, nor what kind of shoes he prefers. The war has exposed the fallacy of Liberia's Americanism. By closing its eyes to the war, the United States exposed Liberians to what had always, in fact, been true – the fact that there was no special relationship. This has been silently accepted in America, among those who know where Liberia is. Meanwhile, on the Liberian side it has been difficult to adopt a public acceptance of something which all along has been secretly known – that Liberia is no more American than any other part of Africa. But now the severing of these albeit illusory ties is complete. Liberians no longer look to the US as a godfather, whose own forefathers negotiated Liberia into existence.

America has shed a chapter in its own history in a way that only a superpower could do. Meanwhile, Liberia and the West African sub-region in which it lies have seen the opening of an important and decisive chapter which, ultimately, is of greater value to the evolution of a stable Liberia than whatever attachment there may have been to the United States.

Nine months after the eruption of violence in December 1989, regional states led by Nigeria and Ghana launched what has become a test-case for international bodies engaged in conflict resolution. Under the auspices of the Economic Community of West African States (Ecowas), the Economic Community Monitoring Group (Ecomog) was dispatched to Liberia, to step in between the warring sides and oversee a cease-fire.

The arrival of Ecomog in 1990 transformed the Liberian conflict by involving the entire region in the search for a solution. Diplomatically, regional involvement tested the credibility of most of the region's leaders as negotiators and statesmen. They all failed in their objectives. Militarily, the conflict has tested the resolve, skills, training and leadership of the region's largest armies. As a force at times fighting an all-out war against Charles Taylor's army of teenage guerrillas, Ecomog failed in its objectives of either achieving outright military victory or forcing Taylor to negotiate sincerely.

Each of the Ecomog states (Nigeria, Ghana, Guinea, The Gambia and Sierra Leone) had their own reasons for joining the force, aside from the horror stories emanating from Liberia, which had shocked the entire region.

Nigeria wanted to assert its regional pre-eminence; President Ibrahim

Babangida was also under pressure from Nigerian Muslim leaders to halt the attacks on Liberia's Muslims, who were a target for the NPFL. Most were from the Mandingo tribe, which owned 60 per cent of Liberia's wealth and was generally allied to the Doe regime. Ghana distrusted Taylor and during his period in Ghana as a renegade from Liberia in the 1980s had jailed him twice as proof of this distrust. More importantly, Ghana was concerned to stem regional instability. But it did not want to see Nigeria play the pre-eminent role in any regional initiatives. Guinea remained close to Doe until his government collapsed; its agenda was also dictated by concern for Liberia's Muslims. For The Gambia and Sierra Leone the issue was much closer to home. From very early on they were both aware that Taylor had recruited their own dissidents to the NPFL.

The Ecomog force rapidly became as divisive an element in the Liberian crisis as the war itself. Despite Ghanaian and Nigerian claims to the contrary, President Felix Houphouet-Boigny of the Ivory Coast did not share the worry expressed by Nigeria and Ghana that the entire West African region could become divided militarily over Liberia. He would not have risked disturbing the relative tranquillity of his own country if he had felt that Liberia's war would spill over his border.

During the Nigerian civil war Houphouet-Boigny had supported breakaway Biafra throughout the conflict. In this he was steered by the French government's policy of wanting to undermine the power of Nigeria by dividing it, and thereby preventing it from becoming an economic power capable of overwhelming the smaller economies of the French-speaking and French-allied countries. After his defeat, the Biafran leader Emeka Ojukwu was given a home in Abidjan, from where he ran a successful transport company until his return to Nigeria in 1991. In the intervening years French nervousness about Nigerian hegemony had resulted in an entirely new policy. Instead of undermining Nigeria, France invested heavily there, to an extent which gave Paris substantial economic leverage in Nigeria, and, therefore, in the sub-region, which it has viewed until today as its own backyard.

By the time Ecomog arrived in Monrovia in September 1990, France had come to accept the defence pacts that Nigeria had signed with Sierra Leone and The Gambia. But the presence of an ever-increasing number of Nigerian troops in Liberia, a country up for grabs since the US had made it obvious that it no longer cared in whose sphere of influence it lay, began to worry both France and the Ivory Coast, France's closest ally in Africa. As Taylor secured control within most of Liberia, assisted by the willingness of the Ivorians to allow a regular supply of weapons to pass across the north of their country *en route* from Burkina Faso to Liberia, French business interests were to be seen arranging contracts with Taylor's men, and an attempt was made for a French company, BRGM, to take over production of the world's largest iron-ore mine at NPFL-controlled Yekepa on the Liberian border with Guinea.

As had been the case with Nigeria, France sought to influence non-Francophone Africa from within, and readily encouraged a sympathetic attitude towards Charles Taylor, in whom they saw a potential ally. Leading France's strategy was its long-serving ambassador to the Ivory Coast, Michel Dupuch, a close personal friend of Houphouet-Boigny.

Dupuch has consistently refused to comment on his role. But it is clear that he was regarded as a hero in NPFL territory, which he visited despite having no diplomatic accreditation outside the Ivory Coast. Such was Dupuch's importance that on one occasion when the US ambassador to Monrovia, Peter De Vos, made a visit to the Taylor-held port of Buchanan in early 1992, the Americans found the town decorated in red, white and blue banners. They assumed this was in their honour, until discovering that it was in expectation of a visit by Dupuch later that day.

Such foreign interference has prolonged the Liberian conflict. Throughout the war, all attempts to negotiate an end to the slaughter have been hampered by personal agendas and business interests, in which outsiders – Europeans, Americans, Lebanese, Israelis – have played as much of a role as Liberia's own protagonists.

For Charles Taylor, the agenda has been one of replacing Samuel Doe with himself. In 1989, Taylor's politics were those of the cold war, during which half-baked ideas and vague promises coupled with proof of military prowess and effective propaganda mattered more than real ideas. It was these credentials that gained Taylor his Libyan support during the 1980s. But by 1990 the old power blocks of the cold war were crumbling. Tiny countries like Liberia – a cold-war side-show similar to Somalia – were in need of political philosophies free from the cold-war paradigm. At their heart, the new politics of such countries required the recognition that they themselves no longer mattered strategically to the superpowers, except as secure votes at the United Nations. They had to see themselves for what they had really been – wild cards in a superpower game of imperialist poker.

The cold war had a significant impact as a lever on the practice of power. The Reagan years provided regimes like that of Samuel Doe's with *carte blanche* to behave as brutally as they wished. Doe's US critics were usually isolated senators, easily ignored by the Reagan administration. It is extraordinary that the excesses of the Doe regime did not lead to any decisive action. Reagan held a lever made all the more effective by the fact that he never pulled it. By ignoring criticisms of Doe's rule, the Reagan White House strengthened Doe's resolve immeasurably. Charles Taylor's response, after lengthy travails, was to secure Libyan backing for his invasion.

According to one of Taylor's former closest colleagues, who trained in Libya with the NPFL and then left Taylor on the eve of the invasion, the training period at the Mataba base outside Tripoli saw far-reaching agreements being made between the NPFL and the Libyans with regard to the practice of government in a Taylor-led Liberia.

> The American and British citizens would be subject to thorough screening, while the American embassy staff would be reduced to ten and all foreign embassies would be relocated in the OAU village, where they were all going to be bugged ... The [US] Omega [navigation] station would be run by Libyans. Military training camps would be opened for other African revolutionary groups, and Liberian lands which had been given to or taken by Guinea, Sierra Leone or Ivory Coast would be liberated. The Ghanaian government was targeted because it had imprisoned Taylor, and the [left wing] MOJA militants and the leaderships of all the Liberian political parties would be eliminated.

The Libyan link, which Taylor has always denied, was a complicating element in a war which might otherwise have been more straightforward. The Libyan link gave Doe an added card to play and the Americans, who maintained regular contacts with Doe up until his death, could not ignore it. Taylor had to be secretive about it: to have admitted it would have been difficult in view of the poor US relationship with Libya. But by attempting to conceal the link Taylor appeared dishonest. Either way, it soured the wholesomeness he wished to project. What Taylor did not realise – as a Romanian firing-squad executed Nicolae Ceauşescu almost at the hour the NPFL was crossing into Liberia – was that the stakes had all changed even as his invasion was launched. Overnight, there was no cold war. Almost overnight Liberia disappeared off the US strategic map. It no longer mattered to State Department planners whether Charles Taylor of Liberia had spent time in Tripoli. The US did not care.

If Taylor had come clean, and had been open about his backers, his motives, and his planning, then the war would not have raised suspicion across the region. Instead, Taylor behaved like a cold-war dinosaur, unable to reassess his task of ending the Doe tyranny as one which had changed dramatically with the end of Liberia's strategic role. Taylor remained intent on stepping into Samuel Doe's shoes, refusing to acknowledge that Doe had only survived in power because of his importance in relation to American strategic thinking. Without American military and financial aid, and the kudos of being received at the White House (while in Liberia his bullies beat, raped and murdered with impunity), Doe would not have survived. But instead of using Doe's changed status in the eyes of his American backers as a lever to force him out, Taylor pursued his original plan, ultimately failing to project a radically different view of leadership to that of Doe, while his army certainly never acted in a way which distinguished it from Doe's army. Only their aims were different. Taylor's aim was to take power. Doe's aim was to hold on to it.

Now the war is over and a new president has been installed, though the country remains deeply scarred. An explosion of the most grotesque violence in central Monrovia in April 1996, led and inspired by the faction leaders, which left the city littered with beheaded corpses, revealed how close to the surface the option of violence remains. None of Liberia's faction leaders, who were the main contenders in the democratic contest, is capable of healing the wounds which the war opened. For the faction leaders, Liberia remains a prize over which they have fought, and which they now believe they deserve to be handed. Meanwhile, the peace-keeping force continues to provide the only real security, and even its success has only been appreciable in terms of degree: some lives have probably been saved, some destruction probably averted. But peace has been a long time coming.

Liberia was not a name on everybody's lips when I arrived in West Africa in late September 1989. I had left a job as a parliamentary correspondent at Westminster, having decided that I had to see the world before I could believe with confidence that I had anything worthwhile to say about it. At 1am on a hot night I arrived in Abidjan, Ivory Coast, at the dawn of a new life, my suitcase in my hand, feeling vulnerable, young and alone. I had arranged to contribute stories to the *Financial Times*, as well as some other newspapers. I found a small room in the centre of the city and began to write about cocoa and coffee, and to wonder what lay beyond the city in which I was effectively imprisoned, because I had no money to travel beyond it.

A month after I arrived a newspaper asked me to write a story about ritual killing. It had been reported that a child murder had taken place, that a senior politician was accused of involvement and had been imprisoned, and that the killing had been an attempt to determine the outcome of an election. The country where all this had taken place was Liberia. There was no budget for me to go there, so I had to write about it from Abidjan. I wrote the piece, and knew that it was to places like Liberia, of which I knew nothing, that I must go if I was to experience what I had set out to see.

Several months later I did go there, and, as the war began, I was swept inexorably along in its current. I discovered that the world I had left behind in England, and from which I rapidly became isolated, was exceptional, and that the land in which I was now living bore the scars of secret histories generating emotions and behaviour which, as with the country whose story I have tried to tell, left me spiritually broken, but then gave me the strength to rebuild myself. Perhaps I can say that I have lived and grown with the war in Liberia. It is a profound part of me. And, perhaps now it is over, the rich red earth of Liberia will once more nurture the green shoots of spring after a long, dark winter, and give me a new beginning.

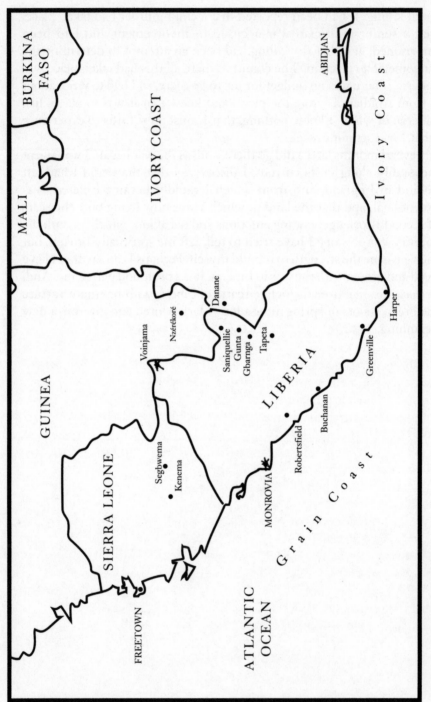

Map of Liberia and neighbouring countries.

1 Soldiers, Priests and Beer Money

MONEY SLID from hand to waiting hand. Only small amounts of money. Notes or a few coins. It slowly made its way inside the passports, or more openly, straight from one hand into another. There was no money in my passport as I handed it to an enormous woman wearing a New York Police Department-style uniform, who sat, Buddha-like, inside a small cubicle five feet above floor level at one end of the airport terminal. My passport joined a small pile on the desk, and she took the next handsomely-loaded document from the person behind me and stamped it. Eventually I was the only person in front of her. I held out my hand. She looked me in the eye, then slowly began flicking through the pages of my passport.

'You go' nothin' fo' me?' she said. I smiled. She did not.

'Wha' i' the purpo' o' your mission?' I told her I was there to visit Nimba. She shrugged, continuing to flick through the pages. After a few moments' pause the stamp thudded down onto an empty page where she scribbled some illegible instructions.

'Repor' to I'gration wi'in fordy-eigh' hour,' she said, thrusting the passport over the counter at me.

A man in a sports jacket and sunglasses took my passport from me when I walked behind the cubicle.

'We have been expecting you,' he said. Then he said I could go, handing me the passport without looking through it.

In the next room the customs officers rubbed their hands. 'Wha' i' the purpo' o' your mission. D'ya have any gold, diamonds abou' your person?' They told me I could go. Then, around the corner of the customs hall, one came after me.

'You ha'n't had your baggage marked. Now, that' ain't allowed. So, what d'ya ha' fo' me? Wha' d'ya ha' fo' me? Just a small thing.'

'No. Nothing,' I mumbled nervously.

He shrugged and daubed my bag with pink chalk, then disappeared.

It was a hot morning in January 1990. This was Liberia.

On the flight from Abidjan I had met a reporter for Agence France Presse, an American living in Abidjan. He told me he was going to

1

Monrovia to pay his correspondent. He was keeping two thousand dollars strapped tightly to his chest and was nervous about it. He would not be going to the north to where the rebels were. That was not the purpose of his visit. He was from the mid-west of America and he should have felt at home in Liberia. Liberia was just like America, I had been told. But I later realised this was a myth people used, to pretend that Liberia had been raised by a responsible godfather. It had not taken long before this American also sensed this was a myth. He wanted to pay his stringer and get out.

'But you have to go to the north. That's where the story is,' I told him.

'Well, sure. But that's naat part of my mission.' He was in his mid-twenties, but had grown a beard because he looked so young. 'I look about twelve without a beard,' he told me. 'But even with it I don't look much older.'

Taxi-drivers descended on us outside the airport terminal, all wearing fake Ray-Ban aviator sunglasses, stone-washed jeans, sneakers and an array of logo-daubed baseball shirts. They refused to fight for our custom, because to do so was clearly not cool. Eventually one of them deigned to take us.

'This is the voice of E-L-W-A, broadcasting from Monrovia.' The broadcaster's voice rose smoothly out of the taxi radio. He played slow reggae tunes before the news came on. 'And now E-L-W-A brings you the latest national and international news with our programme "Window on the World",' said the voice. The stories were about the finalising of the budget. Then came appeals from 'prominent citizens' for the rebels in the north to lay down their arms. The smooth voice never wavered. The national legislature had authorised President Doe to take whatever money he needed to finance the army campaign against the rebels, so he had diverted five million dollars from the voter registration fund, which was to have led to the creation of a register in the run-up to elections scheduled for 1991. The report continued:

> In a statement, the nation's legislators, and I quote: 'categorically, unequivocally and emphatically deprecate, condemn and denounce the vicious, atrocious and seditious invasion by Charles Taylor and his cohorts on 24 December 1989' ...

Then Samuel Doe's voice came on, saying that Liberia was one nation and that it should not be divided by 'Charles Taylor and his clique of rebels'. Then there was more soft reggae.

The road from the airport passed between fields and then along the perimeter of the Camp Schieffelin army base before approaching the suburbs of Monrovia at Red Light Junction. The taxi-driver told us these names as we drove towards the city.

'Schieffelin. Thaa the home o' the Ar' Force' o' Liber'a. Now we approachin' Raa Laa Junctio', whi' mark' city limi',' he told us, his shoulders and head swaying slightly from side to side with the music. Just before the junction the traffic was being directed off the road onto the verge, around a ceremonial arch which was being built to commemorate a planned visit by the Pope.

'O'er there, Pres'ent Dorr buildin' hisself noo house,' said the taxi-driver. At the top of a long hill the president had flattened the ground to build a new home. The site had a commanding view over the city and was ideal for a siege. But as yet no building had begun. 'JFK on thaa' side,' the taxi-driver told us, nodding his head towards the John Fitzgerald Kennedy Memorial Hospital. 'Thi' Sinkor distri'.' The houses and buildings were smart. Palm trees swayed in the breeze as they rose out of the shrubberies of well-kept gardens.

And on the roadside were hundreds of advertising signs for airlines flying to Europe and the rest of the world, signs for car showrooms, signs for printing works, signs promoting the government's environmental programme: 'Support the Green Revolution', they said, with an intricately painted illustration of farmers at work in a luxuriant tropical setting. Other large signs, similarly hand-painted, advertised the country's national parks, with large animals prowling through jungle. Small cafés, workshops and restaurants stood beside the road or were signposted off it. And churches. Everywhere churches. Methodist, Unitarian, Catholic, Lutheran, Baptist, Seventh Day Adventist, Jesus Christ of Latter Day Saints, spiritualist, new churches of Africa, Pentecostal churches and Presbyterian churches – they all advertised their presence, alongside the signs for soap and toothpaste and menthol cigarettes, with arrows directing the faithful down small dirt tracks to chapels beside the beach or in amongst the palm-shadowed houses.

'Pres'ly the Pres'dent live here. Thaa' the Exec'tive Maansha. Ju' pa' the statue o' thaa unknow' sol'ja.' We passed the statue of an African soldier dressed in a First World War uniform. 'Yeah, thaa's where the Pres'dent live now. Thaa's the Exec'tive Maansha.' Behind trees, down a road with a sign saying no entry, was the multi-storey office block occupied by Liberia's heads of state since it was built by new-found

3

Israeli friends in 1964. We took the public road past the national police headquarters and the law courts and drove down the hill into the city centre to the Holiday Inn Hotel.

'The war can wait. There are always wars, anyway,' said the Lebanese owner of the razor-blade shop. The banks had closed for the day, and I had asked somebody at the hotel where I could change money. Cadillacs prowled the streets between the razor-blade shop and the Holiday Inn, a hotel as gaudy and decadent as the hotel chain from which it had stolen its name was bland. Besides razor blades, the shop's shelves groaned under the weight of rice sacks, chewing gum, buckets, packet mashed potato and, under the counter, black market money. Thousands of dollars. The new Liberian five-dollar note, crisp and green.

Until a few months previously the country had run on coins, or on American dollars. People used to help each other carry money in sacks from the banks. Then they began to complain about the weight and the security risk. So the government introduced the 'J. J Roberts', a five-dollar bill depicting the country's first president as an upright, white Victorian in a wing collar and frock coat, who led the freed slaves of America into African nationhood. Now he was consigned to the clenched and sweaty fists of the buyers, sellers, officials, armed guards, customs officers, baggage checkers and civil servants slipping and sliding their share of the J. J. Roberts into the wallets, pockets, desk drawers, cubbyholes, dashboard ashtrays, grubby money-boxes and shirtfolds of liberal, libertarian, liberated Liberia's economy.

I changed my money and returned to the Holiday Inn Hotel.

'I think I'll try the prawns,' said the American correspondent with whom I had arrived. James, his stringer, had met him in the hotel room we were sharing. The American had handed over the two thousand dollars, but James had begun to moan that it was not enough. The discussion had gone on and on, until in the end James had been forced to accept that it was all there was. Eventually he had left, saying that he would meet us the following morning to arrange press passes with the Ministry of Information, to allow us to go to Nimba county.

By now the American had been convinced that a visit to the area of fighting might be a good idea. But he still had his doubts about his safety. Then it dawned on him that perhaps he should just tell everybody he was American and they would consequently treat him better. Convinced of the wisdom of this strategy, he relaxed over dinner and worked his way through prawns and fish and dessert and coffee, beneath the yellow and red light bulbs of the Holiday Inn's dark, wood-panelled and windowless restaurant.

It was nearly seven o'clock. I had finished eating, so I left him sitting in the restaurant, saying I was going to go downstairs to watch the news.

In the entrance hall, beside a trickling fountain in a grotto illuminated with blue lights beneath the stairs, the Lebanese owner of the hotel, Mr Gawhary, sat with his children watching television. He was vast. His children made lots of noise. On the screen President Doe, squeezed into a shiny grey double-breasted suit, looked straight past the camera and made the speech I had heard earlier on the radio:

'We have a nation. We will not be divided by Charles Taylor and his clique of rebels.' The newsreader said that a group of Taylor's rebels had secretly arrived in Monrovia the day before, armed and planning to launch the second prong of a two-pronged offensive. But they had got drunk in a city bar and bragged that they were going to overthrow Doe. Then they had been arrested. They would be paraded on television the next day, the report said.

Doe finished his speech. His audience clapped. The people watching in the hotel lobby had listened silently. They didn't talk even after Doe had finished. Doe claimed, some months later, that he had been victim of 38 attempts to overthrow him, and that he would diffuse this attempt as he had done all the others. I wondered whether the people in the hotel were asking themselves if this was any different from the previous attempts to get rid of the government. They didn't say. Mr Gawhary went on meeting the needs of his customers, introducing himself to his guests as if they were all old friends.

Later, the lobby became the prostitutes' catwalk. They wore tight vests and skin-tight trousers or satin shorts and high-heeled stilettos. Their hair, make-up and bright lipstick, and the way they carried their gold-strapped patent leather shoulder bags, gave them the appearance of over-done male transvestites. They wandered up and down, grimacing in the blue light of the fountain grotto, until the elegance of their parade was undermined by a power cut. Candles were lit, but the aura of Caesar's Palace had been lost, so they sat down and smoked with everybody else.

I went up to the room I was sharing with the American. The air conditioning had stopped with the lack of power and the heat had risen. I lay on my bed and stared up at the ceiling. The telephone rang and a woman's voice said: 'Are you coming round then. I'm in room 305.' I put the phone down. It rang again almost immediately, just as my room-mate came through the door. I told her to stop ringing, and put the phone down.

'You must have pretty good contacts, if y'already got people ringing you up,' he said, concerned about the competition from another reporter.

'Yes,' I said.

The phone rang a third time.

'I'd really like to see you. I'm waiting in room 305.' I put the phone down without saying anything.

'You must have real good contacts,' he repeated.

'Actually, that time it was a prostitute from down the corridor. Fancy a night with her?'

'Gaad no. What would my wife say? I don't do that kind of thing. I hope you don't either. After all, we are sharing a room.'

'No. It's okay.' I lay on my bed as the room grew hotter and steamier.

Early next morning James arrived and we went to the Ministry of Information, where two plaster lions stood sentry on either side of the entrance. An official in a shiny brown suit said that the documents necessary to take us to Nimba would take a while. The minister had to sign them. At one o'clock he had still not arrived. The official took us to the ministry office from where the Liberian News Agency, LINA, operated, churning out government propaganda using equipment supplied by the German government.

At four o'clock a gleaming white Mercedes pulled up in front of the two plaster lions. The minister, Mr J. Emmanuel Bouwier, alighted and swaggered up the stairs. The brown-suited official told us the minister was coming. We followed the man and his entourage along a corridor to a double door at the end, where we were swept aside and had the door closed in our faces. The brown suit went in, then emerged. The minister would not sign until we had another signature from the chairman of the Press Union of Liberia. The shiny brown suit hung around. We went through town to the offices of the press union, and had the document signed just before dusk. The Ministry of Information, when we returned to it, was about to close. The white Mercedes was still there. Inside the brown suit told us to wait in his office while he took the forms into the minister. He then returned five minutes later with the forms signed.

'Now,' he said, peering over his desk. 'For me?' He patted the forms on his desk, right there, within sight of the Executive Mansion, down the corridor from the minister. He took five dollars, handed over the forms. Now we could go to Nimba.

The following morning James, the correspondent, was late. The city was humming with life before he arrived at the hotel. We followed him through the streets down towards the waterfront, along a road which looked over a wide sweep of grey-brown water and mangrove. This was where the slaves had come to be free. In 1822 they had landed on Providence Island, which stands in the centre of the sweep of water. A road bridge soars over the island where there are small buildings and some trees. People know it is where the slaves from America first landed. It is a kind of birthplace for the country. A site. But one which nobody ever goes to. I wanted it to be something special; but it is just an island with a small, brick house at its centre, under the bridge.

James argued with some taxi-drivers who, from behind their imitation Ray-Bans, refused to appear tempted by the possibility of making money out of the long trip to Nimba.

'Too expensive. Too expensive. Too expensive,' one kept saying. 'The checkpoints are too expensive.' They all said they would have to charge us double – the fare there and back – even if we didn't come back with them. They would lose money if we only paid one way. James began to agree with them and became blasé about the money, now that he had his own.

'How much yo' pay?' one then asked. One hundred dollars – American.

'Okay,' we said, and, as we pulled out of the city, I wondered if I would ever return to spend ordinary days with the people there.

We had been driving for over an hour before we reached the first check-point on the boundary between Montserrado and Bong counties. There was a bar across the road and a sign saying: Welcome to Bong County. We had to drive off the road to the checkpoint and go through different rooms where different officials stamped our forms and asked questions about the purpose of our mission. They were calm and didn't ask for money and hoped we had a safe journey to Nimba county.

The road passed between the trees of rubber plantations, endless lines of tall trees, silent, orderly, disappearing into a distant darkness at the end of each row. Memories of school geography lessons and rubber tappers passed through my mind, in a fleeting reminiscence of the way I had been prepared for the outside world.

At the next checkpoint the army had taken control. A soldier forced us out of the taxi with his automatic rifle trained on the windscreen. The world began to change, as this reality carried me along in its arms, and I wondered how easy it would be to become a victim of those lessons intended as my preparation for real life.

'Ge' dow'. E'e'ybody ge' dow',' the soldier shouted. 'Mo' 'way fro' the car. Mo' 'way.' He yelled his orders with total purpose, and we got out of the car. Of course, the natural reaction was to do what he said and go where he told me to go, because of who he was and who I was. I had to believe that the situation demanded my acquiescence so I could begin to understand what was going on and be sympathetic and be able to write about the reality. Over the months that were to follow I learned that the only thing to write about was the horror of no longer knowing what the reality was and what it was not.

The American approached the soldier.

'Hello, there. I'm an American,' he said. The soldier kept his gun trained on the windscreen of the car, even though there was now nobody inside it. Then he pointed with his gun to an office, from where people on a verandah were watching him wield his authority.

We went into the office. There were soldiers and civilians. The soldiers watched and listened attentively as the civilian customs officers, whose post this was, asked us for details.

'Wha' is the purpose o' your mission? Wha' d' you hope to find? Wha' is your nationality?'

'Well, now, I'm an American,' said my companion.

They flicked through our passports, looked at the press passes given to us by the brown-suited man in the Ministry of Information and gave us pieces of paper on which to write down all the details of our visit. I assumed they would turn us back. I have never understood why people in authority ever allow journalists access to their crimes. And these people, perhaps, knew what had been going on in the villages, even if their knowledge was only scanty and ours, at that time, non-existent.

'You gotta tell it like it is. Thaa's raa man. Tell it like it is. You press can tell the world just how it is,' the civilian official looking through our passports suddenly blurted out, wanting to make us see that he not only knew why we were there, but that we should understand what was going on. Not just report another bloody African affair. There was more. Much more. But what? He knew. They all knew. From that moment it was clear that everybody knew that something was happening which would be unstoppable.

He kept repeating: 'Tell it like it is. Tell the world,' and I wondered whether the world would care.

After two hours we were told we could go. We walked around the barrier where the soldier who had stopped us with his gun told us he wanted a ride and that he would be coming along with us. The taxi-driver was waiting on the other side of the barrier. Before we got in, he started to exclaim about how much he had had to pay the officials, the soldiers, to get the car through the barrier.

'Faa' daalar'. Faa' daalar'. Fo' each one o' us. Faa' daalar. It's too baad. Too baad. Life too hard i' Liberia.' He clicked his tongue on the top of his mouth. He was angry. This was not for our benefit. He directed himself at the soldier, whose colleagues had exacted the money from him. But the soldier said nothing. He just sat on the front seat of the car and propped his gun between his legs and we set off, with the taxi-driver shaking his head until his foreign passengers gave him a refund. I wondered about the wisdom of having a soldier in the car as we headed to where the rebels were, past villages deserted by all but the few goats or chickens left behind to amble among upturned pots and into huts whose doors had been torn from their hinges. None of us spoke, and along the road there was complete silence.

Liberians remember that in 1959 the then president, William Tubman, met with the then Ghanaian prime minister Kwame Nkrumah, in the northern town of Saniquellie, the principal town of Nimba county. There, they set in motion the events which led to the founding of the Organisation of African Unity. For Liberians the town has a special significance because the meeting put it on the map and established its international importance.

The soldier in the front seat directed the taxi-driver to a two-storey government building, just past the ceremonial arch which welcomes visitors to Saniquellie on one side and bids them goodbye on the other. The soldier advised us to meet the general whose name, he thought, was Smith, though he thought he may have been replaced by a General Craig since the fighting began. We were escorted inside the building, taken upstairs, told to sit down. The soldier stood staring at us through the sunglasses he had never once taken off.

'I wan' you to wraa' to me. Gi' me your address,' he told me. 'Gi' me your call card.' I gave him my card, and then he told me to take down his name and address. 'Maa' naa' is Sergeant Kpue. You ca' wraa' me a' the barra' in Saniquellie.'

'I'll do that,' I said, wondering if now he had started talking I could ask him more about the war. Then a group of soldiers came up the stairs. With the group was a white man in uniform. He walked past us, pretending not to have noticed we were there, and disappeared into a room. He was red from the sun and, along with his Liberian colleagues, dusty. We asked Sergeant Kpue if we could speak with the white soldier. Eventually he appeared from the room and walked over to us.

'Yes, gentlemen. How can I help you?' he asked. He was wearing a pistol in a holster at his waist. Above one breast pocket was the word: Ranger. Above the other a name tag: Newman. Sewn on his shoulder was an American flag.

'Well, you could start by telling us your role here.'

'I'm afraid I'm not at liberty to identify the purpose of my presence.'

I asked him whether the United States was providing military assistance to the government forces.

'Not as such. Though the United States is honouring its long-standing role within its advisory capacity to the Armed Forces of Liberia.'

'Is this a response to the belief that the rebel forces are backed by Libya?'

'It is generally believed that the anti-government forces have received assistance from the Libyan regime.'

'So what is your role here? I see that you're armed.'

'The role of the US military is purely advisory. We have no intention of becoming involved in an internal Liberian affair.'

'Does the role of Libya make it more than an internal Liberian affair?'

'I'm not at liberty to say. Thank you, gentlemen,' he said, raising both his hands against further questions before walking off. The Liberian soldiers prevented us from following him by using the same raised hands gesture.

Sergeant Kpue led us outside, where General Craig was passing in his jeep. Kpue went to the general and asked whether it might be possible for us to speak with him, but his answer was no. The general drove off. Then a car with four white nuns pulled up outside the building. A big American woman, who was driving, opened the window. The American journalist called her 'sister' and asked what had been going on.

'Oh, it's all excitement today,' she replied. 'The whole town has been queuing-up to look at the bodies the soldiers brought back. They dumped them down at the lake, just across the bridge past the mission. Can't say I'm very keen to see them myself. You should go and call in on the brothers while you're here,' she told us as she pulled away, and the three laughing nuns waved frantically at us from the passenger seats.

The sun was hot. It was mid-afternoon. Sergeant Kpue disappeared and we never saw him again.

We walked down the main street. A tall, smartly dressed man of around thirty walked up to us and said he was the Saniquellie correspondent of the national news agency, LINA. We went into a dingy café together, where the owner's son came back three times from forays in search of beer, only to tell us that none had been found. There were no soft drinks either. Nor any food. We talked to the reporter and everything seemed to get quieter in the already silent café. The owner's children were hurried away. We sat and listened.

'There's been fighting every day, and at night too. Heavy, heavy guns. I saw them,' said the LINA reporter. 'They brought the artillery through the town yesterday, the army, and they' bin firing it unstoppably. Boom. And then a few minutes later, boom. The Mandingo are coming here, frightened, very frightened. They all came from the villages. From Kahnplay. From Bahn. From Butuo. All the Mandingo. They are here now. Many of them. All frightened.'

'Why the Mandingo?' I asked.

'Because they are so close to the Krahn. That's Doe's tribe. They are so close. And the war has forced them to flee. Many hundreds of them. Come to Saniquellie. They know it is all finished for them with the rebels. They know they can never go back. Never, never go back home.' He slowed his speech, then offered to take us to where the bodies had been dumped.

We walked into the centre of the small town. At the main crossroads a large group of people was gathered in and around a house, standing on the verandah, leaning on the window sills.

'They are the Mandingo from the villages,' the LINA reporter said. We went to talk to them. The reporter translated their mixture of English and dialect.

'Char' Taylor people killed many,' the headman kept repeating, over and over again. 'Many die, many people die.'

The previous day they had come from Kahnplay where, they said, the government and rebels had fought a fierce battle. Then the government troops had rescued them, all the Mandingo, and told them to leave the town and go to Saniquellie.

His young daughter was crying as he spoke. Tired of consoling her, the girl's mother threw up her hands in despair and wrapped her long, coloured shawl tightly around her shoulders and passed her to an older woman. The people on the verandah watched the girl as she cried herself to sleep in her grandmother's arms.

'They came at nine in the morning. They surrounded the houses and started shooting at everything. Then they began burning our homes. They used gas to set fire to the thatch, and when we could no longer stand the heat inside we had to go out into the street. And as we left our homes the rebels fell upon us. I saw five, maybe six bodies. My neighbours. They had their throats cut. And then we ran. We all ran. Everybody was running.'

The LINA reporter found a small van to take us to where the bodies lay. On the way we had to go through an army roadblock, close to the road which led up to the barracks. I expected the soldiers to ask us where we were going. Why should they want us to see their victims? Instead they waved us through without even looking to see who was inside the van. A few minutes later we stopped and got out. The reporter led us down a grassy path between trees towards a small pond. Beside the reeds, where dragonflies hovered on warm airwaves, three bodies lay, disembowelled, their throats cut, dumped in the tall grass, flies buzzing around the shining red and pink and purple organs which were spilling out where their bellies had been sliced open. A rusting car-jack lay on the chest of one of the bodies. Blood had oozed from head wounds and dried. Perhaps the car-jack had been used to kill them, because there was blood on it too.

Saniquellie's water supply had been contaminated by more bodies which were lying in the river that fed the pond, so people had stopped drinking it. The reporter told us we should go back to town in case the soldiers came. He left us talking to some missionaries, who asked not to be named. They invited us to stay with them as we would not be able to leave Nimba county before the 6pm curfew came into effect. Over dinner we listened as they tried to explain what had happened, always trying to avoid any suggestion that their own mission had been exposed as a failure by what they knew was going on.

'Since the soldiers came they have been pillaging shops, and stealing goats, rice and money from the local people. And they have been killing indiscriminately. The three bodies you saw near the pond, they're not rebels. Doe is trying to eliminate the opposition, and he may even have rigged the whole uprising for that purpose. But now the soldiers have arrived, and many of them spend their time drunk and scared. I heard about two children who were playing outside after curfew. When the soldiers arrived they chased the two children into their house and shot them in the legs. They are usually around ten thousand people living in Saniquellie. But most of them have fled into the bush, or to Guinea. But it's to get away from the army, not from the rebels.'

The radio station, usually a source of information, played only music.

'No dedications tonight,' said one of the missionaries. 'The disc jockey is Gio. He doesn't want the army to know where he is.'

Next morning a taxi-driver demanded $115 to take us back to Monrovia. He was scared. He gave money to soldiers at all the checkpoints we went through, which we had been through for free with a soldier in the car on the way to Saniquellie the previous day. 'The money for the soldiers – it's all in the price,' he said, but otherwise he was silent, nervous, intent on getting us to the airport.

He took us straight to Robertsfield airport, avoiding the centre of Monrovia.

'The Republic of Liberia forbids the exportation of all Liberian dollars and foreign currency. You have to leave it here with me. How much ya got?' a customs official demanded, his hand outstretched. 'I see that bunch o' notes. Gi' me some.' I handed him five dollars, wanting to be let out of this place. 'Have a nice day,' he said. 'I hope you enjoyed your stay in Liberia.'

After him the baggage-checker made small talk, having watched the customs man from across the room. Where did you go, he asked? Where are you from? How was Nimba county? He saw the notes I had put back in my pocket after the previous hand-out.

'Gi' me faa daalar. Put it in the tray there,' he said, pointing to a wooden tray littered with the stern, soiled face of J. J. Roberts. 'A man's gotta drink.'

2 A Prize for the Gambler

MYSTERY WAS a key element in the story, though for many Liberians it is not mysterious when something inexplicable happens, because explanation is not the same as truth. Explanation is really justification, and if the justification for something is based on a lie its value as an explanation does not diminish. Much of what happened was caused by people lying. Lying, or the accusation of it, is one of the most potent forces in Liberia, and the purpose of politics is to weave tales which will allow people to prevent the exposure of their lies.

Some say Charles Taylor did not personally lead the invasion of Liberia that Christmas Eve in 1989, as was reported a few days later. At that time it hardly mattered to me or anybody else whether he did or not. His name did not emerge for a while after the invasion. I was in England for Christmas when the invasion happened. The entire incident was small, of a kind that, to the Western television audience preparing for Christmas, was unremarkable in the wilderness of West Africa. To Liberians it marked the logical, understandable, rational build up of events which have forged Liberia's tragic history since its foundation. The war had started, but the question of who had led it remained unanswered. Charles Taylor's role was not known, and the reality about him was one of the truths I would go looking for.

On 12 April 1980, the night of the coup which brought Samuel Doe to power, Taylor hid in the bathroom of the Holiday Inn hotel out of fear. Ten years later I was staying in the same hotel when I heard Doe denounce Charles Taylor and his clique of rebels as their invasion engulfed the north of the country.

There was heavy gunfire from the direction of the Executive Mansion that night in 1980. President Tolbert was in his bed being disembowelled by a non-commissioned army officer named Harrison Pennue, who had managed to reach the building's bullet-proofed sixth-floor residential apartments. Out in the grounds of the mansion, Master Sergeant Samuel Doe was hiding behind some bushes, while Tolbert screamed in agony and the coup-makers spilled the history-making blood. By morning, the streets of Monrovia were filled with the low-ranking soldiers from the native tribes who had overthrown 146 years of corrupt, pompous rule by the Americo-Liberians. People celebrated, and two weeks later flocked to the beach to see what would happen to their old oppressors now that Tolbert was dead.

'Charles was shocked by the execution of the Tolbert ministers. He cried. He hid in the bathroom where he went to cry when the executions went on,' said Tupee Taylor, his former wife. 'I told him to hide himself, because the soldiers might think that he was sympathetic to the Congos,' Tupee told me.

Now, when Liberians watch the film of the ministers being executed on the beach, they stop it before the first drunken executioners open fire, missing several of their targets and sending bullets whizzing out into the Atlantic Ocean. The horror befalling the fat old men tied to the poles is not lost on the country, now that it has fought a war with itself. Now, audiences do not want to see the second round of slaughter, when the rifles are replaced with machine-guns and the old men watch as their executioners, their drunkenness deeming them incapable of aligning their targets, approach them and pull the trigger.

Taylor had arrived in Monrovia before the coup, on a visit financed by Tolbert, who had invited his Liberian critics in America to see the country and his reforms for themselves. Taylor's wife Tupee has no reason to know exactly what Taylor did on the night of the coup, because she was not there, though she joined him soon afterwards, when he related his account of events to her.

On the night of the 1980 coup (an occasion which Liberians often treat as similar to the assassination of John F. Kennedy, during which everyone supposedly remembers what they were doing when they heard the news) Taylor was out nightclubbing in Monrovia with Blamo Nelson. Nelson, who was also on the free trip from America paid for by Tolbert, drove Taylor to the Holiday Inn hotel at around 2am, when the sound of gunfire could already be heard.

Next morning Nelson went back to the hotel, but Taylor had gone. Two days later he saw Taylor outside the Ministry of Finance in a jeep with eight well-armed men. They stopped and picked Nelson up and drove to the Barclay Training Centre to see Thomas Quiwonkpa, the new army commanding general, whose troops were looting the houses that belonged to the old regime, arresting their occupants and laying the groundwork for Doe's rule.

Quiwonkpa asked Taylor and Nelson which government posts they would like. Without any consultation with Doe they were sent to run the General Services Agency (GSA), which put them in charge of the allotment of all government property to the ministries.

Taylor and Nelson had been in Monrovia for two months by the time Doe seized power. Tolbert had invited them after they had been arrested in New York, following their occupation of the office of the Liberian ambassador to the United Nations, whose General Assembly Tolbert was to address as chairman of the Organisation of African Unity. They, along with numerous other Liberians – all of whom, except for Taylor, were members of the native Liberian tribes who had been excluded from power in Liberia during the long reign of the Americo-Liberians – were protesting against a new Liberian treason bill and sedition law which banned criticism of the government, and were arrested.

The protesters were grouped as the Union of Liberian Associations in the Americas (ULAA). Taylor was chairman of the ULAA board of directors. President of the organisation was Moses Duopu. Blamo Nelson was secretary-general. Other board members included Gbai Bala, who later replaced Duopu as ULAA president, and Tom Woweiyu. Within a few years of the UN protest they would all be on different sides. Some with Doe because they were from the Krahn tribe, others with Doe because they scented financial profits, others, like Taylor, clashing with the new regime because of jealousy, fear and insecurity. Civil war would leave whatever common purpose they had in tatters. Their split after the 1980 coup was the clearest sign of a future tragedy.

Taylor's arrest in New York on 11 May 1979 was the high point of his career in Liberian politics while in America. According to a fellow board-member, Joseph Geebro, Taylor had recommended buying arms and burning down the Liberian embassy in Washington, during an outbreak of rioting in Liberia in protest at a rice price-rise the previous month.

Taylor had been in America since 1972 when his father, an Americo-Liberian Monrovia judge, sent him to Chamberlain Junior College in Boston, Massachusetts, and then to Bentley College, also in Massachusetts, to study.

In America Taylor did the rounds of parties along the east coast, where Liberian exiles, students and others lived on meagre scholarships. To pay for his studies he worked changing lightbulbs in a Philadelphia apartment block, then as a salesman in Zayre's department store in Philadelphia, then on the production line of a Boston toy manufacturer called Sweetheart Plastics. In 1975, aged 27, he met Tupee at a party in the Mattapan district of Boston, at the house of a friend called Constance Barcon.

'The parties we had were fabulous. Charles was going out with somebody else at the time. And he had another girlfriend called Beatrice Bowen. It took him eight months to court me. I was only sixteen,' said Tupee, who now lives in a smart, expensive house in Abidjan with Taylor's two legitimate children. 'He took me to a restaurant once, in Wildwood, New Jersey. He used to buy smart suits rather than pay the rent. One day we won $1,000 on the dogs, and we went all the way to New York to spend the money. Charles bought some drinks with a $100 bill. Then he bought more drinks, but instead of using the change from the first $100 bill he used another $100. And he told me: "I did that to impress you".'

Equipped with three credit cards and, according to his lawyer, American former attorney-general Ramsey Clarke, an overdraft which eventually rose to $16,000, Taylor travelled from political meeting to political meeting, moving himself into a position of dominance within the Liberian community, capable of exploiting his articulacy and energy to overcome the reticence of his countrymen.

Political manoeuvring within the ULAA provided the Liberians in America with the opportunity to wield the power they were deprived of back home. In 1979 while President Tolbert was on his visit to New York, Moses Duopu, then holding the ULAA's rotating presidency, met the head of state. ULAA rules had forbidden such meetings since the rice riots in April. Duopu, whose victory against Taylor in the ULAA's 1978 presidential elections had created a rift between the two men, was impeached by his fellow board-members, led by Taylor. Duopu had not been trusted since failing to provide a financial report to the ULAA board the previous year. He had said the report was unfinished, and excused himself from a meeting where it was to be discussed, on the grounds that his wife was sick. Board members later visited his wife, who was in perfect health, and it was generally assumed that the money had been salted away. Ten years later the mistrust between these exiles was allowed to explode and Duopu was murdered by Taylor's men after the civil war broke out. He was killed, despite being married to Taylor's sister-in-law, Tupee's sister – a fact Taylor uses when denying that he could possibly have been responsible for Duopu's death.

Internal resentment within the ULAA simmered before and after Doe seized power in 1980. But the coup gave the self-exiled political players in America a real country to play with and real money to gamble. Gbai Bala, a Krahn who became one of Doe's closest advisers, was with Taylor on the Tolbert-funded visit to Liberia in 1980. Bala says that throughout the visit Taylor's half America-Liberian background was the main influence on the way he behaved. Bala even claims that Taylor became a member of Tolbert's ruling True Whig Party during the visit, a claim which has never been proved and which is unlikely, given Taylor's strong criticism of the Tolbert government throughout his trip.

Few people in Doe's Peoples' Redemption Council government liked Taylor. His links with Quiwonkpa, Tupee says, were strong partly because she was herself the chief of staff's niece. On taking over the GSA Taylor adopted the trappings of power which had in the past just brought him a bank overdraft. His critics describe him as travelling in the back of chauffeur-driven government cars clutching a small dog, with up to 12 armed bodyguards, looking more like a tycoon than a minister in a country whose economy had not grown for years. He ran GSA like a fiefdom and became one of the most powerful decision-makers in the government. But his ability to affect the operations of all government departments, by deciding who should and should not have access to the state property under his control, meant he could fall out with all the most powerful people in the country simultaneously. And he did so.

Determined to exploit the luxuries of office at the expense of the state, ministers in Doe's PRC government used their official cars for nights out on the town. They furnished their offices lavishly, and avoided at all costs making any genuine sacrifices in the name of nation-building. Meanwhile, torture and abuse carried out by the army were given free rein. Civilian ministers were subject to military justice, after each received military rank. Major Charles Taylor steadily fell foul of the PRC by remaining outside the coterie of hard-liners which surrounded Doe and for whom the revolution heralded an undreamed-of bonanza of self-gratification.

In January 1981 Taylor was linked with an anti-PRC document and, Tupee says, army thugs came and ransacked their house on 16th Street, Sinkor. Taylor was taken to the Barclay Training Centre, where one of his captors, Geoffrey Bartu, tore the watch from his wrist. Tupee tried to get a note to her uncle, Quiwonkpa, about the arrest, but he was in hospital on the Firestone plantation having an eye operation. Upon his return, however, Quiwonkpa angrily reprimanded the soldiers and ordered Taylor's release. Taylor later told Ramsey Clarke that he was dragged naked through the streets of Monrovia during his arrest, though there are no eyewitnesses to this.

Politically, Taylor also fell foul of Doe and his henchmen by criticising the arrest of students. By government decree 2a, issued in 1982, students were banned from all activities which 'directly or indirectly impinge, interfere with or cast aspersion upon the activities, programmes or policies of the People's Redemption Council'.

Doe, illiterate, greedy and above all totally without real authority over his pack of scheming ministers, was powerless to control the avarice of his regime. Meanwhile he complained about his poverty, relative to his billionaire fellow-members of the club of African dictators. Resentment intensified of an increasingly powerful Taylor, who retained remnants of the desire at least to see a functioning government, long after the bulk of the PRC had sunk into an orgy of theft, drunkenness and systematic human rights' abuses.

Government cars became an increasingly thorny issue. Taylor and Nelson at one point decided that all government vehicles, the main status symbol enjoyed by officials, should be parked in official compounds after working hours. Doe approved, but few if any officials acceded to the order. In January 1983 Doe wanted to go on a nationwide tour, but he complained to Taylor that there were no cars. Taylor replied by saying that he would have a fleet of cars ready in three hours, and ordered soldiers to mount roadblocks to stop and commandeer all government cars in good condition. The vehicles, some of which belonged to members of the ruling PRC itself, were then taken to the Executive Mansion where three hours later Taylor handed Doe a bag of car keys. Meanwhile, numerous government officials were telephoning the mansion with their complaints.

On the potent issue of office furniture, Taylor created a powerful enemy in the form of the deputy minister of commerce, Clarence Momolu. Momolu wanted a new rug for his office, to be supplied by Taylor's GSA. Taylor refused, on grounds of austerity. Momolu complained to the members of the PRC who were from his native Lofa county in north-west Liberia. The get-Taylor campaign started, with the Lofa members lobbying for Momolu to replace Taylor as GSA director while Doe was on a visit to Lofa county. Doe, whose vice-president Harry Moniba was also part of the Lofa lobby, agreed.

The clash led to Momolu replacing Taylor as GSA director in November 1983, and Taylor was demoted to the post of Deputy Minister of Commerce. At the same time Quiwonkpa, Taylor's effective guardian, fled. Quiwonkpa, whose relative popularity, particularly in the army, worried Doe, had been frustrated by the president in his attempt to play a more political role in the government beyond his position as army commanding general. However, he refused the post of PRC secretary-general on the grounds that it was a demotion from his position in the army. As was normal when Doe was met with insubordination, Quiwonkpa was accused of planning a coup and was placed under house arrest at the home of an aunt in Centre Street, Monrovia. From there he managed to escape. On 23 November an armed group raided the Yekepa iron-ore mine in Nimba county. Quiwonkpa was accused of responsibility, though he was not involved. Among the seven people who died was the son of the mine's security chief, Charles Julu.

On becoming GSA director, Momolu immediately launched an inquiry into the agency's finances. Coupled with Quiwonkpa's departure and the heightening tension in the country following what became known as the 'Nimba raid' , the inquiry could not have come at a worse time for Taylor. It centred on investigations into a Taylor-inspired policy of bulk purchasing of goods for government departments. The aim was to buy in bulk in order to cut the cost of ministerial supplies, which had amounted to $40 million in 1980. The practice had centred power on the GSA and reduced ministerial control over the awarding of contracts – the area where financial kick-backs were potentially most lucrative for government officials. Deprived of kick-backs, the officials directed their anger at Taylor. The result of Momolu's inquiry, which involved Blamo Nelson listing all 143 transactions made by GSA since 1980, led to Momolu supplying Doe with evidence of supposed financial impropriety in Taylor's GSA. Momolu held a press conference at which he accused Taylor of impropriety, using the report as evidence. Taylor also held a press conference and called for an audit of GSA.

According to Tupee, who was then in America having a baby, Taylor's friends in the security services were advising him to leave the country from mid-October onwards. Tupee added her voice to their suggestion when she returned to Monrovia. Taylor told his former assistant at GSA, Grace Minor, who would later become a financier of the civil war, that he was leaving. On 25 November he drove east towards Cape Palmas, took a boat to Tabou in the Ivory Coast and then travelled on to Abidjan. From there he flew to Paris. Tupee flew out of Robertsfield International Airport two days later, unhindered because Taylor's absence had yet to be noticed, and met Taylor at the Paris Hilton Hotel where they stayed for two days before leaving for America.

'Of the 143 transactions, only the last one was potentially suspect,' Blamo Nelson told me. That deal, worth $900,000, involved the purchase of spare parts from a company called International Earthmoving Equipment

Inc. (IEEI) of Iselin, New Jersey. The company was to provide the spare parts for machinery through Dhillon Brothers, an Indian firm that was well established in Liberia and whose chairman, B. S. Dhillon, was president of the Indian Businessmen's Association in Monrovia.

Previous government contracts with Dhillon Brothers had led to the company already being owed thousand of dollars by the state. This led Dhillon Brothers to stall in providing the goods until previous bills were paid. Despite Taylor's prompting, they had still not provided the goods by the time he was removed as GSA director, though a government cheque for $900,000 had been paid to them through the Bank of Credit and Commerce International in Monrovia.

The non-arrival of the goods gave Doe's henchmen the evidence they thought they had been looking for in order to pin corruption charges on Taylor; it looked as though the money had been spent without the goods arriving. Momolu wanted to impress Doe. He initially refused to hand over documents listing the companies which had done deals with Taylor's GSA to the bureau within the National Security Agency that was investigating the corruption allegations. One NSA official involved in the inquiry said that the NSA told officials of the GSA that they were all suspected of involvement in the scams and that they were banned from leaving the country. A list of their names was pinned up at Roberts-field airport.

But a full-scale inquiry, like that being conducted by the NSA, was not the idea at all. The whole plan was to get Taylor alone. This would do wonders for Momolu's career, and lead to endless preferment from a grateful Doe, who was at that time embarking on an anti-corruption drive in a bid to attract more foreign aid with which he could enrich himself and his cronies.

According to the NSA official, the agency discovered three cheques amounting to one million dollars at BCCI in Monrovia, crediting IEEI and another company, Grain Coast International. Edwin Holder, a long-time friend and later a business partner of Taylor's, presented himself as Grain Coast International's representative in Monrovia. According to the NSA official, Holder, who was interviewed by the NSA during the investigation, said the cash was withdrawn and handed over during a meeting at the city's Ducor Palace Hotel to company representatives who had arrived from America and thence departed with it.

Nelson, who remained at GSA for some time after Taylor fled and was one of those assumed by the NSA to be involved in the corruption, claims Taylor did have a business relationship with Grain Coast

International, though not with IEEI, and that Holder was certainly behind the company:

'When your friends get into office here you see power and you can cash in,' said Nelson, candidly. 'In the process of doing this some people overlook some of the simple details of protecting your own ... The whole concept of conflict of interest in Liberia doesn't exist. If people aren't angry about your dealings then they're not illegal. It's a crazy country. But I don't remember seeing Holder's or any other Liberian's name in connection with International Earthmoving Equipment Inc.'

The real, political reason for the Liberian government's pursuit of the case was only made clear in confidential letters between the key players who hoped they could gain at Taylor's expense. The tone was reflected clearly in a letter of 8 December sent to Doe by the Minister of Justice, Jenkins B. Scott, in which he refers to 'the subvert attitude of Mr Charles Taylor'. Doe, keen to appear as articulate as his more educated ministers, replied in a similar vein, referring to Taylor's 'subversive attitude'.

In his reply, Doe wrote that the government's efforts to pin the corruption charges on Taylor would be futile unless the US government also assisted. Unknown to Doe at the time this was already happening. The American Federal Bureau of Investigation had launched an inquiry into Taylor and had discovered that he had indeed received money through the transaction. Not the entire $900,000, but $100,000 which, according to the FBI, had been deposited in an account in Taylor's name at Citibank, 399 Park Avenue, New York, by Dhillon Brothers on 13 January 1983, the day after receipt of the first of the planned three $300,000 GSA payments to IEEI.

A briefing paper drawn up by Taylor's lawyer Ramsey Clarke, explained that this Citibank account was

> ... maintained by Taylor in the US to cover unrelated moneys they had received from Taylor in Liberia for transfer to his account in New York. These moneys belonged to a number of people whom Taylor refused to identify because their lives would be endangered in Liberia if the government knew who they were and that they were transferring money out of the country through Taylor. Apparently Dhillon Brothers had retained $100,000 received from Taylor in Liberia, or transferred it elsewhere, and replaced it with $100,000 from the $900,000 on the parts contract. The government of Liberia never claimed the $100,000 was illegally transferred to Taylor. It claimed Taylor took the entire $900,000, a fact disproved by bank records.

The Liberian government was not, officially, able to use the FBI evidence of the $100,000 transfer as part of its own evidence. However, Ramsey Clarke was clear that the Liberian government, America's closest ally in Africa, had its case against the dissident Taylor 'bolstered later by bank records secured by the FBI in an unprecedented effort to assist a foreign government'. Despite the FBI evidence, however, Taylor refused to say where the money had gone or whom it belonged to.

'It's pretty clear to me that Charles was set-up. The FBI knew the money did not go to him. It's possible that some of it was being used to oppose Doe,' explained Ramsey Clarke. Clarke said Taylor never told him who the $100,000 was destined for.

> Charles was bringing money out, but he couldn't identify the people whose money it was as it would have endangered the people in Monrovia. His motives weren't wealth. They were political. They were in order to finance opposition to Doe. This accounted for $100,000 of the money sent through Dhillon. We were able to prove, if it became necessary, that there were accounts to which the money went. But that would have exposed the owners of the money. Anyway, the Dhillon bank account shows they did receive the money they were owed. Also the FBI did acknowledge that the money had gone to where it was meant to go, and the records should show that Charles remained in Liberia for eight months after the cabling of the money. It would have been foolhardy if he had been stealing the money while staying in the country. But the spare parts didn't come. That was the rub.

Clarke admitted that he never saw the Citibank records which proved the destination of the money. He also acknowledged that the money itself did not go ultimately to Dhillon Brothers, but to IEEI, a company he believed had been created for this single transaction and in which Taylor never fully clarified his role, not even to his lawyer.

Doe approved an arrest warrant for Taylor on 19 December 1983, though it was not formally lodged until 2 February 1984, together with an extradition request.

On 10 January 1984 Taylor had written Doe a confidential four-page letter, revealing his determination to take power for himself while effectively blackmailing Doe and his government on the issue of the corruption allegations. This only intensified the Liberian government's determination to get Taylor at all costs.

In a melodramatic attempt at gaining the sympathy of the president,

Taylor explained to Doe that he had left Liberia 'on a health mission abroad in an attempt to prevent my health from further deteriorating as the gravity of the situation was approaching crisis level.' He did not specify the disease, but Tupee told me he was suffering from a skin complaint. The letter continued: 'As I recovered from my hospital bed I had the privilege, thanks to the love of friends in and out of certain areas of Government, of receiving newspaper and other intelligence briefings from Liberia, that revealed information that was a direct threat to my life and existence ... The evidence was clear that my life was in immediate danger.'

In a statement that would have echoes in the future, Taylor went on to say:

> On many occasions we discussed the revolution in detail and disagreed on several issues, especially the mechanism for return to civilian rule. I still remember when you took a decision that persons having political ambitions for [the planned civilian elections of] 1985 should resign their positions with the government. I met with you on three different occasions during the period involved (and you can' t deny this), and made it clear to you I had political ambitions of my own but didn't think I should resign and insisted that you withdraw the statement, but you refused to do so. I knew then that the vast differences in our political view could cause immense problems between us and I would have to prepare for the worst.
>
> There is no question in my mind about my services to the Government of the PRC ... You know very well that I did nothing without specific verbal or written instructions from you or a member of the PRC and now everyone is trying to play 'MR. CLEAN', which you and I know very well is a lie ... Up to this point I have behaved responsibly as I think an ex-official serving in such sensitive position should. I have kept my mouth shut while newspapers have hypothesised and made guesses as to what happened at the agency over the three years under my leadership. You and I know what happened and why. I am not prepared to become the whipping boy, just because I fled to save my life.

Taylor then wrote that Doe should end the extradition proceedings against him, end the block on his diplomatic passports, recall the 'death squads organised to assassinate me', and end the accusation that he was involved in the November 1983 raid on the iron-ore mine at Yekepa. (The secret trial of 22 defendants following the Nimba raid ended on 6 April 1984, with death sentences being passed on 13 people, some of whom were judged in absentia.)

Taylor's letter concluded by saying that if these accusations against him were not withdrawn 'I will have no alternative but to fight back by making public to the world everything I know about the PRC, about your own activities, financial transactions, and that of every council member and all the many corrupt actions that you know I know of. I would not want this any more than you would. You know that I never embezzled any money and also you know that I served [you] well. This is not a threat of blackmail as some may suggest, it is what I will do if you don't put a stop to these lies, just to protect myself and my image.'

Taylor was clearly placing himself as the supposedly innocent accomplice in corrupt activities which he refused to take responsibility for. From the course of the extradition proceeding one thing stands out: the Liberian government never demanded the return of the $900,000 from Dhillon Brothers, nor did it pursue the extradition of Mr Dhillon after he left Liberia in 1983, even though the spare parts were never delivered. This tends to confirm the theory that it was specifically Taylor whom the government was after. His threat to expose their own corruption gave added impetus to their quest.

On 17 February 1984 the Liberian foreign minister Ernest Eastman sent a telex to the Liberian embassy in Washington confirming some of the details in the letter by cancelling Taylor's two diplomatic passports and announcing the government's intention of seeking his extradition: 'As we have been reliably informed that Mr Taylor is deliberately floating around Europe to avoid extradition the government, in an attempt to restrict him his movement thereby making extradition possible, has cancelled his diplomatic passports no D/05379-83 and D/04952-82 rendering them null and void for all intent and purpose.'

Eastman became Taylor's foreign affairs spokesman in 1990 after it became wise to jump from Doe's sinking ship.

In January 1984, soon after the extradition proceedings were under way, Taylor returned to West Africa, to carry out some business transactions during a four-week stay in the Ivory Coast. Tupee said that he was also looking for dissidents from Liberia. The 'political ambition' referred to in his letter to Doe was already emerging. On his way back to America he was apprehended at Heathrow airport in London, where officials had received the extradition request alleging theft of public funds. The British immigration authorities reviewed the case and, on deciding that it was an internal Liberian matter, the country which had in fact been the first to establish diplomatic ties with Liberia after its foundation, released one of Liberia's then most wanted dissidents.

Taylor returned to his smart house at 322 Willowbrook Drive North, Brunswick, New Jersey, where, Tupee explained, they were 'living off savings'. Despite the warrant having been issued in December 1983, Taylor continued to avoid arrest, though without any obvious attempt on his part to conceal his whereabouts. Aware of the likelihood of legal action being taken against him, he prepared the ground.

'One night we were watching Nightline with Ted Koppol, and we saw Ramsey Clarke campaigning for Jesse Jackson. And Charles thought – he looks like a nice man. Maybe I should tell him of my problem,' said Tupee. Taylor contacted Clarke, who was a strong critic of US foreign policy in Africa, and who had been aware of Taylor owing to his involvement in other Liberian cases. On 24 May, a full three months after the first request by the Liberian government, Taylor was arrested by United States Marshals in Boston and imprisoned in Plymouth County House of Correction.

On 6 June an affidavit was posted in support of Taylor's extradition by the then Liberian solicitor-general, J. Laveli Supuwood. Like Ernest Eastman, Supuwood later jumped ship and became Taylor's legal affairs spokesman after the outbreak of the war.

3 The American Way of Life

Had we been candid about the standards of government in Liberia it would have been very damaging to US interests ... Great powers don't reject their partners just because they smell.

CHESTER CROCKER, *former US Assistant Secretary of State for African Affairs (1981–88), Georgetown, 4 February 1993.*

I believe that Liberians had a perfectly legitimate reason to believe that we had a responsibility to take a role in the war.

HERMAN COHEN, *former US Assistant Secretary of State for African Affairs (1988–93), Washington, 9 February 1993.*

We are very concerned about the Liberian situation. We have a strong historical relationship.

WARREN CLARKE, *former US Deputy Assistant Secretary of State for African Affairs, Abidjan, 23 March 1990.*

IT WAS an early evening in February 1993. A Cadillac taxi had swept me from the bland order of Washington to the quaint streets of Georgetown. I was dazed by the normality. This was where most of what had happened in Liberia had been decided, I thought, as the Haitian taxi-driver turned the enormous car towards Georgetown University. I was going to see Chester Crocker, who has retired from the business of diplomacy, his experiments with Africa now reduced to diagrams on a faculty blackboard.

'We had the Executive Mansion pretty well wired. So we knew what was going on in the mansion. Womanising until 3am,' Crocker told me, as we sat in his office. Students wandered across the neatly kept grounds. One had directed me to the university's new red-brick multi-storey block, where courses for high-fliers, potential diplomats, leaders and policy-makers are held in bright rooms with newly varnished desks facing blackboards upon which the intricacies of American foreign policy are outlined and discussed.

'I don't believe in trust in diplomacy. I look at performance. I never trusted Savimbi. But with Liberians one had a quality of dialogue because they really thought of themselves as honorary Americans. This meant that it was very candid. On both sides. During the cold war, diplomacy with third-world states was something like running a singles' bar: they come to New York and go shopping.'

He never once paused, except to say how busy he was, that I could not keep him long, and to ask if I had read his new book.

The post of US Assistant Secretary of State for African affairs is reputed to be more like the post of President than any other within the US government. Because nobody else really cares about Africa, the Assistant Secretary can really do what he likes. Gun-running to right-wing rebels, propping-up criminal dictators, overthrowing leaders with poisoned toothpaste or mercenary firepower have all, at some point, been within the Assistant Secretary's armoury.

On 12 April 1980, when Samuel Doe emerged from behind the bushes in Monrovia's Executive Mansion grounds, and Harrison Pennue had finished dousing himself in the blood of the disembowelled President Tolbert, America had made some new friends in Africa. They might, in Crocker's words, 'smell', but it was a smell that could be doused to keep it from leaving its scent on anybody who got too close. Crocker had to wait another year before being given the fiefdom of the American State Department's Africa office. Meanwhile the beleaguered administration of Jimmy Carter kept the channels of communication open with Doe, so that the cold-war warriors of the Reagan years could inherit a continuity of policy with which they could work or not, as they pleased.

'Liberia was not the object of coveting by anybody. It wasn't as if the Soviets were waiting to come in,' Crocker said. At its height the US embassy in Monrovia had the largest staff of any US embassy in sub-Saharan Africa. The combination of the apparent absence of an outside threat, as asserted by Crocker, with the importance, reflected in these staffing levels, that Liberia obviously held for America (whether or not it was vulnerable to being 'lost' to the Eastern bloc), suggests the nature of the US relationship with Liberia.

'Liberia was our own colony,' said a senior State Department official with long experience of the country. 'We wanted this place to work. Part of it was military assistance. We wanted to professionalise the military. It was a failure. It was an unmitigated failure.'

America's Liberian colony was really born on 12 April 1980. While previous Liberian presidents had enjoyed a special relationship with America, some had also established themselves, to varying degrees, as leaders of note. By the time most African countries were fighting for independence during the 1950s, the Republic of Liberia was already over 100 years old. Tolbert and his predecessor, William Tubman, presided over their aristocratic system of government for a combined total of 36 years, preserving the privileges of the Americo-Liberians, running it through the masonic lodges from which the indigenous tribes were excluded, and oppressing dissent with ease.

But Doe was different.

'He was always a little concerned about his own status,' said Crocker, clearly determined to avoid any hint that it was perhaps reasonable the illiterate, low-ranking and highly vulnerable 28-year-old who became president of Liberia should feel insecure. Doe's problem, and the roots of what have to be seen as the tragedy he created, was that there was no reason to accord him any status.

Like Charles Taylor ten years later, Doe was able to manipulate his way into a position of power, largely due to the absence of another leader. Unlike Taylor, however, Doe learned nothing about politics. Instead, he attempted to develop a personality cult about himself, which had its climax in annual celebrations of his birthday, as a way of compensating for the absence of any real achievements. For Doe, ending 136 years of Americo-Liberian minority rule was something for which he had to believe the country owed him personal gratitude. He had no other claim to fame. While many of those who became Doe's enemies throughout the 1980s continued to feel that Tolbert's overthrow was the necessary prerequisite for their political aspirations, the pain that followed pushed even some of the most ardent opponents of the old regime to feel, within days of the 1980 coup, that everything was going very wrong. It appears to have been relatively easy to slit open Tolbert and to slaughter his ministers. But what then? In fact, due to the absence of any kind of plan on the part of the coup-makers, Doe was really owed very little for his part in the coup. The lust for power among his confidantes resulted in the kind of disputes which forced people like Taylor to run away, and quickly isolated Doe from the more educated people who supported him – people with ideas about how to develop the country.

Unfortunately for Liberia, Ronald Reagan's America did not see things this way. America did not care who was in power in Liberia, as long as he served the American interest. American policy-makers like Chester Crocker are keen to portray this as reflecting a charitable attitude on their part. Their attitude is intended to give the impression that despite the earnest struggle they have in keeping their allies within the limits of humane behaviour, they will sincerely continue to try to work with them. But if, as Crocker appears to believe, there was no East–West battle for Liberian hearts and minds during the cold war, if the risk of 'losing'

Liberia to the Soviet Union did not exist, why was there a need for America to accept Doe and his atrocious regime? What is clear from Crocker's statements is that his judgement of performance did not extend to the performance of America itself. At every step US policy failed. It did not create a democracy in Liberia (which was originally given as the condition of American aid), but in the meantime propped up the Doe regime and continued to give Doe money, pay the civil service, repay the IMF and finance the military.

'We were basically subsidising the government. Every month we would be running around trying to pay for Liberia's fuel imports and arranging bridging loans,' said former American ambassador to Monrovia, James Bishop. Meanwhile, appalling, public displays of the abuse of human rights were being perpetrated and the ground was being prepared for the war that was to come.

'I consider the revolution of 1980 to have been a revolution, and the previous regime to have been an aristocracy. It was the first experience of democracy for Liberians,' Crocker claimed. After the bloody and, many would say, undemocratic slaughter of April 1980, and the subsequent murder of opposition figures and students during the next five years, it is hard not to feel that American policy-makers on Liberia were attempting to justify state criminality on the grounds that it was being carried out by the 'people' as opposed to the 'aristocrats', and must therefore be democratic. Until well into 1990, after Doe's soldiers had committed the most atrocious human rights' abuses ever seen in West Africa, America kept talking to him. After all, he was their partner, even if by the end he was smelling pretty bad.

For America, during the 1980s, Liberia's importance lay almost solely in the form of strategic installations. Diplomatic communications throughout Africa were relayed to Washington via a communications station outside Monrovia. The transmission station for the *Voice of America*, the US government radio station, was sited in Liberia. It has now been moved to Sao Tome. The Omega transmission station, which allowed ships in the Atlantic and aircraft to navigate using triangulation, was in Liberia and was essential, largely owing to its geographical position. From the military point of view, Liberia was perfect. American airplanes flying arms supplies to the Angolan rebel movement UNITA stopped for refuelling at Robertsfield airport *en route* to bases in southern Zaire. Twenty-four hours' notice was supposed to be given for such arrivals, but this became routine. To facilitate this operation, Robertsfield was modernised and the runway improved. Finance for these improvements did not come in the form of foreign aid but from the US Department of Defence. Militarily America could also call on Liberia in other ways. By agreement, the entire Liberian-registered merchant fleet – the biggest in the world – could be called upon to assist American forces in time of war or national emergency.

In return, America had no concrete obligations to Liberia. The military assistance agreement between the two countries did not actually oblige the Americans to do anything. However, following the 1980 coup the desire to prop-up its new partner in West Africa led the US to grant $60 million in military assistance. While $42 million was to pay for improvements in the living conditions of the armed forces, the rest went on military supplies. According to James Bishop, these included 4,000 M-16 assault rifles, light weapons, mortars and light artillery, as well as communications, trucks and the refurbishment of navy patrol boats. Bishop's confirmation undermines claims made during the height of Doe's terror, when American officials would only identify military assistance as having been spent on the improvements in living conditions at the barracks. Possession of 4,000 M-16s, in addition to previous weapons stocks, essentially meant that most combat troops within the 6,300-strong Armed Forces of Liberia had access to a gun, should they be distributed. However, the bulk of US military assistance went to Doe's Executive Mansion Guard – his private militia and personal bodyguard – and the First Infantry Battalion. Both were dominated by Doe's Krahn tribe, and both used their superior equipment, numerical strength and the fear they instilled in the population, to protect the evolution of Doe's regime on its path to criminality.

Meanwhile, the idea of 'popular redemption' professed by Doe, the meaning of which he and his co-plotters could never really claim to understand in any profound way – it was merely their propensity to use terms and theories as an opiate to divert attention from the awful reality – had also to go beyond favours to the military. For this he needed more money.

It poured in.

Soon after the Reagan administration took power, Secretary of State George Schultz met Doe in Monrovia.

'Schultz said after the meeting: "Perhaps I made a wrong career choice if it was people like that I was going to meet. Doe was unintelligible".' This was the way James Bishop related Schultz' account of the meeting. Nevertheless, that year America granted Liberia $52.4 million in economic support, development assistance and subsidies on rice imports.

31

In 1982 it was $62.3 million, making Liberia Africa's biggest per capita recipient of American aid. From then on the Doe regime settled in to a luxurious period of pillaging, funded largely by its cold-war partner. Philip Banks, a lawyer who held the position of justice minister during the 1990–94 interim government, estimates that Doe and his cronies stole $300 million during their ten years in office. Doe kept thousands of dollars in cash in a six-feet high safe in a corner of his office in the Executive Mansion. He also had $5.6 million in an account at a branch of the Bank of Credit and Commerce International in London, which was lost when the bank went under in 1991.

The money, conflict over who could steal most, and the increasingly violent guarding of their own power by Doe and his accomplices, ultimately lay at the heart of the conflict which would defeat them. While Doe employed other tribespeople in his government, their power meant little because real influence lay in the hands of the military, whose key posts were occupied by the Krahn after Thomas Quiwonkpa's departure as commanding general. From day one of the 'redemption' regime, Doe and his cronies killed to survive, and spawned a world of real and imaginary enemies, whose deaths would ultimately be avenged.

'We go by the army law,' Doe told the people from his native Grand Gedeh county during a meeting with Liberian expatriates at the Washington Waldorf hotel while on an official visit to America in 1981. The comment worried his 'countrymen', as the Krahn and most other Liberians call their fellow tribespeople, as they were concerned about what would happen to them if the tide turned against Doe. Accounts of summary executions under Doe are numerous and well documented. But specific events contributed directly to the growing enmity between the regime and other tribes, and steadily created the conditions for the war. In doing so, these events exposed the unstoppable nature of tyranny, drawing the regime further and further along a road towards inevitable self-destruction.

The Nimba raid of 21 November 1983 revealed for the first time since 1980 the urge within the ideologically bankrupt regime to explain its own insecurity; it peeled away any pretence of differences of opinion with its enemies and identified a cause of conflict everybody could understand – tribe. The raid was organised by Samuel Dokie, a former Minister for Rural Development, who fled the country after falling out with Doe in 1983 when he refused to transfer $3 million from his ministry into Doe's personal bank account. Dokie was sacked over state radio and fled to Guinea, from where the raid was launched. Doe's accusation that the by then estranged Quiwonkpa was involved was intended both to discredit Quiwonkpa and also to identify the raid as tribal. Quiwonkpa was a Gio from Yekepa in the largely Gio county of Nimba. Dokie is a Mano from Saniquellie. Quiwonkpa had gone to Yekepa, the town attacked during the abortive Nimba raid, after refusing Doe's offer of a political position. When the raid took place, Quiwonkpa, though he was not involved, realised he would be a suspect. He fled the country, eventually ending up in America.

The raid left seven people dead. As well as forcing Quiwonkpa to flee, the event created an enemy for all Gio in the form of Charles Julu, the head of the Yekepa iron-ore mine's plant protection force, who was also chairman of state security in Nimba county. Julu's son was one of those killed and uninhibited revenge was what Doe would later be able to offer him. At the time, those allegedly involved, 22 of whom were charged with 'Treason, Mutiny, Murder and Conspiracy', were all found guilty, but all but those found guilty of killing were pardoned and duly left the country to become the nucleus of the next coup attempt.

Following the Nimba raid – which Dokie had been warned by sympathetic friends was bound to fail – the next serious attempt was launched by the Americo-Liberian nephew of Clarence Simpson Jr., until 1980 the treasurer of President Tolbert's ousted True Whig Party, Elmer Johnson. Johnson, who had fought with the US Marines in the 1982 invasion of Grenada, arrived at Robertsfield airport with a gun hidden inside a video tape-recorder. He and an American, William Woodhouse, successfully entered the country, but were then betrayed. The house in which they were staying was surrounded by the AFL and there was a shoot-out during which Johnson lost an eye. He was arrested but relatively soon pardoned by Doe. Johnson gratefully accepted the pardon, then left the country in a bid to plan his next coup attempt, just like his Nimba raid predecessors.

Doe's desire to pardon his enemies was part of his attempt to create a statesmanlike impression of which he believed largesse was an important element. According to his former vice-president, Harry Moniba, Doe failed to learn anything from the coups mounted against him.

'Doe was always finding himself in conflict because of the way he had come to power. The executions of 22 April 1980, turned public pressure against Doe,' said one former senior minister who was with Doe until almost the end.

In 1985, a third attempt was launched, this time by the then deputy commander of the Executive Mansion Guard, Colonel Moses Flanzamaton.

Flanzamaton opened fire on a car Doe was driving, but failed to hit his target. He escaped but was captured on 4 April, and in televised interrogations said that three opposition leaders had hired him to carry out the assassination; he also implicated an American working as an adviser to the security forces as being part of the operation. Flanzamaton claimed he had been promised $1 million to kill Doe, to be paid half now, half later. Lack of evidence led to the hasty release of the opposition leaders, while the government said Flanzamaton was to be tried before the Supreme Military Tribunal. In fact, no trial was held. He was executed by firing squad on 8 April 1985.

The event was a blow for the Americans, because State Department officials have now admitted that Flanzamaton was spying for them. They now had nobody in the Executive Mansion to feed them details of with whom Doe was womanising until 3am. Asked about Flanzamaton's role, Chester Crocker said: 'Any great power has both technical and human sources of intelligence. And probably has more than one. That's the way the world is organised. By regional standards in West Africa, Monrovia was a serious mission for the CIA.'

Occasionally, secret intelligence resulted in disclosures which necessitated action to steer their friend and ally away from paths that might undermine American self-interest. And, of course, money was the only way to do this.

In August 1982 Doe had executed his vice-president, Thomas Weh Seyn, after accusing him of leading a Libyan-backed coup attempt. (Weh Seyn himself had murdered President Tolbert's son A. B. Tolbert who had been arrested after the 1980 coup.) He had been critical of close links with America, while Doe regularly slammed the Libyans, because he knew it pleased America. But in 1984 the US learned through intelligence channels that Doe had decided to pay Colonel Gadaffi a visit, with the possibility of renewing diplomatic relations.

A senior Liberian government official at the time said:

> The US was very sensitive to the Libyan presence. In 1984 Doe was invited by Libya to make a state visit. Doe accepted the Libyan invitation. The US didn't like the idea and Reagan sent Vernon Walters to discourage the visit. Walters promised $5 million to Doe immediately without conditions. Doe knew that he could get more from Libya. His officials were already waiting for him in Tripoli. The trip may have led to the re-establishment of diplomatic relations. But after Walters' visit Doe cancelled the Libyan visit.

Crocker said he and his colleagues portrayed Libya to Doe as being unreliable. 'We made it pretty clear to him that Libya just wasn't on,' he explained.

The American tactic to prevent this link being established was unashamedly admitted to by a senior state department official: 'Libya was important. We told Doe: this is the wrong thing to do. It might give these guys a foothold in the region. With regard to Libya we bought Doe off. There was a direct link [between aid and foreign relations].'

The essence of Doe and his cohorts' concerns about the US are reflected in a memorandum sent on 22 March 1983 to Doe by his then Minister of State, Major John G. Rancey, intended to advise Doe on measures he should take if he wanted to keep power after the promised return to civilian rule in 1985. The note read:

> As you requested, per our discussion regarding possible strategies for remaining in office beyond 1985, it is my opinion that several essential steps will have to be taken if we are to minimise the effect such a decision will have upon your credibility as Head of State. Since it is obvious the greatest opposition will come from the Americans I think we should do everything humanly possible to placate them into supporting you, economically and politically. For this to happen however, the following moves must be considered:
>
> 1. Remove all known MOJA and PPP sympathisers from the public eye through reassignment or dismissal from the Government and private positions.
> 2. Re-establish diplomatic ties with the state of Israel.
> 3. Adopt a sharp stance in both domestic and international arenas against Soviet policy.
> 4. Dissipate all domestic opposition through strategy if possible; crush with force if necessary.
>
> It would be expedient to denounce Socialist philosophy and those individuals and governments associated with it including the Ethiopian and Libyan friendship with the Soviets. Condemn all Soviet expansion in Africa, especially Chad, and you will convince the US that ideologies other than Western-based capitalism have no place in Liberia. It may be helpful to label any internal activists as Socialists.
>
> To be totally convincing in the 'pro-American' attitude, it may be necessary to acquire a Foreign Minister with whom the US will be comfortable, a distinction that Mr Fahnbulleh does not enjoy.
>
> Once Liberia receives her blank check of support form [sic] America it

is possible to begin the last, but the most formidable task, the total elimination of potential opposition. As we agreed in our discussion, it may be anticipated that the most vigorous opposition to your staying on will come from Nimba County. You may be assured that the leading voice will be that of your 'friend' Thomas Quiwonkpa ... I am convinced that they are troublemakers who do not hesitate to organise themselves. You may recall that Nimba was the strongest base of the PPP. Nimbaians seem to love politics, thus, the removal of Thomas and supporters from the Army and positions of Government must be gradual and most carefully planned ... Regardless of the risk, I believe you will agree that Thomas and the other 'Nimba heroes' must be totally discredited, if not totally eliminated ... I have no doubt that once these critical steps are taken it is certain that the people of Liberia will overwhelmingly support a continuation of your leadership in 1985.

The letter reflects the complete absence of any kind of political philosophy in the regime, other than the philosophy of clinging to power. The readiness of the regime to do absolutely anything to please the US, knowing that Reagan's America would only see what it wanted to see, meant that Doe could portray his domestic enemies as the 'socialist' enemies of America, and thereby oppress and 'eliminate' them almost in the name of the United States. This repeatedly allowed the Reagan administration to flaunt Doe as an ally when the administration's critics in Congress attempted to distinguish criminality from American national interest.

By 1985, however, Liberians opposed to Doe were reacting with increasing disbelief to the continued American support for the monster they had watched take power. Rumours abounded that secretly America would like to see Doe overthrown, but that it was not acceptable for the US to be seen to be involved. This was not the case. It was the wishful thinking of a population which was losing hope. The hope of many Liberians that secretly America was on their side against their oppressor was not true. America wanted Doe to remain in power.

A key American policy-maker told me:

> We were getting fabulous support from him on international issues. He never wavered in his support for us against Libya and Iran. He was somebody we had to live with. We didn't feel that he was such a monster that we couldn't deal with him. All our interests were being impeccably protected by Doe. We weren't paying a penny for the US installations.

The Reagan administration's contentment with Doe had its most memorable moment when Doe honoured his promise of holding civilian elections. This he did on 15 October 1985.

'I have photographs of the cheating. The ballot boxes were filled before the voting,' says Doe's former vice-president Harry Moniba, who retained his post as a result of the malpractice. 'The Liberian Action Party, which declared itself the winner, was also cheating. [Doe's] National Democratic Party of Liberia cheated more carefully,' he said. This did not matter to America.

Crocker, testifying to the US Senate Foreign Relations Committee's Africa sub-committee on 10 December 1985, said: 'There is now the beginning, however imperfect, of a democratic experience that Liberia and its friends can use as a benchmark for future elections – one on which they want to build.' His comments came after two political parties had been banned and prevented from running in the election, after a year preceding the poll when opposition leaders had been imprisoned, after a massacre of students on Doe's orders at Monrovia university on 22 August 1984 following agitation against Doe by students and academics.

American acceptance of the election result contributed to the view among many Liberians that the country it looked to for guidance must have a hidden agenda which eventually would save them from Doe, but which in the meantime it was necessary to conceal until the time was right to rid them of him.

After the election Chester Crocker said, in a statement to a joint session of the US Congressional Subcommittees on Africa and Human Rights and International Organisations on 23 January 1986, that 'we learned that Doe was considering appointing to important positions in his new civilian government Liberians of proven talent who were not members of his party.' It didn't seem to matter to the US government that officials such as Rancey were throwing democratic titbits to the US, solely in order to prevent any public breakdown of relations while Doe secured another mandate to commit murder and mayhem.

Thomas Quiwonkpa did not understand that fundamentally the United States was happy with its ally in Monrovia, as long as Crocker could continue to find a balance between what he called in his 1986 testimony the 'plusses and minuses' of Doe's conduct. Crocker said that 'no outside observer could be certain who won those elections', yet the US accepted the result. A month later, on 12 November 1985, the very people Rancey had identified in his 1983 letter to Doe as 'troublemakers' arrived in Monrovia, and for six hours Doe was overthrown.

After fleeing to the United States in November 1983, Quiwonkpa had enlisted as a student and lived outside Washington DC, while spending much of his time in Aberdeen, Maryland, a town dominated by American military personnel. Among the leading Liberian dissidents who met Quiwonkpa during the subsequent two years, there is not one who did not believe that Quiwonkpa felt he had US support to stage a coup against Doe. On the part of some, this was wishful thinking. For others, it was used as a way of recruiting supporters for the coup attempt. Boima Fahnbulleh, Doe's education and foreign minister before falling foul of Rancey's campaign to oust officials perceived as unsupportive of American policy, was told by three of the plotters that the US was in favour of the coup. Fahnbulleh, a left-of-centre politician who had been a key member of the pressure group the Movement for Justice in Africa (MOJA) before the 1980 coup, was to have become a presidential candidate if Quiwonkpa's attempt succeeded.

'There were friendly governments interested that something should happen in Liberia. They were looking for somebody to lead it. Quiwonkpa's name came up, and he was keen. There were agencies in the US government who wanted to see something happen in Liberia,' said Tonia King, a former customs officer who fled Liberia after being arrested by Doe in 1982. 'The US wanted Doe overthrown, but they wanted Liberians to do it. By 1984 the US had realised that Doe was bad, and asked Liberians whether they had any organisation which could overthrow Doe. They responded very positively to Quiwonkpa. They sat up to him,' said King, who told Fahnbulleh in June 1985 that he had spoken with and received approval for the coup from the CIA representative in the Ivory Coast.

Fahnbulleh also said King had received approval from Israel, whose forces were training Doe's Executive Mansion Guard in Israel as part of a defence agreement. Fahnbulleh's scepticism about the potential for success was intensified by the mention of Israel, a country he was ideologically at odds with, but which, more importantly, was unlikely to be party to a coup against a leader whose Executive Mansion Guard it was training.

Fahnbulleh's doubts about the Americans' readiness to play a role in the coup were entirely accurate. According to the former US ambassador James Bishop, American officials heard in the spring of 1985 about the possibility of a coup against Doe and that Quiwonkpa was involved. 'We understood that it was going to be much earlier than when it happened. The report was that it would be staged in the summer. We gave the report credibility,' said Bishop.

A senior state department policy-maker has now confirmed that American embassy officials in Monrovia then went to Doe and informed him of the coup plot. 'Because we had reason to believe that he knew we knew and would therefore think that if it took place we were a part of it. We also tried to get word to Quiwonkpa to knock it off,' the official said.

Tonia King initially tried to interest the Ivory Coast authorities in allowing the coup-makers to launch their insurrection from their territory. The Ivorians refused. In Sierra Leone, Fahnbulleh introduced King to the future Sierra Leonean minister of state for presidential affairs Dr A. K. Toure. Toure introduced them to Major General Joseph Momoh, the future president but at that time army force commander, who in turn introduced them to President Siaka Stevens. 'Stevens was very keen to be involved,' said King. But the immediate problem was getting resources. According to Fahnbulleh, the Sierra Leoneans provided all military supplies, and Liberian dissidents living in America raised $75,000 to finance the operation. Quiwonkpa arrived in Sierra Leone, where he soon ran into the head of the American military mission accredited to both Liberia and Sierra Leone, Colonel Vair. As the American military mission in Monrovia is situated in an office inside the defence ministry, the two men had seen a great deal of each other before Quiwonkpa fled from Liberia. Vair, who Bishop described as 'an idiot, who ran the military mission like a brothel', asked Quiwonkpa what he was doing in Sierra Leone. It is not clear how specific Quiwonkpa was, but Vair would have known from earlier intelligence reports that the coup was being planned and that Quiwonkpa was behind it. Given that Doe had already been alerted to a possible coup, it seems highly unlikely that Quiwonkpa's presence in the Sierra Leonean capital Freetown was not known to him. However, Quiwonkpa's meeting with Vair was used by some of the coup-plotters as proof, if only to boost their own morale, of US approval of the coup. In fact, this was not the case and precisely the opposite was true: America was trying both to prevent the coup taking place 'because it would have caused a lot of deaths', and informing Doe of his enemies' intentions.

Fahnbulleh drove the coup-makers to Sierra Leone's border with Liberia on 11 November 1985. 'It was a suicide mission. Quiwonkpa was hesitating, but he was pushed by King [and other planners] who claimed US support,' said Fahnbulleh. At the border there was confusion among the 35-strong group when their logistics officer, James Beah, approached the others in the dark and was not recognised. Two of the invaders, Joe Wiley and Lawrence Wales, opened fire on Beah and killed him. Wiley denies that he deliberately tried to hijack the coup attempt to secure sole power for MOJA, of which he was a member, by undermining Quiwonkpa. 'But most of us thought that Quiwonkpa would be the same as Doe,' Wiley said later.

'From then on Quiwonkpa lost control,' said Tonia King. Within six hours of arriving in Monrovia, where it was intended that Quiwonkpa would go to the Barclay Training Centre to attract the support of the men he used to lead, the plotters had been rounded-up. Quiwonkpa was captured, tortured, castrated, dismembered and parts of his body publicly eaten by Doe's victorious troops in different areas of the city. The plotters who had remained in Freetown fled. America's ally was safe.

A mass slaughter then took place. In reprisal for the coup, Gio and Mano civilians, soldiers, government officials and police officers were rounded up by the Executive Mansion Guard and slaughtered. The US embassy, in a bid to downplay the slaughter in a way that was to be repeated in future Liberian massacres, said 400 people were killed. The figure is reckoned by numerous Liberian eyewitnesses to have been as high as 3,000. Civilians who celebrated in the streets of Monrovia when they thought the coup had been successful were later rounded up by Doe's troops and driven to the beaches outside the city and massacred. Truck-loads of bodies sped through the city from the grounds of the presidential mansion, from where Doe could observe the slaughter, to mass graves outside Monrovia on the road to Robertsfield airport.

Following the coup attempt, Charles Julu was given the chance he had been awaiting to avenge the death of his son during the 1983 Nimba raid. Julu rounded up Gio civilians in the compound of the Lamco iron-ore mine and ordered soldiers to flog them. He used Lamco trucks to transport Gio soldiers and civilians to the Sika valley in the Nimba mountains near Yekepa, and slaughtered them before throwing them down a disused mine shaft. Lamco security guards, whom Julu commanded, led the slaughter. The company, which at that time was partly owned by a Swedish company, Grangers, in a joint venture with the Liberian government, did not even dock the pay from their employees for the time they had taken off to murder and mutilate. As proof of the vengeful motivation Julu had borne, two of those murdered were James and Lewis Dokie, brothers of Samuel Dokie who led the 1983 Nimba raid for which Julu was now exacting his revenge. Similar acts of revenge were carried out against Gios in Doe's home region of Grand Gedeh county.

The hundreds who were arrested but survived the slaughter were both victims of and witnesses to the criminality of the regime. In Monrovia numerous leading opposition politicians, notably those involved in the election a month beforehand, were imprisoned, stripped, beaten, and some of their houses burned to the ground by Doe's troops. In Nimba county, Julu led the torture of the Gio and other tribes assumed to have been sympathetic to the coup-makers. For days, scores of people were systematically beaten with ropes made of electric wire inside the offices of the iron-ore company. In Grand Gedeh, scores of Gios, Manos and Grebos were arrested, stripped and beaten by the detachment of the Executive Mansion Guard which is stationed at Doe's home town of Tuzon. Nobody knows how many were beaten, but everybody who was knew what had happened. They, just like Julu, would wait for revenge.

'In the short run, President Doe's government seems to have the power to govern,' Chester Crocker said two months later, in his January 1986 statement to the Congressional committees. 'A key lesson of the November coup attempt is that the military units that counted – the first battalion and the Executive Mansion Guard – were loyal and effective.' He went on to say,

> There is in Liberia today a civilian government based on elections, a multiparty legislature, a journalist community of government and non-government newspapers and radio stations. An ongoing tradition among the citizenry of speaking out. A new constitution that protects those freedoms, and a judicial system that can help enforce those provisions. The [Liberian] government is committed publicly to that system.

US State Department statistics show that in the financial year after the rigged election and the post-coup massacres Doe's government was accorded $55.9 million in US aid. Doe had reneged on his promise of free elections, but had held a charade which let both him and his financiers – the Reagan government – off the hook. On paper an election had been held, and the Reagan administration could satisfy itself that democracy really had blossomed, despite being condemned in the US Congress, and, later, by victors in the contest such as vice-president Harry Moniba, as one of the most rigged elections in history. For both Reagan and Doe avoidance of the truth was in their mutual interest: 'I don't think we made any special effort to point out what our relationship [with Liberia] was. But here was a guy, Doe, who believed the US was right and the USSR was wrong,' said a key American policy-maker.

America's problem was, of course, that having nurtured its monster, there was the problem of keeping it under control. One of his former confidantes said that 'Doe used to complain to me sometimes that he was just not getting as rich as some of the other African heads of state. He used to say: look at Houphouet-Boigny [of the Ivory Coast]. He has all that money. Why am I not getting that rich?' His annual presidential salary of $35,000 was minuscule beside those of the habitual diverters of foreign aid he took to comparing himself with. He wanted more for himself, and also for his cronies, otherwise they would stop supporting him.

Corruption, of the kind in which Charles Taylor implicates himself and the rest of the Doe regime in his letter to Doe of 10 January 1984, began eventually to irk America. Liberia's corruption was an issue for the American tax-payer; human rights were not. By the time of the 1985 election, the US had given Doe $400 million. By the outbreak of war in December 1989, this had risen to $500 million. This was still less than the cost of relocating all the US installations sited in Liberia, but came to be seen as an increasingly expensive price-tag. Even though human rights' abuses in Liberia were not playing a significant role in the cat and mouse game of the cold war, pressure within the US opposition-led Congress eventually resulted in an attempt to stem the corruption which was proving such a waste of American money.

On 26 August 1987, Doe, the US State Department and the United States Agency for International Development signed an agreement allowing 17 American-appointed Operational Experts (Opex) to take over financial control of government accounts in the Liberian Ministry of Finance and at the National Bank of Liberia. Opex officials were also to be present in the revenue, customs and data processing offices of the Ministry of Finance, the Bureau of the Budget and other key government offices. The Opex team, which produced its final, unpublished report in May 1989, worked on the basis expressed in the report of being 'a last ditch effort on the part of the US to assist Liberia out of its financial crisis'. The report also said that Doe had 'requested outside assistance to help control fiscal disarray in Liberia, and gave the team operational authority to implement management and policy reforms'. Doe was to act as arbiter in any disputes which might arise during the operation of the Opex team.

Overmanning in the public sector as a result of favouritism by ministers keen to employ family members, as well as the total disarray of national accounts in the Ministry of Finance, were criticisms made by the Opex team. But such criticisms are not peculiar to Liberia, and prevail in most critiques made by Western economists when describing the economies of Africa. More significant is the evidence in the report showing how decision-making was carried out, and how, having apparently invited the Opex team in, Doe and his cronies then developed elaborate methods of diverting funds from the ministries under inspection directly to the Executive Mansion.

The Opex report, which looks at the process of decision-making within the government rather than tracing where foreign aid money has gone, identifies the close relationship between members of Liberia's largely expatriate business community and the Doe government. This relationship meant that businessmen, mostly Lebanese, Indian and Israeli, were able to use personal contacts with Doe's 'kitchen cabinet' to strike business deals which circumvented any budgetary controls the Opex team may have been trying to instigate. The report said:

> Lebanese businessmen were among the most influential at the Mansion. A Lebanese-owned construction company obtained the first loan guarantee that specifically by-passed the Ministry of Finance and Opex. This deal established a precedent for other construction companies ... An Israeli firm obtained payments for the construction of a new Defense Ministry directly from the Mansion, financed by diverted forestry revenues collected by the Forestry Development Authority ... The vendor community in Monrovia, dominated by the Lebanese and Indian businessmen, also contributed to the budgetary problem. The vendors who provide goods to the Government often overcharge by two to three times the normal price. The Government was in arrears to most of them, dating as far back as 1984, and the vendors rationalised the over-billing as compensation for lost interest and for the risk of not being paid at all. In this environment, vendors have a strong incentive to offer bribes to get early payment.

It identified eight different ways in which the economic reform team was by-passed and decision-making and finances remained in the hands of the Executive Mansion staff. This led the team to conclude that its failure was due to the fact that Doe's Liberia 'was managed with far greater priority given to short-term political survival and deal-making than to any long-term recovery or nation-building efforts ... The President's primary concern is for political and physical survival. His priorities are very different from and inconsistent with economic recovery ... President Doe has great allegiance to his tribespeople and his inner circle. His support of local groups on ill-designed projects undercut larger social objectives.'

It is rare that outsiders are able to get so close to the centre of power in a tyrannous regime. The report is understated, but the unilateral termination of the Opex project by the US government after one year was conclusion enough of how it had failed. More important than its failure, however, was what it actually revealed the degree to which the regime was rotten, with its finances in disarray and the government apparently at the mercy of the foreign businessmen, who readily exploited both the corruptibility of the government and its vulnerability. While the evidence of Doe's determination not to allow economic reform is made obvious by the Opex report, the issue itself only played a contributing factor in his overall decline.

This decline became impossible to hide after the Opex team departed in November 1988, though the absence of a published report from the team deprived Doe's opponents of a weapon with which to discredit him further. It is unclear why the report was not published, though evidence from the leaked copies suggests that to have done so would neither have served to improve Liberian government finances, nor would it have helped America help its ally.

As Crocker said: 'Had we been candid about the standards of government in Liberia, it would have been very damaging to US interest.'

4 Return of a Renegade

Real power you take. It's not given to you.
CHARLES TAYLOR *in conversation with his fellow dissident,*
Tonia King, Abidjan, 1987.

TUPEE ORDERED herself lunch at the American-style BMW burger bar opposite her house in Abidjan where she now lives. 'It was a Sunday. 15 September 1985. I was nervous,' she said. 'Charles called me and asked if I was coming. You have to come, he told me. He thought I had forgotten. I was really tired, and two-year-old Camille had an ear infection so I took her to the hospital. While I was there Charles called again and spoke with my sister Lucia and told her that he had broken out of jail. She didn't believe him. He rang her back again. Lucia rang me at the hospital and told me in Gio that Charles had escaped and that he was waiting for me at a telephone booth at the Howard Johnson rest-house, on the 15th exit of the southbound side of the Boston to Rhode Island highway, Interstate 95.'

Tupee, who had moved close to Plymouth County house of correction in order to visit Taylor where he had been held for the previous 16 months on the extradition charge, did not turn up to meet him. For five months they had planned his escape, she said, but then the idea began to frighten her. She collected $4,000 as payment for two other prisoners, an American and a Cape Verdian-American, both from Massachusetts, who said that for a price they would take Taylor along with them if they escaped.

Tupee had been to meet her uncle, the renegade General Thomas Quiwonkpa, in Maryland earlier that month. He had insisted that she travel to see him in person rather than talk over the telephone. He had told her then that he was about to leave for Africa. It is unclear whether he told her he was planning a coup attempt for November. Even though he had spoken with Taylor by telephone during the latter's incarceration, it is uncertain whether he included Taylor in his coup plot, despite the timing of his eventual escape which gave Taylor two months to reach Sierra Leone. Whatever the case, Taylor played no part in Quiwonkpa's attempt to seize power.

'My guess is that if the United States' government was helping Thomas Quiwonkpa, then they wanted to help Charles Taylor. Taylor didn't realise that the US was getting him out. But that's what it was,' Taylor's lawyer, Ramsey Clarke, told me in New York. 'Doe was very necessary to the United States, and they wanted to thin out Doe's opposition in the US by getting Taylor out. The CIA want deniability. Charles escaped from jail, came to Staten Island, then went to JFK airport and flew to Europe direct. Friends got him out. I don't think he escaped. I think he went to people who wanted him on that adventure. And the US government couldn't accuse Charles of escaping if they actually helped him escape.'

Taylor's versions of events, as reported to the people he subsequently spent time with, are as varied as the relationships he shared with those people. Taylor told Tonia King that he and his accomplices sawed through the bars of their prison cell for several days, lowered themselves to the ground on a rope made of bed-sheets and escaped into the night. The two other escapees had expected Tupee to be waiting with a car on the outside, and threatened Taylor with his life when she failed to arrive. The three men split up, Taylor then making his futile telephone calls to Tupee. He then went to the house of a Liberian, Eric Scott, where he inserted his own photograph into Scott's passport to allow him to travel undetected. Then he drove to the apartment of one of his Liberian girl-friends, Agnes Reeves, where he hid in the block's underground car park. According to the version Taylor gave King, the FBI visited Agnes and took her for interrogation to the local FBI office. Agnes said she did not know where Taylor was, so they let her go. Taylor and Agnes then drove across America to the Mexican border. Having crossed the border using the doctored passport, they lodged with a Mexican drug-dealing family.

Boima Fahnbulleh, the former Doe minister who fled Liberia when the head-count became too high and who, in November 1985, had driven Quiwonkpa to the Liberian border at the start of the ill-fated coup attempt, said that Taylor telephoned him in Paris from Mexico in January 1986, saying that he had bought an air ticket for Spain. Fahnbulleh suggested that Taylor fly to Ghana, on the grounds that it was unlikely the Ghanaians would extradite him to Liberia. Fahnbulleh, who said Taylor told him he had paid his fellow fugitives $50,000 to get him to Mexico (where his passport stamp was backdated to make it appear that he had crossed into Mexico legally), went to Ghana to meet Taylor on his arrival.

Tupee omitted from her account of events that she was arrested a few days after the 15 September escape, along with her sister Lucia. On 23 September they were both charged with driving the getaway car which allowed Taylor and his 'four' other inmates to escape. An affidavit charging the two women said that they had indeed picked Taylor up, along with 'three' of the other escapees, in the grounds of Jordan Hospital, Plymouth, Massachusetts, less than a mile from the prison, and had driven them to Staten Island. One of the escapees, Thomas DeVoll, was recaptured within days of the escape after checking into a hotel on Staten Island. He identified Tupee and Lucia as the women who drove the car. Another escapee, Frederick O'Connor, who was in prison for assault, battery and breaking and entering, was arrested after getting into a fight after leaving Taylor. Reports of the case do not mention a Cape Verdian. Tupee and Lucia were held overnight, and were then put on probation while their movements were restricted to Rhode Island and Massachusetts. They were to pay $10,000 each if they broke the terms of their bail.

The failure of the Quiwonkpa coup attempt on 12 November 1985, had scattered Doe's opponents. Three camps were slowly emerging, with varying degrees of political and tribal bias dominating the endless debates between the dissidents. From Lagos to Conakry, Doe was steadily amassing enemies who would garner support for their efforts. Months and then years would pass. Relationships between the dissidents would fray. Power play, similar to that which had dominated the debates among many of the same people during their protesting years as students in America before the 1980 coup, would forge the character of Doe's opposition. What was lacking was leadership in the struggle against the regime. The Americo-Liberians had failed to do what US policy-makers had predicted: they had failed to overthrow Doe and return to power. The old aristocrats had proved their impotence. Doe had proved his brutality. A new grouping was necessary, which would reflect the response to Doe's oppression.

'We were moving in the shadows. A lot of people came and went,' said Tonia King. Dissidents in America, mainly Americo-Liberians, contacted each other and affirmed their support for any available moves against Doe. Clarence Simpson, the former True Whig Party treasurer, enthusiastically became the dissidents' America-based fund-raiser. King, who in early 1986 was in America, organised a meeting of dissidents in New Jersey, but key players he had been expecting did not arrive. King was given $5,000 which had been collected, most of it from Simpson. He flew to Abidjan, where he gave the money to a dissident Gio businessman and former director of the Liberian Electricity Corporation, Harry Yuen, who had been one of those sentenced to death then pardoned following the 1983 Nimba raid. The money was to be used to organise the armed invasion which, after the failure of smaller-scale efforts, it was clear had become the only way to oust Doe.

Taylor arrived in Ghana to find the majority of Liberia's leftist exiles – mostly members of the MOJA – entrenched in various plots against Doe. Taylor, according to Fahnbulleh, indulged his taste for high living and spent much of his time in the nightclubs of Accra meeting Liberia's dissident élite. Among those he met was Abayomi Kangor, who, it transpired, was a close associate of Doe and who the MOJA members viewed as a spy for Monrovia. Such were the MOJA connections with the Ghanaian regime of Flight Lieutenant Jerry Rawlings, that Kangor was arrested. Under questioning he said he was a friend of Taylor's, who was also duly arrested. Fahnbulleh, who held the same left-of-centre political views as the Ghanaian leadership, said that he was contacted by the Ghanaian security service regarding Taylor's arrest. He recommended Taylor's release, and he was set free. But a subsequent dispute between Taylor and other Liberian dissidents in Accra led to him being arrested a second time.

By this time, Fahnbulleh had organised for Agnes Reeves, who had helped Taylor flee America to Mexico, to join Taylor in Accra: 'It was all part of my plan to undermine Doe by any means,' Fahnbulleh says. 'Agnes made contact with the ambassador of Burkina Faso in Accra, Mamouna Ouattara, who was a cousin of the future Burkinabe president, Blaise Compaore.' According to Fahnbulleh, the Burkinabe government successfully pressured the Ghanaians to release Taylor.

From Ghana, Taylor went to Abidjan, where a second, less politically leftist group of Doe's opponents was steadily accumulating resources which could be used by a viable opposition movement. Moses Duopu, the former student activist with whom Taylor had fallen out in the 1970s (and who, like Harry Yuen, was sentenced to death then pardoned following the Nimba raid), as well as Yuen, Tonia King, Cooper Teah and one of the soldiers who had staged the 1980 coup with Doe, Major General J. Nicholas Podier, were just some of those already in Abidjan. Most were unemployed, living off occasional United Nations' handouts, drinking coffee and smoking on the terrace of the city's Pam-Pam bar in Abidjan's central district of Plateau.

Taylor went to Moses Duopu's house at Rue Sassandra in the suburb of Marcory, where he asked Duopu if he could arrange a meeting with Tonia King and Podier. Taylor stayed at the Hotel Sielike in the suburb of Koumassi, living under the pseudonym of Robert Williams. King and Podier, along with two other dissidents, Alfred Mahn and William Obey, arrived at the hotel and engaged in another of the numerous, circular discussions about how to overthrow Doe. They agreed to meet regularly. Agnes joined Taylor from Ghana and they moved into another hotel, the Bamfoura, in the St Michelle area of Abidjan's squalid Adjame district. Taylor's modest living at the time led the other dissidents to wonder why he did not seem to have the money that everybody assumed he had stolen when he fled Liberia in 1983.

'All of the people there were poor. Taylor was known to have fled Liberia with money, so he was needed in order to provide finance. But even he arrived without money,' said one of the dissidents with Taylor in Abidjan at the time.

Podier gave Taylor a gold bracelet to pawn, with which he was supposed to have raised 300,000 CFA francs to provide the dissidents with food. Despite handing the bracelet over to Taylor, Podier and Taylor barely trusted each other, and their growing discord reflected the desperation which was typical of the isolated, power-hungry and insecure group of dissidents.

Taylor moved into the house of a Togolese dissident, Armand Julian, in Abidjan's Vridi district. This move brought Taylor into closer contact with the West African dissident underworld. Julian, an associate of the exiled Togolese opposition leader Gilchrist Olympio, had been languishing in Burkina Faso waiting for an opportunity to overthrow the military regime of the Togolese president General Gnassingbe Eyadema. The Burkinabe government was under pressure from Eyadema to deport Togo's dissidents back to Togo. Instead of meeting this request, it encouraged Julian to join Taylor, freeing itself from the responsibility of harbouring foreign exiles at a time when it was in need of friends, particularly among the Francophone countries of the region.

Taylor began to gather his own supporters around him as the distrust between he and Podier grew. He began recruiting a force among the pool of non-Liberian dissidents swilling around the region. According to one of his former closest aides, he revisited Ghana and was arrested after attempting the recruitment of an anti-Rawlings group called the Boys' Brigade. Unbeknown to Taylor, one of the people who had ingratiated herself into the Abidjan group was an informer for Ghanaian Intelligence, known by the group as Ophelia. She had heard about the attempted recruitment of Boys' Brigade members living in the Ivory Coast. A telex from her to the Ghanaian intelligence service, outlining Taylor's intention of recruiting them, was discovered in her handbag by Podier. As Podier was a supporter of Rawlings, he refrained from telling Taylor that the Ghanaians knew what he was doing, thus allowing Taylor to return to Ghana and be held briefly for a third time.

Distrust between Taylor and Podier had further intensified when Doe contacted Podier while he was on a visit to Paris. Doe, who by 1987 was growing paranoid about the number of his enemies grouping together in neighbouring countries, asked Podier to return to Liberia and promised him his old job – that of vice-president. Doe sent Podier an air ticket to Paris, which was handed to Podier by a Lebanese businessman, Victor Heikal – a friend of Podier, who also maintained close ties with Doe and his cronies in the Executive Mansion. Podier went to Paris and spoke with Doe by telephone.

'Doe was pathetic and just begged Podier not to try and kill him and then promised him that he could return to Liberia as vice-president,' said one of the Abidjan-based dissidents who spoke with Podier after his conversation with Doe. Doe later tried to arrange a meeting with Podier, but Podier rejected the idea. He was at that time financing himself through a complicated transfer of payments on the rental of his house in Monrovia, as well as using funds from Heikal, and remained determined to launch an attempt to seize power.

The intrigue was not just confined to Podier. At one point Taylor sent his servant Kwame to spy on Podier. Podier was alerted to this, and he demanded the return of the gold bracelet or its value in cash before he finally split with Taylor. At the same time, Taylor was being harassed for money by an Abidjan shopkeeper, who had allowed him to make international telephone calls for which he had not paid. The shopkeeper, a Togolese called Ekru, had Taylor imprisoned for two days in Adjame police station until his release was arranged thanks to the payment of a 300,000 CFA cheque to police officials. The cheque bounced, but by then Taylor had left for Burkina Faso.

On 13 July 1987, Podier crossed the border into Liberia with another dissident, George Mansua, as well as two Americans. Doe's troops were waiting for him. It is generally thought that he was warned in advance of Podier's intentions, possibly by letter, by the latter's rivals in the Abidjan group of dissidents, though it is not certain by whom in particular. Podier, along with his fellow conspirators, was subjected to the traditional beatings and torture for which the regime had by then become famous. Podier was duly executed and the two Americans, Vietnam veteran Sergeant James Bush and civil rights activist Curtis Williams, were eventually freed under pressure from the US State Department.

In August 1987, following Podier's well-publicised torture and killing, the Liberian government demanded the extradition from the Ivory Coast of Tonia King, Taylor and Yuen. Senior Ivorian officials were used by Doe to pressure the Ivorian government. Members of Doe's Krahn tribe with contacts across the border in the Ivory Coast, and Guerés within the Ivorian government, warned the Ivory Coast president Felix Houphouet-Boigny of the danger of harbouring dissidents from a country with which the Ivory Coast shared a long border. Doe, whose parents had emigrated to Liberia from the Ivory Coast, attempted several times to use this cross-border tribal link as a path to Houphouet-Boigny, but the border Guerés were less than warm in their response and Doe eventually gave up. However, the Ivorians grew nervous about the Liberian dissident presence and took to harassing Liberians in Abidjan.

To add to the pressure on the dissidents, disputes over future strategy continued to divide the leaders, even after Podier's death. Taylor had made his first contact with Libya through the Burkina Faso ambassador in Ghana, who had helped in having Taylor released from prison there. Taylor began visiting Libya and, according to Tonia King, was given up to $5,000 each time he visited Libya in 1987. However, the Libyan link worried King and Yuen, who regarded it as bound to strengthen US support for Doe at a time when Libyan–US relations were at an all-time low.

The dissident group disintegrated into three, one each led by Taylor, Yuen and Moses Duopu. Intense pressure from the Ivorians, as well as the internal disputes, led them all to flee before the Ivorians decided to take action against them. Taylor went to Burkina Faso, Yuen to Guinea-Conakry and Duopu to Lagos, Nigeria.

All these groups needed money, and with varying degrees of ingenuity went about trying to raise funds.

Yuen visited the Algerian embassy in Conakry and appeared to secure support for an insurrection in Liberia. But, without warning, this support disappeared. Internal Algerian concerns and the absorption of that country in its support for the Polisario Front's war against Morocco over the Western Sahara edged Liberia off the map. Yuen, a trained electrician, and Samuel Dokie then looked for legitimate jobs to bring in money. They revamped a defunct company called Soprocig, which maintained generators, and bid for a maintenance contract at the US embassy in Conakry. Just as the deal was about to be clinched, Doe heard about it and told the US embassy that the proceeds from the contract would be used to finance his overthrow. They lost the contract, and Doe demanded both men's extradition. The Guineans refused, and Doe sent seven members of the Israeli-trained Special Anti-Terrorist Unit (SATU) to Conakry to kill them. Yuen and Dokie were taken into protective custody by the Guineans, who intercepted the SATU agents, but they then expelled the dissidents after accusing them of carrying out activities 'incompatible with their status'. In August 1988 they arrived in Dakar, Senegal.

Taylor spent the year following the group's departure from Abidjan collecting a fighting force largely by pretending he had the support of tribal leaders like Yuen. Yuen, whose status within the Gio community has led to him being accused of a very negative, conservative and tribalistic political outlook, could certainly have drawn support from the Gio and Mano in Nimba county. But following the about-turn in support by the Algerians, Yuen had nothing to offer his own people, while Taylor was able to flaunt his offer of training in Libya, from where he was by then receiving sufficient funding to advance substantially his plans for an invasion.

In early 1988, according to Yuen,

> Taylor sent people to Danane [near the Liberian border] to tell the people there that Harry Yuen was with him and that they should join him and be trained in Libya … Then in May 1988 Taylor came through Conakry in his search for a country from which to launch the invasion, without telling either myself or Dokie. The Guineans asked Taylor about me and Dokie, and he criticised both of us, and told the Guineans that he was the real NPFL.

The first Liberians to be enlisted by Taylor were a 40-strong group assembled by Cooper Miller, a former soldier who had gradually brought his followers into the Ivory Coast from northern Liberia by telling the border guards on both sides that they were taking part in a football competition. They were taken to Danane and then transported by bus to the central Ivorian town of Bouake. From there they took the train to Ouagadougou and were installed at a military base outside the city. From there they were transported by plane to Tripoli. When he arrived back in Ouagadougou, Miller was given funds by the Libyan ambassador, with which he returned to Abidjan. There he learned of Taylor's latest arrest in Ghana, following the discovery of his attempts at recruiting the Boys' Brigade. Taylor sent Miller a message from his prison cell in an Accra military camp, instructing him to 'continue the operation'.

A second group of 30 Liberians, led by former Liberian soldiers Prince Johnson and John Duoe, was moved from Danane to Abidjan and then took a train to Ouagadougou and on arrival were flown to Libya. A third group was assembled in Danane in November 1988, following the same route, led by another former soldier, Paul B. Harris, who had been a member of the deposed Liberian president William Tolbert's personal bodyguard before Samuel Doe's 1980 coup.

These three groups were added to by 13 would-be trainees sent from Ghana by one of the ex-MOJA stalwarts and Fahnbulleh confidante, Joe Wiley, who had been blamed for the failure of the Quiwonkpa coup attempt. Wiley had himself been trained militarily in Ethiopia when, in 1980, the Marxist government of Haile Mengistu Mariam had offered the new Doe regime educational scholarships for promising students. Pupils sent to Addis Ababa found themselves on highly doctrinaire courses which led Doe, always sensitive to US feelings, to recall them. Some, Wiley among them, did not return, and they were given military training in Ethiopia. Wiley's past relationship with Quiwonkpa, as well as his military experience, aroused Taylor's suspicions. When Wiley's 13 men arrived in Tripoli, Taylor told the men that Wiley, who had remained in Accra, had deserted them and that they should join him instead. Friction and divided loyalties intensified, until Taylor suggested that one of them return to Accra to see if Wiley had run away. But the Libyans, already exasperated by the Liberians' propensity for power play, suggested that all 13 return to Accra. All but three did so. To rid himself of their presence Taylor, sufficiently confident now to parley with his former captors, recommended to the Ghanaian government that they be arrested on their return to Accra. Consequently they, along with Wiley, were held for seven months without charge before being deported to the Ivory Coast.

Taylor, who had used the pseudonym of Commandant Jean-Michel Some while in Burkina Faso, was in a strong position. His first contacts with the military regime in Burkina Faso had been with Captain Blaise Compaore. On 15 October 1987, by the time his group arrived in Tripoli for training, Compaore had seized power from and brutally killed his former close friend and president, Captain Thomas Sankara. Meanwhile the Libyan connection, established through Compaore, diminished Taylor's reliance on West African leaders, at least for the period of training. It meant he could avoid his accident-prone visits to Ghana, and spend less time irritating the Ivorian authorities, who had become increasingly sensitive to the Liberian dissident presence.

The Libyans opened up their military facilities to the Liberians, many of whom had already trained for the lower ranks of the Armed Forces of Liberia along American lines and who now found themselves increasingly disappointed with what they saw as the shortcomings of the Libyan war machine. The experience of one of the trainees provides a comprehensive account of the training they received:

> While in Libya we did military training at Tarjura base. That included Libyan drill, which most found inadequate, then American infantry drill, supervised by Prince Johnson and Paul B. Harris, done on Fridays when the Libyans were at mosque and the Liberians could do their own thing. Then we did commando training, jumping from multi-storey buildings, and barbed-wire training at the seaside base, which was a former US base before Gadaffi took over. Also we did guerrilla warfare training in Hodrabya, close to the desert. It was where the US had trained soldiers to go to the Vietnam war. US trucks, uniforms and huts had been left behind there when the US left the base, which was commonly called 1st September. At this base the Chadian war prisoners were kept. We gave them some of our green jackets to allow them to escape, though this only became known later on. Taylor wanted to recruit Chadians to fight with them against Doe and some of them did go with Taylor back to Liberia. When we weren't training some of us spent time in the base library reading books by Che Guevara, Karl Marx, Mahatma Gandhi and Fidel Castro.
>
> There were 29 nationalities training there, among them Madagascans, Haitians, Brazilians, black South Africans, Central Africans, Zaireans, Sudanese, Ugandans doing aviation studies, Gambians, Martiniquans, Congolese, Sumatrans, Colombians from the M-19 organisation, Sri Lankans (led by a colonel who was planning to overthrow Rajiv Gandhi), and Tamil Tigers based at Mataba, which was the revolutionary office and was called Alba by the Libyans. Also at that time Idriss Deby's Chadians were there, some of whom said they were from Centrafrique but were in fact Chadians. Even anti-Compaore Burkinabe were there training after infiltrating the camp. But Taylor helped expose them, which strengthened his friendship with Compaore.

As with the trainees, the nationalities of the trainers reflected the attraction Libya held for dissidents from the oppressive regimes of Africa and elsewhere. While most of the trainers were Libyan, soldiers and rebels from other countries played a major role in training the numerous armed groups who made their way to Tripoli. Head of the Mataba training-base was Moussa Kusa, though most contact between the Libyan hierarchy and their apprentices was made through his deputy, Dr Moktar. The chief training-officer was another Libyan, Mohammed Hassem, a weapons' specialist, also responsible for training Gadaffi's personal bodyguards and nicknamed 'Wicked' by the Liberians. Lieutenant Joseph Magabe, a Zairean, was the second planning and training officer who gave the Liberians lessons in map reading and reconnaissance. The teaching of military tactics and manoeuvres was run by Abudadi, another Libyan, commonly called 'Desert Lion', who had blackened his skin and fought with the Ugandan president Yoweri Museveni during the overthrow of Tito Okello's regime in January 1986. As youthful as some of the Liberians was a 17-year-old Libyan anti-aircraft weapons' specialist named Glada, who had fought the Chadians in the disputed Aouzou strip and wore a black star tattoo on his shoulder which designated him as a warrior. Among the non-Libyan instructors was a Maltese named Amore, who taught sabotage and counter-sabotage techniques, and a Ghanaian known simply as Mohamed who acted as an Arabic–English interpreter.

For battlefield training the Liberians spent their days at the Halaka. As the Liberian former trainee recalled:

> The Halaka was a circle inside the desert camp and was basically used for exercises and learning hand-to-hand combat and barbed-wire training with live ammunition. No Liberians were injured or killed during this, but Sumatrans were killed. Holmes navy base bordering Egypt and near to Saibar military base was where we did naval training. There we lost a man called Ernest Wemer, who drowned when he was dumped from a ship and told to swim back to shore. He was almost on the shore when the instructor deliberately disabled him. He was alive when his body was retrieved but he bled from his nose when brought on the shore. He died in hospital, where his body has been preserved.

Despite having secured the backing he needed for his group, as well as an apartment for himself in the Mataba base, a room at Tarjura and a new pseudonym, Charlie Liberia, Taylor was still fighting rival Liberian dissidents for unchallenged leadership of the eventual move against Doe.

Another Libyan, Mohammed Tallibe, was in charge of the 200 Sierra Leoneans who had drifted to Libya, as well as having overall charge of the Liberians. Taylor preferred to deal with Dr Moktar, whom he had convinced that he was the rightful leader of the planned insurrection against Doe. For Taylor the main irritation was the arrival of 100 of Boima Fahnbulleh's supporters, who were eager for the same type of training upon which Taylor's 168-member group had already embarked. Tallibe fell out with Taylor because the Libyans accepted the Fahnbulleh group. This annoyed Taylor enormously as he knew that Fahnbulleh had substantial political credentials, as well as credibility in the eyes of other regional regimes, to whom Taylor himself was a relative unknown.

'Taylor had told the Libyans that he would be in Liberia by September 1988 to launch the invasion. Taylor was frustrated. The Libyans were frustrated. They were already frustrated by [the Gambian dissident] Samba Sanyang having been in Libya for seven years,' said Fahnbulleh, who met Taylor in Libya during the training period. According to Fahnbulleh, the Libyans wanted all the Liberian groups to join as one. This they refused to do. 'The Libyans wanted to give Blaise [Compaore] the impression that they saw Taylor as the next president of Liberia. The Libyans needed to show Blaise that they supported him after he had got rid of Sankara, who they saw as too independent,' said Fahnbulleh, who eventually pulled his group out of Libya. His supporters remain, in 1997, spread across West Africa in preparation for a possible future conflict.

Taylor visited the trainees sporadically, though they never saw him doing any military training. 'He already knew about how to assemble arms, and would come into the classes to see how the training was going,' said one of his former aides.

> He always wore military dress, and would stay for a month or a few weeks and then disappear, sometimes travelling in a 6-seater Peugeot with a Libyan driver. Taylor met Gadaffi on the Revolution anniversary, along with Compaore, Sam Nujoma and many others. When he arrived it was with Tom Woweiyu, who used the pseudonym of Bill Smith or Thomas Smith and travelled on a forged Liberian *laissez-passer* with the forged signature of the Liberian consul in Abidjan, which meant he did not have Burkinabe or other stamps in his passport. Woweiyu lectured us on socialism. He visited Libya twice using discount air tickets he got from a brother-in-law who works with Panam. He gave lectures both times he came, but he was very paranoid about being there. He stayed a week each

time and was interested in looking at the remains of the US presence at the base, particularly an oil pipe which showed that the US had been illegally drilling oil within the perimeter of the base.

Intrigue also threatened to undermine Taylor. While he was in prison in Ghana during 1988, following the exposure of his attempted recruitment of Ghana's anti-Rawlings Boys' Brigade, some of the first group of Liberians to arrive in Libya began plotting his overthrow. The 40 Gio recruits from Nimba, notably Prince Johnson, Cooper Miller, Augustus Wright and William Obey, swore allegiance to their plot by killing sheep, removing the hearts, pricking them with 40 needles and covering them with 40 kola nuts. They swore to the sheep's hearts and kola nuts and marked their arms with a star using a red-hot poker. The 40 men informed the Libyans that Taylor was not their rightful leader and that he was connected to the CIA, but the Libyans refused to believe them. A document drawn up by the 40 men, accusing Taylor of being in the CIA and of not being their actual leader, was passed on to Taylor by a Libyan named Yusuf, who was told that Prince Johnson had written it. However, further investigation revealed that it was written by a former lay preacher who had joined the rebels named Enoch Dogolea.

Taylor, after his release from Ghana and arrival in Libya, heard about the attempt to overthrow him from William Obey, a cousin of Prince Johnson. Taylor insisted that he would be president, and made Cooper Miller future vice-president and Augustus Wright future public works minister in a Taylor-run Liberia in order to keep them quiet.

All the Liberians graduated from the Libyan training course on 6 May 1988. But the plans for the invasion were still barely off the drawing-board. Most of the 168 stayed in Libya for another year to do naval training and to act as personal bodyguards for Gadaffi and his henchmen. Taylor's initial plan was to transport his troops by boat from Sierra Leone to Robertsport in Liberia, and then to meet up with a cousin who was stationed at a military barracks at Tubmanburg. Taylor returned to Burkina Faso, where Compaore provided him with a villa, a telephone and a listing in the Burkina Faso telephone directory under the name of Charles Taylor. From here he began looking for a convenient springboard from where to launch the invasion.

Using a Burkinabe passport in the name of Jean-Michel Some, he first travelled from Burkina Faso to the Guinean capital Conakry with Cooper Miller and Augustus Wright, and then went overland to Sierra Leone in order to ask President Joseph Momoh whether the invasion could be launched from his territory, as Thomas Quiwonkpa's had been in 1985. But he was prevented from entering Sierra Leone when border guards grew suspicious about the large amount of American dollars he was carrying in a suitcase. He returned to Conakry and then went to the airport. There he, Miller and Wright were spotted by Harry Yuen's wife, who knew Miller and Wright. Aware that Taylor was using fighters recruited by her husband, she told Yuen. Taylor heard that Yuen knew of his presence and panicked because he did not want Yuen and Dokie to know what was going on behind their backs, and flew to Freetown, Sierra Leone before they could catch up with him.

They were driven from Freetown airport in a hired Mercedes by Prince Barclay, another Liberian dissident who was living in the city, who said he would put Taylor in touch with the head of the Sierra Leonean state security division. During a meeting, Taylor told the police he wanted to see President Momoh, but this raised suspicion and they were all, including Prince Barclay, imprisoned at Pademba Road jail and then deported to Abidjan.

Taylor told his accomplices not to mention their imprisonment to the other dissidents. But Miller told Tonia King, who went to see Taylor and told him that he should listen to advice and that he should not have gone to Sierra Leone. Taylor was angry with Miller, and the lack of trust between them resulted in Taylor's request to the Burkinabes that they arrest Miller on his return to Ouagadougou. After his arrest, Miller wrote to the US embassy in Ouagadougou saying that Taylor was going to fight against US interests in Liberia. The letter was intercepted and both Miller and Augustus Wright were apparently tortured in an underground prison in Ouagadougou. Both were left in prison and were only released in May 1990 at the request of the United Nations representative in Ouagadougou. Meanwhile Taylor returned to the Tarjura base in Libya.

The Liberians remained in Libya until July 1989. Taylor's problems in finding a friendly country bordering Liberia mounted. In 1989 he revisited Freetown, along with Tonia King and one of their Libyan contacts. They met senior Sierra Leonean officials and, according to King, gave the impression that they were working with Fahnbulleh, who was close to the Sierra Leonean hierarchy. This was not true, and the Sierra Leoneans brought Fahnbulleh to the meeting from his house nearby:

'The problem was that Fahnbulleh could not be informed of our plans because he wasn't involved,' said King. 'Taylor didn't want Fahnbulleh involved. It was then that I realised that Taylor didn't want a democratic organisation, and in fact just wanted something for himself.' Taylor left Sierra Leone determined to have his revenge on Momoh by eventually allowing the Sierra Leonean dissidents who joined him to invade their country from the territory he came to control in Liberia.

Despite the absence of a final destination, the recruits in Libya began leaving. Some flew from Tripoli via Paris and landed in Burkina Faso in July 1989, others flew direct to Ouagadougou. Officers of the National Patriotic Front of Liberia (NPFL), as the rebel group was by then being called, stayed in Ouagadougou's City Number Two district, while ordinary recruits stayed at the Stadium Hostel until they were told to move toward Liberia for the invasion. During the stopover, Taylor exploited the obsessive fear of 'juju' prevalent among the Gio and Mano tribes by demanding of 25 key commanders that they swear allegiance to him. At a ritual, which was overseen by Taylor and Agnes Reeves, a sheep was killed and its blood mixed with an unknown black powder as well as gin, which all those present had to drink while saying 'If I go against you I will die in war.'

All the NPFL had left Burkina Faso by the first week of November 1989, though more recruits were still being brought from the Ivory Coast. The police in the central Ivorian town of Bouake at one point stopped and arrested 25 of the new recruits from travelling because some of them did not have identity cards. They were forced to sweep the floor of the police station before eventually being released. They stayed in Bouake for another day 'to enjoy themselves before going to die', one of the recruits said. They were then taken immediately to Danane in north-west Ivory Coast where the NPFL commander Moses Black gave them money so that they could disperse among the border villages.

Meanwhile Taylor had gathered his commanders in Abidjan, among them Prince Johnson, Samuel Varney, Targan Wantee and Joseph Kayzoh. In all, 40 had arrived by plane at Abidjan's Port-Bouet airport from Ouagadougou on 22 November 1989. At Port-Bouet they successfully bribed the customs officials and police to let them through the airport without being asked any questions. From Abidjan they left for the Liberian border, arriving at the village of Bin Houye in early December.

The idea was to push on two fronts, from Bin Houye and Guinea. In Bin Houye, on 21 December, as they prepared for the push, Taylor ordered all his troops to take a stone and swear over a pan of water that 'If anybody goes against me or plans to kill me, they will die.'

That day 14 of the rebels, including Paul B. Harris, crossed unarmed into Guinea from the Ivory Coast. They were to receive weapons when they arrived at the Liberia–Guinea border, where the Guinean district commissioner had promised Taylor weapons and was expecting a large pay-off in return. By nightfall on 21 December the 14 had reached the Guinean provincial capital of N'Zerekore. They waited for Taylor, but he had been stopped at the Ivory Coast border and did not arrive with the money for the district commissioner. Instead, he sent orders to Harris, via a go-between named Michael Pagay, that they should continue to move towards Liberia even though they had no weapons.

Next day, at a village near the Guinean town of Diecke, the group heard the sounds of a meeting of the secret Poro society (a secret brotherhood which has its own spirits, history and rituals through which communication is made to spiritual ancestors). John Dolo and Saye Boayou, both members of the Poro society, were sent to the village to see what was going on. Dolo and Boayou talked with the village chief, who gave them food and asked them what they were doing. They said they had been passing with some friends, and that they were going to see the district commissioner, not knowing that the commissioner was in a village they had already gone through. This aroused the suspicions of the chief who sent somebody to tell the police about 14 lost Liberians on their way to the border. The police arrived from the town of Yomou and arrested them all. At Yomou police station one of the 14, Samuel Lartor, confessed that he was a soldier. Guinean soldiers were called and they were taken to Yomou military barracks where they were tied up and beaten before being sent, on 26 December, to the military barracks at N'Zerekore.

At the barracks the commander apparently asked them: 'Are these the footballers?' and everybody said yes. The commander appeared not to have been part of the pact with the district commissioner, who had agreed to provide the NPFL with arms in the deal arranged by Taylor's confidant, the Togolese dissident Armand Julian, and a Guinean–Liberian businessman, Moussa Cissé. All 14 were taken to the police station where they were squeezed into a small room, photographed, asked for their documents and then escorted under armed guard back to the Ivory Coast.

While the 14 were attempting to pierce through Liberia's border with Guinea, Prince Johnson led a small group across the border from the Ivory Coast straight into Liberia. They crossed from Bin Houye with two single-barrel shotguns and made their way towards the town of Butuo, where the AFL had a barracks and a plentiful supply of weapons.

Key to Prince Johnson's success in pushing into the country was the support he secured from the Gio villagers. The Gio tribe is divided into three. The pure Gio comprise the largest group, second in size is the Gio-Yorm group, and third is the Gio-Bewally. All three were represented in the NPFL, but by heading for his home area of Gio-Yorm, Prince Johnson was able to appeal to his own people for support. This they did, allowing him to push to Butuo, and thereby almost cut himself off from his supply route in the Ivory Coast. The plan had been to reinforce Johnson's group, but within days of crossing the border Johnson effected the split with Taylor which he had threatened since the coup attempt against him in Libya.

Simultaneously, the third prong of the offensive upon which Taylor had finally decided, collapsed as disastrously as the push from Guinea. As well as the invasion from outside, Taylor had decided to infiltrate people into Monrovia. They were all arrested after giving themselves away. Paul Weahya, Jesse Gbuargnue, J. Wemmie Zota, Wemem 'Zaizee' Karpeh, Alfred Some, George Nueh and Morris Kolliewood were made to confess who they were on Liberian state television, when they denounced Taylor and his Libyan connections to the delight of the Doe regime which, at that time, had little idea of what was really happening along its northern border.

The 14 fighters deported from Guinea returned to Danane, where they tried to contact Taylor by going to Moussa Cissé's house in the town. They discovered that Taylor and others had been arrested by the Ivorians after cross-border shooting had erupted near the Ivorian town of Zouan Hounien and AFL (Armed Forces of Liberia) soldiers had fired at rebels retreating across the border. Somehow Taylor had managed to escape and flee, though not before leaving behind a briefcase which contained maps, operational documents and photographs which were handed over to the Ivorian authorities.

Taylor fled to Abidjan with Armand Julian, leaving some of his troops with the view that he had deserted them in panic. From there he went to Burkina Faso and sent Agnes with 200,000 CFA and some shotgun cartridges to Danane on New Year's Day. Meanwhile in Danane the Ivorians, fearing that fighting would spill across the border, were arresting scores of Liberians, among them some of the NPFL's main commanders including Putu Major, James 'Border Patrol' Quiyee, Samuel Lartor, Benjamin Cooper and other new recruits. Agnes fled to Bouake and then joined Taylor in Ouagadougou.

The shortage of weapons then became Taylor's major problem. The Libyans had waited for him to prove that he could launch an invasion.

Now they had some degree of proof, though the arrests by the Ivorians and the failure of the Guinea and Monrovia attacks threw the whole escapade into doubt. Prince Johnson had driven AFL troops back as he had advanced. The surprise attack on Butuo had provided the NPFL with arms from the barracks, and given Prince time to consolidate his positions while fighting eruped in villages close to the border.

It was not until early March that Armand Julian went to Ferkesse-dougou to pick up the first batch of arms from Burkina Faso. The arms were hidden inside a lorry filled with yams which Julian told the Ivory Coast customs were for refugees at the Liberian border. The consignment was arranged without the knowledge of Compaore, and was provided by Jean-Pierre Pane, the military commander in the southern Burkinabe town of Bobo-Dioulasso. The shipment included 57 AK-47 assault rifles, 157 Berretta machine-guns, 150 hand grenades, 42 General Machine Guns (GMGs), and 27 Rocket Propelled Grenades (RPGs). These weapons were taken to Zouen Hounien and hidden behind the village's Catholic mission before being taken into Liberia by NPFL troops who had secured areas just across the border around Gborplay, a small village which became Taylor's base when he himself entered Liberia.

5   A Journey to the North

IRON-ORE trickled then poured then thundered from the goods wagons. A steel hawser pulled the wagons one by one along the rail track, into the grip of a circular vice which lifted them off the ground. Pistons hissed as the wagons were dragged into the grip of the vice with a deafening bang. Locks clicked shut around the wheels as the wagon began to turn over and the ore inside spewed out into a funnel, feeding conveyor belts which rose thirty feet above ground and clattered out over the long grass and derelict huts and red-earth road of the goods yard, to a ship waiting at Buchanan's quayside. The ship, already weighed down heavily with Liberian ore, lay ready to steam out onto the Atlantic Ocean, which was calm and clear to the horizon, unmarked by the lights of ships steaming along the West African coast. Away from the emptying goods wagons, the ore conveyor squeaking overhead broke the silence of the warm, damp night, and cast a long silhouette across the darkening sky.

'What the fuck are you doing in Liberia? I have spent the last twelve hours trying to find you, and then I am told you're in Liberia – only after I ring around the other newspapers of London. Who the hell do you think you are, going off like that? It's the first rule of journalism that you never, repeat never, go off without first telling the desk where you are going, and only then if they approve. What do you think you're doing there anyway? It seems to me that you are irresponsibly intent on playing the war correspondent in another nasty little African conflict, without asking anybody's permission and without telling anybody where you're going. Now, what do you have to say?'

Michael Holman, my editor at the *Financial Times* in London, waited for my response. A waiter in the café which adjoined the Holiday Inn hotel had come to find me. I was sitting in one of the café's American diner booths when he came to say there was a telephone call.

'International,' he said, to hurry me. I followed him to the hotel reception, where three months earlier I had sat watching television with the hotelier and his children, a week after the Christmas Eve invasion. Now it was 3 April 1990, and a Sunday newspaper in London had asked me to go to Liberia to see what had happened in the meantime. I had not thought to tell Michael that I was going, as by then he had made it clear that neither he nor the *Financial Times* were interested in Liberia, where the war was now raging. When another newspaper asked me to go there, I had leapt at the chance of being able to leave Abidjan for a while, to see something else.

I could not reply to Michael. I had no idea what to say. All my reasons for being in Liberia, for not thinking to tell him I was going there, were reasons that have only come clear since. I had no idea what he could rightly expect of me, or what I could rightly tell him. I was new to this. I was brought up to believe that people in authority should be deferred to. I was speechless and humiliated.

He asked me who I was there with, and I said that two other correspondents had been on the same plane from Abidjan and that they were hiring a taxi to Saniquellie and the north.

'As you are there you may as well stay there. But you will not be going anywhere by taxi. It's far too dangerous. What I have decided is that you will go to Yekepa iron-ore mine and write me eight hundred words on the joint venture project. But you will not be going in any taxis with the other correspondents. I will arrange for you to be taken there by the iron-ore company. I will organise this from London, and will ring you back in one hour, when I expect you to be at this telephone number.'

The line went dead.

I felt numb, and was glad that I was alone in the hotel. I went back to the café to finish my plate of food. I thought of ordering beer and getting drunk, but instead I ordered Coke and sat staring into the long, dark space of the café. Somebody sat down opposite me, even though there were plenty of empty seats. I could barely talk, and eventually she said 'well, I'm going now,' and left me alone again.

Angry and confused, I asked myself what I needed to do to feel the confidence that would have allowed me to reply to Michael. I felt like crying, but people would have stared, and the whores would have taken it as a cue to pounce. I waited for the telephone to ring, and then it did and the waiter came over and said 'International', and I went up the three steps to the reception.

'You will contact Mrs June O'Connor at the Limco iron-ore company office which is at Pan-African Plaza in Monrovia. From there you will be taken to Buchanan to the company compound where you will stay overnight. Then you will be taken on the iron-ore train to Yekepa. And

I expect eight hundred words on the issues we have discussed. Is that clear? And you will not be taking any taxis.'

His words have remained etched on my mind ever since, because, rarely with words, they changed everything. I replaced the telephone receiver. It was as if somebody had decided to drive home the message that whatever I tried to do with my life, I was always going to be stopped. Do not think that just because you have read about other people doing what their imagination tells them, that you can do the same; this seemed to be the message. It was a blast of cold English air, which no distance seemed great enough to escape.

I called June O'Connor and then took a taxi round to her office. The building, owned by the Libyans and one of the tallest in Monrovia, overlooked the Executive Mansion and the sea. A driveway looped round to its entrance, and I walked up the stairs to the wood-panelled offices of the Liberian Mining Company. Chauncey Cooper, assistant to the company chairman Cletus Woterson, met me, sat me down, talked about iron ore, his plans for my trip, and introduced me to Mr Woterson. We agreed that I would come back the next day at 2pm to drive to Buchanan.

In the evening I met the two correspondents who were taking a taxi to the north, Elizabeth Blunt of the BBC and Robert Mahoney of Reuters. We met in a restaurant and ate with the *Daily Observer* editor and local Reuters correspondent, Stanton Peabody, and a delegate from the International Committee of the Red Cross. Peabody smiled and laughed a great deal, which unnerved me. The rebels were advancing through the country. Monrovia was awaiting news. There was nothing to laugh or smile about. I told Blunt and Mahoney that I was going to the mine and that my editor had no interest in the war. I felt sick with despair as I told them. Next day I left by car to Buchanan with Chauncey Cooper, and Blunt and Mahoney took their taxi to the north.

After night fell we left the groaning wagons as they edged along the length of the steel hawser which dragged them to be tipped and emptied. Up some wooden steps on the edge of the harbour a lone wooden building adorned with fading Coca-Cola flags stood out white against the sky. The windows glowed a faint orange. Curtains covered the windows. Inside, tables were set for scores of diners, but only two were taken. We sat, Chauncey Cooper, the gruff engineer, Ulf Henig, who had shown me round the yard, and some Indians. The restaurant was run by some Chinese, who displayed the menu, listed the evening's specials, smiled, said welcome, in this place where I did not want to be. Later,

Chauncey introduced me to Alexander Kuilu, who was going on the train to Yekepa to start a new job at the mine. After dinner we were both shown to a stark company chalet in the compound, and given beds, and slept.

I woke at 5am. The train was due to leave at six. Chauncey was still sleeping and Alexander and I went to his chalet which was next to ours to wake him. We drove to the rail terminal. It was cold. The track stretched to infinity. The wagons were being moved by an engine we could neither see nor hear, but which sent a domino rumble down the line as it tugged at the empty, rusting wagons. We sat in the red-brick station, then the engines appeared along the track and the driver told us to get into the last of the three cabs which, attached together, pulled the massive weight of the train.

At six we left, the train pulling out of the silent station into the trees. We perched, still half asleep, on the swivelling driver-seats, looking out over the thickening forest as the compound floodlights grew dimmer and the train's horn boomed through the early morning.

I slept, and dreamed and day-dreamed. I felt lost. In my mind I talked to the person to whom I wanted to tell this story, but I knew she was neither listening, nor even caring where I might be. Nor did I care; I was just on a train, in the hands of somebody three engines ahead of me, blasting through the forest. I rested my head against the rocking window, looking blankly into the trees where I saw nobody, feeling my mind lose control as it fought to reconcile the reality of being on the train with the hopes that had brought me to West Africa.

The railtrack passed beneath a small bridge. I looked at my watch and it was 8am. I leaned against the window and saw Alexander lying on the floor. Outside I heard the air crackling. Alexander beckoned me down onto the floor. I leaned forward from the driver's chair to kneel beside him, and the window I had been leaning on exploded in a spray of fine glass. The train shuddered and slowed and groaned. Then everything went silent. The train stopped completely. I could hear the birds outside, but that was all, except for the occasional hiss of the train. We lay on the floor, where glass from the shattered window lay as fine dust on our bags. We lay without moving, without talking, barely able to breathe, barely able to blink, listening for a sound, waiting, waiting, waiting for something to break the silence.

After a time, Alexander slowly raised himself off the floor and crawled towards the back of the cab. Small windows gave a view towards the rear of the train.

'They're coming,' he whispered, peering out of the window just above the lower sill. 'I can see them.'

As he watched from the window I heard slow, stealthy footsteps on the gravel. He moved back towards where I was lying, and as he reached the centre of the cab a barrage of gunfire exploded all around us, from all sides. Bullets buzzed through the cab and glass exploded from the instrument panels and shards of glass covered us where we lay, our faces buried in our bags. There was glass flying through the air, bullets spinning above our heads, and then the boom of a bigger blast nearby sending tremors through the tons of metal which surrounded us like a tunnel, in which I dreamed of the happiness I might feel when the shooting could no longer be heard, as long as the end was sudden and there was no time to feel its pain.

But that moment never came. Time was playing no part in this. But after the shooting stopped we saw the wild eyes of a man who stared at us for a second through one of the shattered windows and then disappeared. We lay, less afraid to breathe, gasping, whispering that they, the people outside, knew we were in the cab. We should get out. What were we thinking then? Who had we become? The victims of an ambush?

We slowly stood, picked up our bags and opened the door at the front of the cab which opened onto a gangway with a railing along it. Alexander went first. He was brave. I was nervous about going out of the door, and he didn't even ask me if I wanted to go first. I followed him slowly, raised my head and saw the gunmen standing beside the railtrack below the big, hissing engine. They had machine-guns trained on us, and were yelling at us to hold our hands high and get down from the train. We threw our bags down onto the gravel beside the track. There were greasy iron steps to climb down. The gunmen, with red bandanas, I noticed, round their heads, and chubby faces, I saw through my fear, took the bags and turned them upside down without opening them. They ordered us to strip and we did quickly; they watched us, half smiling, stopping us before we could stand before them completely naked.

'Who are you. Wha' you doin' o' tha' trai'?' one after the other they asked. 'Wha' yo' doin' here? Who are you?'

I told them I was a journalist working for the *Financial Times*, on the way to write about iron ore.

They told us to empty our bags, and I reached inside and took out notebooks, clothes, radio, money, passport, tape-recorder. One of them, the man whose face we had seen at the window of the train, 'confiscated' the money and passport. Another asked if he could have the tape-recorder, and I gave it to him. We were ordered to put our clothes back on and pick up the bags. A boy with a gun came from the cab of the front engine, where he had been hacking rubber pipes on the underside of the engine with a machete, and asked me if I knew how to stop the train's engine. I followed him to the cab. Inside, excrement covered the floor.

'The driver go' scared,' the boy said, looking round the empty cab, which gave no hint as to where the driver was.

I said I had no idea how to stop the engine, and we returned to the group beside the railtrack. As we did so an aeroplane passed overhead. The gunmen suddenly became agitated and formed into a line with us in the middle, and we snaked away from the heaving train and into the bush.

'Tha's the gov'men' plane. Now they mu' kno' we ha' attack' the trai',' said one. 'They' be sen' in' troops fro' Ganta.'

They took us to a small hut at a crossroads, close to the bridge we had passed under just before the attack. They said they were going to set an ambush for the government troops they expected to be sent to attack them as soon as news of the train ambush reached the nearest army post. We sat there for half an hour, as the grey government aircraft flew a few thousand feet overhead. Nothing happened, and then we were joined by ten more young men with guns, and we formed two lines with ten feet between us, on either side of the sandy road. It was 10am. The road followed a curve, then opened out in front of us, and the gunmen fanned out across its width along the verges through which it had been cut.

We walked under the hot sun, weighed down by our bags. My imagination ran wild as I tried to come to grips with this 'new' reality. What were we? Prisoners, perhaps even hostages, survivors of an ambush? Fleetingly I saw myself as a survivor, then as a captive. New labels, new identities – identities beyond profession and upbringing and birthright. There was a tension between the immediate present and the need to have a perspective on what was happening to me. I had to imagine explaining this new persona I had been given to somebody on the outside, to prove that this was indeed the world of the unknown.

After an hour or more we turned off the red-earth road and onto a soft path between tall green grass and trees which led down to a stream where the gunmen rested. One of them handed us a bottle of fruit juice to drink. It felt cool inside and made me realise how dry I had become walking under the sun. After a few minutes we continued on the path, going deeper into the trees which grew in a thick wood on the left of the path, but which were interspersed with patches of grass on the right. Some of the gunmen returned to the road. There were perhaps ten who walked with us. They did not say where we were going. We followed them. We stopped a few minutes later and sat beneath some trees. We ate grapefruit which Alexander had brought from the company chalet in Buchanan. I took photographs of the gunmen, looking at them properly for the first time, talking, telling them who I was and asking them about themselves, asking where we were going.

'We are taking you to our leader. To see Charles Taylor,' one said.

We were rejoined by some of those who had left us earlier and continued along the path. We had barely walked out of the shadow of the trees when a massive barrage of gunfire burst out from the right side, where the trees and grassy patches stretched back in the direction of the railway track we had left behind. The gunmen ran into the thick trees on the left, breaking a path through the dense undergrowth as bullets, their source out of sight, buzzed among the tall tree trunks. We found a narrow winding path and ran. The gunmen in front gradually pulled further away, unencumbered by bags. The people behind dispersed into the forest, but we kept running and the bullets whizzed past us as if those firing were close by and knew we were there.

Breathless, Alexander stopped and we crouched down among thick bushes as the bullets continued to fly over our heads. The tall trees cast shadows over the forest floor. The bullets became more occasional. We lay among thorny branches, listening for bullets and hearing the birds. Our guides were gone. There was not a sound of a human being. No movement, no voices. We lay, talking softly.

'We could go back to the train,' Alexander said.

Neither of us had any idea where we were in Liberia. We had seen no signs to suggest that there was a town nearby. We had followed an unknown road in we knew not which direction.

After perhaps minutes, perhaps an hour, we stood and retraced our steps. We stepped out of the forest, onto the path, walked slowly past the clearing where discarded skins showed where we had eaten grapefruit, crossed the stream where we had rested, and then found the road. It was deserted in both directions. Where have they gone, I murmured quietly? The idea of surprising anybody with our presence on the road, or of meeting people who had no idea how we had got there, became more unnerving than the emptiness and silence. We walked past deserted huts I had not noticed when we were with the gunmen walking away from the train. Clay pots lay upturned near the dead grey ashes of fires on the flat-trodden brown earth outside the closed doors of abandoned homes.

We walked in the heat of the midday sun, barely a shadow from the trees swaying in the slight breeze along the roadside.

When the sun was directly above us, after we had been walking in silence with nothing left to say to each other, feeling no need or purpose to express our doubts about which way we had decided to go after leaving the forest, we saw a group of people in the centre of the road a few hundred yards ahead. We walked slowly in the centre of the road until we came close to them and could see they were armed. From the roadside another man appeared. His was the face we had seen at the window of the train. He would need no explanation as to why we were there. I was glad he was there.

'We came under attack after we left the road,' I told him. 'The people we were with disappeared, so we decided to walk back in this direction to see if we could find you.'

A tall young man in a shiny silver jacket stepped to the front of the crowd. He was wearing sunglasses and had long hair, though it could have been a wig as it was blond.

'Wha' were doin' on the trai'? Te' me. I wanna know now. You explai' yusself to me raa' now,' he yelled. He was standing less than a yard from me, and he took his gun from his shoulder and held the barrel to within a foot of my belly.

'Te' me raa now. You' a damn spy,' he said.

The man whose face we had seen at the train window stepped in. He calmed the man with the gun who eventually withdrew to the back of the group. Then he introduced himself.

'I am Alfred Mahn. I'm in charge of this unit of the National Patriotic Front of Liberia,' he said, leading us off the road and into the yard in front of some huts. He sat us down and told us that the NPFL had warned the iron-ore company not to send trains up and down the line, because they were liable to be attacked. Then he went to speak with his fighters, and we were beckoned onto the road. A boy took my bag and carried it on his head, and we walked back along the road, away from the railway, for two or more hours.

They had hidden a large truck under trees beside the road, and covered the cab in branches so it was completely hidden from view. It was on a wide bend in the road, close to another of the empty villages we had walked past. It was long into the afternoon, and orange light softened the harsh brightness which had pounded away throughout the day. I became aware of time passing and of having been oblivious to it until then. I now remembered the past hours, of waking into darkness in the company compound in Buchanan, of leaving the goods yard behind as the sky turned from black to grey, as the forest opened up beside the railtrack, as the morning light filtered through. Now it was mid-afternoon. The day was passing. There was no sign of an end to what was happening. These young, gun-carrying fighters, whose character and presence I had hardly begun really to notice, and who I had so far hardly tried to make real contact with for fear they would think I was prying or spying, were dragging me with them into the evening, the night, and maybe into tomorrow. The awareness of time passing slowly began to focus the reality which, until the evening light softened the harsh sun, had been a blur of noise, forest and the empty road.

Alexander and I climbed into the cab of the truck while the young fighters held on to the rim of the open back. The engine roared, too loud to talk over. The gunmen in the back began to sing, I don't remember what song, and the road and the forest began to slip by quickly as we drove with the sun behind us.

We drove fast, through villages either empty or occasionally inhabited by a few women and young children. At around 5.30pm we roared into a larger village, where the main street gave off onto narrow lanes between small houses. Everywhere there were young people, some with guns, most without, young men wandering in groups who peered at the lorry, then saw me inside and stared harder.

'So,' a shirtless officer in army fatigues and flip-flops said quietly, as he laid a machine-gun on the table in front of him. 'What were you doing on that train?'

He did not seem surprised to see us. He sat on a low-slung chair on the muddy verandah of a faded pink-painted bungalow. I went into a long explanation. He did not look up, or even appear to be paying much attention to my fear, my desperate need to explain, my uncertainty as to whether my life was in my hands or not. Occasionally he nodded, but as I embarked on my explanation of what had happened he began disassembling the gun, delicately, at points asking the group of armed men with him for advice on which part to take off next. My explanation came to an end long before the gun was fully disassembled. So there was silence, while we watched him as he cleaned and oiled the parts, advised by his young attendants who appeared to know more than he did. For an hour or more we sat there. Then he said Alexander and I should be taken to an office where an NPFL official would ask us question: 'Take down some particulars.'

We walked surrounded by the young fighters, most of them in new camouflage uniforms. They took us to another bungalow, where a young, bespectacled man behind a desk opened up a line of aggressive questions.

'You ha' so' proof o' who y'are?'

Alexander showed his University of Liberia card, and said he was taking a job as an accountant at the iron-ore mine, an explanation which the official accepted. I showed him my Government of Liberia Ministry of Information press card.

'This card means tha' y'are working for the gov'ment,' he told me. I assured him not, that the card was given by the government to visiting foreign journalists. 'Bu' this card say go'ment o' it. So you mus' be working fo' the gov'ment,' he insisted, and I saw my life in my hands again. I realise now, all this time later, that I was glad I knew nothing about Liberia and knew nothing about what did or did not matter there, because if I had known then I would have been imagining my fate. But I had no idea of my fate, so I was free to be honest and deny that I was working for the government.

After 20 minutes we were taken back to the shirtless official, who had finished reassembling the gun but had commenced cleaning a small pistol which had been lying on the table throughout the gun-cleaning process. He said we going to be taken from the town. I asked him the name of the town, the first time I had asked him a question.

'Saklepie,' he said.

A four-wheel-drive Pajero pulled up on the road outside the bungalow. Our bags were bundled inside. We were told to sit in the back. The commander talked to the driver, peered up and down the street, did not look at us or say anything and swung his arm to say we should go. We sped a few hundred yards through the village, now doused in late evening light. We pulled up at a crossroads where a stream of young men, some with weapons, was walking quickly along the road toward an enclosed truck with its back-door swinging open. The crowd blocked the road and we slowed and stopped. Beside the crossroads some pigs were rooting in a ditch crammed with rubbish. As they sniffed, one upturned a stick which then emerged from the rubbish as a bone – a curving human spine, complete from the neck down to the pair of jeans to which it remained attached, with a belt still keeping the trousers tight around the bloated legs and waist.

The driver blasted his horn and the crowd of young men cleared the road for us. As we drove by they ran to the open truck, leaping inside to join scores of others, singing as they went. On the side of the truck a sign was painted advertising the pleasure of drinking 'Aromatic Schnapps' in bright red letters.

'What are they singing?' I asked.

'Oh, they're jus' singin'. They're goin' off to fight. They're goin' to fight Dorr,' said one of the armed guards in the car. We left Saklepie behind and the road plunged into forest; night fell and we drove through the darkness, through villages barred by checkpoints where serious young voices yelled 'halt and iden'ify yusself', before the rope barriers were lowered and we sped on. Finally, past midnight, we reached a series of checkpoints on the edge of a village crawling with armed youths. The driver talked us through. The guards in the car showed us to a thatched hut.

'Sleep,' one said to us. It sounded as though the door was locked from the outside. Now we must be prisoners, I thought, then fell into a deep sleep.

6 Shadows in a Forest

'WAKE NOW. The chairman will see you.'
Two boys in their teens, wearing clean white tee-shirts, clean blue jeans, stood at the open door of the hut, their guns hung from leather straps, high up on their chests. Rays of sunlight broke though the bound stakes which formed the hut walls, spattering the inside with shards of white. Alexander sat on the edge of his bed, anxious, silent, his mouth slightly open, watching from beneath half-closed eyes. Would the chairman be wanting to see him too?

'Jus' the reporter,' one of the boys at the door said. I put on my shoes, all I had taken off to sleep, and followed them.

Would there be a trial, I thought, seriously? Was I now a criminal accused of spying, guilty of being unwitting, guilty of following the advice of my superiors? I followed the two neatly dressed gunmen out of the small round hut and into the sunlight of day two.

We walked, one of them ahead of me the other behind, around the perimeter wire of a small single-storey house. Everywhere there were people, boys and girls, with guns. Schoolchildren, teenage or younger, ambling under the trees of the rain-forest village, fumbling with the triggers of what I was told at some point were AK-47 Kalashnikovs. The finely polished wood of the gun's handle, the matt black metal of the barrel, the magazines loaded with brass-tipped bullets, a spare magazine bound with tape or strips of rubber to the loaded magazine, in place and ready for the day of action. I wondered how these children went through the transition from being pupils in school to being fighters, with guns as their security, who would take their country's future in their hands, and immerse themselves in the wail and clatter and blood and pain of battle? I had never seen a battle, so I did not know how they changed from being schoolchildren, farmers' children, wading through flooded fields to pick rice, climbing the palms to hack at palm nuts for oil to cook the leaves and rice and soup and stew, whose steam mingles with the smoke from the fire beneath blackened pots and pervades the soft calm of the neatly swept village courtyards of Nimba and Liberia and Africa. Changed, into this stern-faced army of children who wandered beneath the swaying shadow of the massive rain-forest trees and who were now taking command of themselves on a wide parade-ground where the trees had been cleared.

I was told to wait at the wire perimeter-fence. Two girls stood sentry at the small dark doorway of the house, their heads wrapped in shawls which revealed only their eyes. They wore uniform tee-shirts which bore the flag of Nimba county and words explaining that they had been printed to commemorate development projects financed by the German government. The girls peered at me sternly, without talking. I was beckoned inside. Three men were laughing as I entered. Two remained seated, one wearing a long white robe sat forward on the edge of a faded golden settee, the other on a dining-chair opposite him. The third stood in a corner of the room.

Whether they said hello or welcome or nothing at all was blurred by my own sense of drifting into a room where all eyes were on me, and where the seconds and minutes of the cool, bright morning ticked by to the sound of birds and the sight of the young fighters passing along the road outside the open shutters. And the three men laughed as I entered and made me stand by not asking me to sit, so I stood and smiled, I think, smiled a great deal and appeared mild and not too confused but also not too certain, not too confident. These people had almost killed me the day before, on what had become day one. They had nearly killed me.

'You were nearly killed. You were very very lucky, 'cos we had been goin' to use mortars to blow that train off o' the track,' said the man perched on the edge of the faded golden-coloured settee, Charles Taylor. I was listening to Charles Taylor's explanation as to why I was still alive, why my journey from Buchanan station had brought me here. Somewhere inside me I was asking why they had not used mortars. 'You were very lucky. We had told the company that if they continued to use the train, we would hit it. We told them three days ago.'

'Well, I have been travelling. I haven't heard the news,' I said. Why did I not tell the truth, that I was on the train because I had been told to be on the train? I didn't want to give the impression that I was in the hands of other people. These were people who would not understand that. They would not understand that my own weakness got me on that train, but that it was a weakness I was trying to work out of myself, slowly. They would not understand about the people who had sent me to where I now stood. They were so far away that to bring them into an explanation, for now, seemed futile. I could forget them. This was where I was. Alone.

Taylor asked me to sit. 'Please, have a seat.' I sat next to the man sitting opposite him on the dining-chair. 'This is Samuel Dokie,' Taylor said. I shook hands with the leader of the 1983 Nimba raid, whose two brothers had been murdered in the revenge meted out by the AFL in Nimba led by the monstrous Charles Julu, the man who had overseen the killings during which one of Dokie's brothers was beaten to death with a rope made of electric cable.

A woman brought in a plate of porridge, laying it in front of Taylor. 'Sorry there's no scrambled egg,' Taylor said, taking a spoon and scooping half the porridge onto another plate which he handed to me. 'Tea or coffee?' he asked.

'You were so lucky. You should not be sitting here with us today,' said Dokie, cackling with intermittent laughter, smiling, staring at me while I sat eating porridge beside him. He went a little too far, as if somehow the attack on the train would have been more of a success if it had been blown off the track with mortars, whatever the consequences. He didn't seem glad that I was there.

Taylor appeared awkward as Dokie continued to say how lucky I was, that the NPFL could have finished me off. I wondered about his sympathy. Perhaps Taylor felt more concerned about my well-being. He didn't seem to feel the need to impress me with his potential firepower more than once. He was more in control than Dokie.

He stood and went into a back room of the house, then reappeared in blue trousers and a matching blue short-sleeved safari jacket, smart black brogues and a pair of Ray-Ban sunglasses.

'They're not just gun-toting women,' Taylor said as we walked out of the small house and into the sunlight, and the two women sentries stood briskly to attention, clasping their Kalashnikovs to their breasts. 'They are highly trained, and have become an important part of our fighting force.'

We walked down a slope to the parade-ground. Hundreds of people, perhaps even a thousand, old and young, lined up, some armed, others standing to attention in muddy clothes, worn jackets, trousers bound with string, hair uncut, shoeless feet, some with plastic sandals. The eyes of those in line followed us as we passed, though they continued to face forward. I wondered if they knew who I was, what I was doing there. I was nobody to them. I was enthused at seeing them brought together to take their future in their hands, defiantly waiting for their leader to bring something better than the lives they had been suffering under Doe. Their leader. Another leader. Another figure in the ordinary poverty of their lives. Another figure who said it was possible to end the rigid mundanity and routine hardship, another leader who would turn the tide, show that no condition is permanent. Is it true, that everything changes? That everything can change? That what seems embedded, solid, protected by armies, protected by fear, can be overthrown? Are such claims simply the war-cries of hungry politicians, who are eager to amass their armies, but who are really unable to change anything other than the personnel holding the purse-strings, while countries drift in their own directions, beyond the powers of the people who try to steer them?

'Our war is a response to the shame Liberians feel at the Doe government,' Taylor said to me as we inspected the parade. We stopped half way down the line of troops. For 15 minutes he spoke, loud and clear and intelligent, about why they were there, why he was there, what they should do to make their lives better. 'A new Liberia. A new Liberia.' Then he warned them: 'Anybody found raping or looting will face a firing squad.'

The gathered troops, encouraged by the armed fighters who inspected them and kept them in line, listened, then responded. 'Major Taylor, he our leader, Major Taylor, he our leader.' Taylor listened and waved as he turned to go back up the slope to his house, pointing out captured weaponry on the way.

'It's capable of bringing down an aircraft,' he said, pointing to an anti-aircraft battery mounted on a swivelling dish with a seat for the operator. A young man dressed in a well-ironed, dark green uniform and peaked army cap sat in the operator's seat; he peered through an eyesight and rapidly swung the gun around 180 degrees, then swung it back and forth while everybody watched. He loaded a bullet belt from a green metal box beside the gun, and we left him peering through the eyesight at the empty, cloudless sky.

Taylor asked me for the telephone number of the British Embassy in Abidjan. He wanted to call them to say that I was safe. It was the first time in 24 hours that I had a sense of the outside world peering in on where I was. I had the telephone number and gave it to him. Where would he call them from, I wondered? He took my business card, to make sure he got my name right, he said. I watched him walk across the yard in front of his house, holding the card up in front of him as he read it.

I sat in an armchair beneath the enormous tree which also shaded the anti-aircraft battery, now covered in a green tarpaulin.

I waited. Nobody came to talk. I walked back to the top of the slope from where I could overlook the parade-ground. On one side there were youngsters crawling on their bellies through the mud, some carrying pieces of wood shaped expertly into the appearance of Kalashnikovs.

I saw Taylor emerge with Dokie from his house, and walked back to the armchair beneath the tree.

'Somebody will be making contact with the British Embassy, so as they can let your family know you're with us and safe,' Taylor said. 'And if you wish, you are free to go.' He paused. I could walk away from here, and it would be over, and this small world in the forest would once again be hidden away. 'But what we would like to be able to do is show you around the area under our control, so you can see for yourself the suffering inflicted on the people by Doe's forces. That might take a few days.'

'I think I'd find that very interesting,' I said, blandly, while in my mind I could see the outside world falling away, and I focused only on where I was, in the small village in the forest, undistracted, unable to consider any influence on my decisions other than the need to move deeper into this place.

'Good,' said Taylor. He told Dokie to find a car and some guards, and within half an hour we were ready to leave in a large, four-wheel drive. Taylor waved us off. Dokie sat in the front, beside an ageing driver. On either side of me on the back seat sat two young guards, their Kalashnikovs ready at the open windows, and in the luggage area behind the back seat sat a third guard.

'I slept there once,' said Dokie. We were standing at the end of a row of pale, mud cracked-wall houses, neat and square, with windows of four small panes. That was what they had been, and hands had worked hard under the sun, patting and shaping the mud onto frames of bound sticks. That was what they had been, until the war and the flames. 'It was a long time ago,' he said, staring, his eyes screwed up, his slightly protruding front teeth forming his closed mouth into an expression of momentary sorrow, then anxiety. 'Before I had to leave.'

Around the top of the mud wall was a fringe of black. The roof of corrugated iron had melted and collapsed onto the floor where already it had started to rust.

'It was the house of a blind woman. The army shut her inside and burned her alive,' said the headman of Butuo, Denis Seue, speaking through Dokie's translation. 'It was 28 December and four trucks of soldiers arrived at about 8pm, and the soldiers came with General Smith and said that everybody in the village was a rebel supporter and that Doe had ordered that everybody should be killed and that all the houses should be burned. They arrested eight people, including a pregnant woman, and stripped them and lay them on the ground and shot them all. And the pregnant woman's husband pleaded with the soldiers that she should be spared and that they should kill him instead. But General Smith told the husband that Doe had ordered that all pregnant women should be killed. The husband, his name was Bolly and his wife was Yanglue Bolly, he was a Krahn. But he had married a Gio woman and so they executed him along with her. And that was where the madman lived. He was killed too. I was shot and hit in the leg and lay there for an hour and pretended I was dead, because the soldiers stood and waited to see if we were all dead. I was the only survivor, and I crawled into the bush and escaped to the Ivory Coast for treatment.'

We walked up the slope that Butuo is built upon as a slight breeze whipped up the ashes and charcoal along the street.

'That was the house of the man who owned the village. We found his body over there. And his head over there,' Seue said, pointing to a patch of grass on the edge of the village, where a group of old men sat at a rope checkpoint with single-barrelled shotguns propped up between their legs, beside a three-feet high pole upon which a skull had been placed wearing an army helmet.

'It's the army commander from Butuo. We killed him and put his head here. That's all there is left of him,' said Dokie

On the road to Butuo all the villages we had passed through had the same checkpoints, the same groups of old men with ancient shotguns. At every cluster of houses, in every front yard on the roadside, there were the same signs of an uprising, of gnarled and craggy faces smiling, and eyes sparkling with the prospect of revenge.

'The single-barrel groups are our front line of defence,' said Dokie. We sat, and they gulped down strong palm wine, these hunters turned militia who had watched their village burn, their families killed, their crop stores destroyed.

'I wanted to die. I tried to kill myself. Six of my family are dead. My home is a ruin. Everything I had they stole,' said the 82-year-old headman of a nearby hamlet. 'The scars are deep. The tribes will never be friends. We want revenge.' He paused and wiped his eyes, an old man crying in front of the people he had to lead. A few years beforehand he had financed the electrification of the village. Now it was all destroyed, and flies swarmed among the charred ruins. 'The flies came when the streets filled with bodies. They never seem to go. Every morning they are there,' he said. We sat with the headman and somebody brought rice, cooked leaves with delicious meat and more palm wine and I began to feel the wine seeping through my veins and making me tired and drunk. I realised that the old men sitting at the checkpoint were delirious, with horror and drink and harsh sunlight, and we fell silent because there was nothing left to say, as the drowsy afternoon hummed with flies.

Around a bend in the sandy road, in the shadow of the overarching trees of the thick forest, a group of people appeared, walking fast. The men at the checkpoint brandished their shotguns, held tight their machetes, adopted fierce expressions which would have been funny if this had not been real. They stood beside the road as the group emerged from the shadow of the trees and into the sunlight at the edge of the village.

'Halt. Stand and be recognised,' yelled a young boy manning the checkpoint with the old men. The group slowed and ambled. They were all young boys, unarmed, sweating, nervous. They said they had been walking for three days. They wanted to get to Gborplay, to the Patriotic Front, to Charles Taylor.

'For me Doe is a dead body,' said a boy who said he was 13-years-old. Dokie listened to their story, where they had come from, what they wanted to do. He was expressionless as he listened. Then the guards at the checkpoint let down the rope barrier draped with red rags, and the boys regained their previous rapid pace and walked on through the village in the direction of the base at Gborplay, from which we had driven that morning.

We walked back to the disused school where we had left the car. It was mid-afternoon. As we approached, there was the roar of an engine and an enormous bulldozer crashed through the bush nearby. We sat on the school verandah and Dokie said that we would spend the night here in Butuo. He beckoned one of the guards who had travelled with us in the car. 'Moses. Moses.' The one who had been sitting in the rear of the vehicle came up to him. 'Go and buy me some cigarettes … Marlboro,' he said. Moses laid his gun down beside Dokie, took the 1,000 CFA franc note that Dokie held out to him, and trotted off into the woods.

'Where is he going?' I asked.

'Ivory Coast. It's only 20 minutes away. They don't mind, the Ivorians, as long as we leave our guns behind in Liberia,' said Dokie.

'How will he get there?' I asked.

'He knows the forest paths. It's all paths to the border. That's how the people who escaped from here managed to get away from the army.'

We were silent for a while.

'After a while war becomes our daily life. You start to enjoy it,' he said, looking out over the village whose capture had marked the beginning of the rebellion last Christmas Eve. He was the most important person in the village, an envoy from the NPFL, a representative of Charles Taylor.

When Moses returned with the cigarettes from across the border, we walked in the tracks of the bulldozer onto a parade-ground where several hundred NPFL fighters were lined up.

'Mayar Taylor, He our leader, Mayar Taylor, He our leader. Down down Doe. Down down Doe,' they sang as Dokie approached; he was flanked by the three guards from the car, with me at his side. The bulldozer roared and, as evening fell, fixed its floodlight on the parade.

Dokie congratulated them, the first battalion, on keeping Butuo secure for the NPFL, but he also had a warning. 'Anyone discovered raping or looting will face the firing squad,' he told them, echoing Taylor's warning to the parade he had addressed in Gborplay that morning. Then he turned to me and asked me to say something to the gathered fighters. I declined, wondering about my role and not knowing whether I could be sincere, so I remained silent.

We slept in the school, the only building not damaged by the arson. We left at around 10 o'clock the following morning. We talked in the car. Dokie became more open, though interjected his comments about his role and about Doe with fighting talk and propaganda about the Patriotic Front, the Chairman, the revolutionary forces that were sweeping the country.

'At first the Chairman said he would want to hand over power after 90 days, but that was unrealistic. So now it will be five years. And, as I already held the ministerial post under Doe, I think the Chairman will want me to go back to rural development. But rural development is a tedious task,' he said, as we bounced and slid and climbed over the dirt roads which are the only roads in this neglected corner of Liberia. 'The problem in Africa is that because of underdevelopment in the regions and the centralisation of power, the only way to make money is in politics. When people don't see politics as the only way to get rich, then things will change.'

Young gunmen, old men chauffeuring rebels, the threat of the firing squad, the Chairman, deserted roads, old men sitting in the doorways of their burned huts, old men and tiny children waving as we pass their enclaves of burned, scarred huts, checkpoints, orders, soft afternoon silence in the endless, calm, beautiful darkness of the forest, the war, or at least the threat of it, and, between the noise and the silence and the action, Dokie's theories about politics and the hungry people who pursue politics and the perks and the dangers and the threats and the prestige. But the lingering question remains as to when and where and into what form all these elements, the symbols of the struggle in the villages and along the roads, emerge from the darkness of their gestation. Will the hungry population watch the new regime slipping into the ways of the old one, and will the death and sacrifice and hope dissolve as the people who fought and lived return to the forests from where they came?

'I'm tired of the struggle, because in the end the country complains that the new government has not come up with its promises. And there's a cycle, with coups which are led by junior ranks who are alienated from power. The new government establishes itself and alienates the same army ranks from power, and the cycle continues,' said Dokie, his high, grating voice seeming to reflect anger, but in fact showing his exasperation, the exasperation of a continent tired of its failure to take hold and shape itself.

The road plunged deeper into the forest. Thick bushes clustered around the roots and veins of the massive soaring trees. The road was new mud, and after an hour or more we stopped just before a bridge of sawn tree-trunks which had been laid side by side over a stream. On the other side an earth-mover was ploughing through the red soil, while men with shovels and pick-axes stabbed the ground and tore at the roots of the trees to clear the way.

'The Patriotic Front is building a new road to make the journey from Butuo to Tapeta much quicker,' said Dokie. We got out of the car. The workmen looked at us, suspiciously at first. Then they were told this was Dokie, and once they knew who we were they bowed and smiled and thanked him for coming to see them. They sweated in their mud-caked clothes as a bulldozer appeared from over a hill and belched black smoke as it drove towards us. The bulldozer pushed another tree-trunk down towards the bridge they had built. The men lashed it with rope and eased it into place and the bridge was finished. The guards from our car walked down to the stream as the driver slowly edged the car down the slope to the logs and aligned the wheels so they would not slip in either direction. He drove across the bridge, which rolled a little as it settled into its red-earth foundations under the weight of the car, and then accelerated up off the logs onto the slope on the other side.

To the tune of 'Oh, Suzanna', 500 trained troops from the NPFL's 1st Battalion marched off the parade-ground at Tapeta singing: 'Oh, my brother, Don't you cry for me, I'm off to the battlefront, Don't you cry for me.'

Dokie walked into the house of the district commissioner, an official long-since gone, his house now a lounging area for the NPFL. As he was mounting the steps of the house an old woman fell down in front of him, wailing and screaming. Dokie smiled and stood over her. He put his hand on her head, and then lifted her so she was standing, still wailing. He smiled more and his face shone, and then he turned and entered the building.

Inside, two frightened 10-year-old boys were standing against the wall. They said they had run 40 miles overnight from Grand Bassa county to say that they had seen three government reconnaissance scouts in their area.

'No information is useless,' Dokie told them. 'You did well.' He instructed a commander to send 60 men south as far as the NPFL territory extended to see if there was any evidence of an AFL advance. Faces revealed nervousness, even fear. Tapeta was the southernmost town in NPFL hands. The AFL had been pushed out only 10 days before, just across the Cestos river which marked the border with Grand Gedeh county, Doe's homeland. The tension in the room increased. The roads in this region were extensive because the logging trucks which had used them before the war had to have access to the most isolated stretches of forest. An AFL advance through the forest would be easy.

I left Dokie talking inside the house. Outside, women soldiers wandered around a small parade-ground and sat on the steps of a pedestal out of which rose an empty flag pole.

'The first day I held a gun i' wa' too heavy. But now I can carry it as if it's packe' o' cigare',' said Korpo Zubas, commander of 28 women fighters aged between 15 and 20. 'Now I ha' killed a lo' o' people. Too many to count,' she said. An older woman, Joanna Mehan, said she had been training 235 women at the NPFL base in Gborplay. She said that her husband had fought and died with Thomas Quiwonkpa in the failed coup of 1985.

'Since then I' bin training. In Burkina Faso,' she said, the first time any of the NPFL had said they had received any training outside Liberia.

From beyond the wall of the commissioner's house came the sound of the singing I had heard when we arrived.

'Oh, my brother, Don't you cry for me, I'm off to the battlefront, Don't you cry for me.' Then, around the corner of a building, old men and children come marching side by side towards the parade-ground. The building, the local police station, was burned down by the NPFL a week before with one policeman inside it, said Dokie, having emerged from his discussions.

'The body is still there if you want to have a look,' he said to me as we walked towards the parade. The smell of the rotting body drifted across the parade-ground, as Dokie repeated the warning that rapists and looters would be shot, and the gathered men and boys listened attentively.

At the Baptist mission, on top of a hill up a muddy road flanked by thick bushes, a sacked employee of Liberia's national radio station who had since joined the rebels was attempting to repair the transmitter of the Radio Voice of Mid-Liberia Baptist Mission – radio ELMBM. The Baptist missionaries, five married couples and two single people, had flown out of the mission three days before. The mission landing-strip stretched into the bush – an exit route from the war. For a few moments I wished I could follow it, walk down the landing-strip and be away from the parades and guns and the exhaustion I was feeling after hours of talking and listening and driving through the forest into the unknown.

Elmer Johnson sat perched on a settee in the dark living-room of Tapeta's rival religious institute, St Joseph's Catholic mission. The three Italian nuns and two American and two British missionaries had left at the end of March. Now the children they had once taught, freed from the religious propaganda which slipped out of the Liberian consciousness within days of the war starting, ambled across the playing-fields with their guns.

Elmer Johnson, who had led the 3 November 1984 attempt to overthrow Doe and had lost an eye in the ensuing gun-battle in Monrovia after his insurrection had been betrayed, was the NPFL's chief military strategist and had been in charge of Tapeta since the last seven AFL soldiers were driven out on 26 March. Elmer had left Liberia when Doe seized power in 1980. He came from a distinguished Americo-Liberian family, one of whom had been a vice-president. He joined the US army as a sergeant paramedic, had a brief spell in Grenada during the US occupation of the island in 1982, and left the army in July 1984.

'I left in order to make plans to set up a force to overthrow the government of Samuel Doe,' he said, raising his voice over the sound of the heavy rain which clattered onto the mission's metal roof. Elmer had a lisp. His directionless glass eye stared through his round, tortoise-shell spectacles with an air of expectation, always awaiting the response of the listener, who he watched with this unnerving stare.

'These men are very determined to defend their local community, because of what the Krahn soldiers have done,' he said, with no attempt to hide his belief, prevalent among the often arrogant Americo-Liberian descendants of the ex-slaves who had formed Liberia's upper class until 1980, that the war was simply a pitching of Liberia's tribes against each other. 'During the national reconstruction, the government of Charles Taylor is going to have to work very very hard to reconcile these tribal differences. Doe created it, and he knew it was going to work, and it worked. We're not out to kill Krahns. We're just out to kill Samuel K. Doe, to remove Samuel K. Doe from office, who happens to be Krahn, and those in the army who are backing him in power,' he said, placing revenge at the top of the NPFL's military agenda in a way that neither Taylor nor Dokie had done.

I asked him about the oft-repeated claim, made by Taylor, that the invasion of 24 December had been carried out with two single-barrel shotguns and some knives. He confirmed the story, but then went much further than Taylor had done regarding their weapons' supplies.

'I know that friends loyal to us have supplied us with weapons ... around 30 per cent of the weapons we are using – the AK-47s and the like – have been captured from the Liberian army. The rest have been supplied. But Gadaffi doesn't decide the terms of operations here in Liberia. We are not hard-core ideologues. We're traditional capitalists. All this rumour about the NPFL being a red organisation doesn't stand, and I have met with Pentagon officials who are very concerned about that, and I continue to reassure them that this isn't the case. In Africa there are a lot of guns. Getting AKs doesn't necessarily imply that Gadaffi is the godfather of the Liberian revolution and that we will turn into a Libyan satellite,' he said, undermining the denials that Taylor had made that the NPFL had anything to do with Libya.

We ate rice and stewed leaves and meat and talked long into the evening. The rain stopped beating on the tin roof of the mission. I walked outside and was approached by a boy in a crisp white shirt and neat trousers, the first I had seen not carrying a gun since we had arrived in Tapeta.

'You are the reporter who was on the train,' he told me. I told him I was. 'E'erybody know' abou' the train roun' here. E'erybody know' about you.' He wanted to walk away from where a group of the NPFL fighters were sitting, eating in the darkness. We walked towards the mission school building. He said he had been left in charge of the mission when the nuns and others left. 'I' trying, bu' the sister' and brother' will be very angry with me, because I can' stop the rebels fro' looting e'erythin' fro' the school. They' take all the pencil' and book' and e'erything. I' tryin' but it' no' easy. They ha' their guns and I try, bu' they jus' steal, and nobody ca' sto' them.' He was anxious, and asked if I could relay a message to the missionaries, who had gone to Monrovia, to tell them that everything was fine and he was trying hard to do the job they had entrusted him with, but that it was proving quite difficult. He gave me his name and I said I would try and relay the message, but that I didn't know when I would go to Monrovia.

He thanked me, and walked off into the darkness, distinguishable only by his clean white shirt, past the bright colours of an illuminated crucifix which hung over the church, the only colour against the black and grey of the evening rain-clouds.

Dokie and Elmer ended their discussions. I was accompanied down a long passageway to a small, pale blue door and told this was my room for the night. Inside, on a small desk, lay a pile of school exercise-books and papers strewn and left unarranged in a room which would normally have been tidy, with the name Sister Maria Carmen on each one. I was an intruder in the private world of somebody I assumed I would never meet, another fleeing victim of the war. I sat on the bed, which was narrow, and felt awkward lying down on the sheets which belonged so clearly to the woman who had made this room her own. A small crucifix hung from the pale wall, a pair of small, women's shoes were neatly placed side by side beneath the bed, a towel hung over a chair, well-thumbed paperback books and health manuals lay on a shelf. In her mind this woman planned to return here, as most of her possessions had been left behind. I closed the curtains, which depicted scenes from Epping Forest, a few miles from the town in England in which I had grown up, where I had walked the previous Christmas, days after the incursion into Liberia, and seen deer darting among the bare winter trees. I switched out the light and half slept, awake to the possibility that Sister Maria Carmen would return while I lay there.

I started to recognise the roads, the turns, the villages we went through. The country seemed less confusing. The red roads through the dark forests became different, with their small details more recognisable and memorable, the burned villages less fleeting. I wanted to be able to walk through it, to hear the forest and the people who must have been hiding in the shadows as our car passed.

We left Tapeta and returned along the road towards Grai. Dokie had brought along a very young girlfriend, who sat beside him on the front seat. The old men of Grai were sitting in a large open-sided hut waiting for Dokie to come. They had waited for three days. They were tall, strong men; they seemed kind, relieved that Dokie had come, looking to the future, hearing about the war from the few people who travelled through the forest to bring news. They asked about what had been happening. Dokie told them that after the attack on Butuo in December the NPFL had fought for nine days, between 27 January and 4 February, with the AFL at Kahnplay and had lost some men, and that after the battle the AFL fled and the NPFL stopped its advance in order to train more troops. The fighting resumed with ambushes at Bahn on 20 March, from where the AFL soldiers fled to Saniquellie and Ganta and the NPFL killed 120 AFL troops and lost only two of its own. On 26 March the NPFL seized Tapeta, then Blor Dialah on 31 March, and most recently, on 2 April, Saklepie.

The old men thanked Dokie for the information, and took us to the telecommunications installation on the edge of the village, which had been wrecked by the AFL as they retreated. They gave us food there, rice and potato leaves and meat, and one of them brought out a two-foot black mask which was lying inside the telecommunications office.

'Would you like a Gio mask?' Dokie said to me. I picked it up and one of the guards in the car put it among the bags, and we drove out of the village, and the old men still sat inside the large hut and talked about what Dokie had told them.

It was around 4pm when we reached Toweh Town, and we stopped to listen to the BBC radio news, the only news which gave Liberians a reasonable account of what was happening in their country. Twice they mentioned the attack on the train and the subsequent message from Taylor to say I was with the NPFL and was safe and would be returning to the Ivory Coast soon.

We sat in a tiny house on the edge of the village. Everybody had left, even the dogs which usually got left behind. There had been no burning, just the signs of desertion. Doors left half-open, shutters closed, no footprints on the dried rivulets which ran down the road between the houses, which would have been bustling with the quiet activity of the village during normal times, no smoke rising from the enclaves of small huts into the beautiful, pale late afternoon sky. Where is the war, I wondered? There were no signs of it here. Just the intangible signs of fear, the emptiness of a village where people have come to know what will happen if they stay, so they leave, and nothing happens to them, and that's the war, until the battlefield is emptied of all but the killers, or those too old or young or afraid to run away.

As we were listening to Dokie's radio, eating another meal of the same rice and leaves and meat, a boy ran up to the house from the crossroads which could be seen from where we were sitting. He said he had walked all day to report to somebody, anybody, that four NPFL fighters had been killed in an attack by bandits at nearby Gbaplay village the previous night at around 2am. The attack had happened in heavy rain, the boy said, in the village. The bandits had bypassed the NPFL ambush but some of the Gbaplay single-barrel guard had shot and killed some of the bandits, though he didn't know how many. Some people had said the bandits were now 40 miles away. Others said they were only seven miles away.

'Who launched the attack?' I asked Dokie. Until then I had felt safe in the NPFL's hands. They seemed to be in control. They had support from the population which had not fled as refugees. They seemed organised.

'Just bandits,' Dokie snapped. 'They use army weapons and are financed by the army, but this is the first time they have killed any of our boys.'

It wasn't until 6pm that Dokie sent our car off with two of our three guards to call for more troops to come and scour the area, particularly the road between Toweh Town and Gbaplay, which was the road we had to take to get back to the NPFL base at Gborplay. Evening turned into night.

I was frightened.

My faith in Dokie's ability as a protector was diminishing as we sat under the stars without our guards. We sat under a full moon talking softly. Dokie could see I was nervous. I could hardly speak, and became afraid of the night and the sounds of the forest which echoed from the trees all around us, and above all afraid of the silence which hummed as soon as the talking stopped. We were waiting for something to happen, hoping it would not, knowing that if we were attacked we would have little chance of defending ourselves. The darkness grew. We had no fire to warm us, as it would have let anybody passing in the forest know that we were there.

'It's the first time we have sat outside for weeks,' said one of the handful of men who had emerged from the apparently deserted village when we arrived. 'People aren't so scared since the army left.'

Dokie told me to follow him.

'We'll be safer here,' he said, leading me to a small house in the middle of the village. 'It's away from the main road.' I had no idea which way the attackers may approach from, if they came here at all. Would they come from the road, or stealthily, through the blackness of the forest, among the small, dark houses? They would reach this small house, I was sure of it.

I lay on a hard bed, my eyes wide open, wrote a note to my family which I hoped they would find if ever my bag found its way out of Liberia, even if I did not, lay my knife beside me in some vain hope that I could defend myself, and listened to the haunting, humming, buzzing sound of the night, imagining that every sound was approaching bandits. I must have slept eventually, because cold morning light filtered through the cracks in the closed shutters as I sat up in another unfamiliar room, wondering whose it was. I walked out into the yard, where Dokie was sitting on a chair wrapped in a sheet, while one of the men who had sat with us the night before clipped his hair which fell onto the red earth of the yard. The girl he had brought along stared out at the scene from a window framed by pale blue shutters and a thick, rambling bush which covered the house.

The bandits had not come.

It was morning.

Time for coffee.

'Now the rebel is shaved,' said Dokie, standing and shaking the clipped hair from the back of his neck. 'It's the first haircut I have had since I was in Dakar in November.' He told me the reinforcements he had sent for had arrived at around 10pm the previous night and were still scouring the area.

We returned to the small house where we had been the previous day when the boy came with news of the bandit attack. We talked, awaited news from the NPFL fighters who had been called in. The morning dragged on to midday.

At that time I knew nothing about Dokie, and had never heard his name until Taylor introduced me to him. As we sat in the small house he told me about his life, how he had led the Nimba raid in 1983 about which I came to know more later.

'After the raid I escaped to Guinea with $25,000,' he said, without explaining where he got the money from. 'And then I was arrested at the border by Sekou Toure's soldiers. Sekou Toure was the president then, and he was a friend of Doe's, and I was taken to Sekou Toure's prison in Conakry, the Camp Boiro. Doe had demanded that the Guineans hand over three other Liberian dissidents at the end of that year's OAU [Organisation of African Unity] summit, held in Conakry. The Guineans didn't hand me over. I don't know why. But the other three were killed, at the end of the OAU summit,' he guessed.

I began to see what I thought might lie at the root of his blasé attitude towards my own survival after the attack on the train.

'They held a funeral for me in Liberia. That woman in Tapeta, the one who fell to the ground when she saw me. She was at the funeral seven years ago. She is the grandmother of my children, and she thought I was dead in 1983. Yesterday, that was the first time she had seen me since Doe sacked me over the radio when I refused to transfer $3million from my ministry to his bank account.'

He paused, and in the silence of the tiny house I felt like a child, with nothing to cling on to, fatigued by the futility, so ignorant of the reality.

'But all that time I was in the Camp Boiro,' he said. 'In the cells there were people who had been there for a long time. They wrote their testimonies in blood on the wall. There was one ex-soldier I shared my cell with. He was put on the black diet, which meant no food or water until he died. Once he asked me to piss into his mouth because he was dying of thirst. But I refused. The man died after 12 days, and I shared my cell with him for one and a half days before the body was collected. Then Sekou Toure died and five days later the military took over and they put me in a military camp for one and a half years, in protective custody. They brought Sekou Toure's wife and children there, into the camp, and everybody knew that the soldiers constantly raped his wife in front of the children.'

He paused.

'Africans can be so wicked to each other,' he said, half laughing, while trying to stifle the horror, knowing that, in his heart, it could be him in the future overseeing some horror in the name of change. He had been released from the military camp in 1985, and stayed in Conakry until his move to Dakar in 1988, where he joined with his fellow Nimbaian dissident Harry Yuen in an effort to amass an army to overthrow Doe.

'When my mother came from Monrovia to Conakry after my release, she arrived at 7pm and we didn't sleep all night. She just sat and stared at me for hours without saying anything. Then she would ask me to stand, and say: "Are you really there in front of me?".'

It was nearly 6pm when we left Toweh Town. The reinforcement troops said they had found no sign of the bandits. We drove down the hill to the crossroads we had been watching for almost two days, turned to the left and a few minutes later nearly crashed into a massive tree-trunk which had clearly been felled to block the road. The driver brought the car to a sudden halt.

'Dammit, they were supposed to have cleared the road,' Dokie screeched.

Perhaps this was where his life would end, after so many years of horror, on a narrow muddy forest lane.

Moses leapt from the back of the car and prepared his gun, walking quickly ahead to draw any potential fire away from the car. There were thick bushes on either side of the road.

We could have been so easily trapped.

But there was no ambush. Moses walked around the felled tree. The two other guards cleared branches and we drove beneath the tree's straggling, unearthed roots. We drove on, through Gbaplay, where we saw the house which had been attacked by the bandits two nights before. Evening turned into night, and we drove silently, nervously, the guards with their hands on the triggers of their guns, for two more hours, before we arrived at the familiar slope and the steep embankment on either side of the road which marked the entrance to the camp at Gborplay.

The next morning I stood on the stones of the camp shower and washed myself down with cool water as the sounds of the army in training echoed through the trees. I wondered what I looked like.

Taylor arranged himself at a table under the tree where the anti-aircraft gun lay covered by its tarpaulin. He wore white. He laid maps out on the table in front of him, his guards in their German co-operation tee-shirts posing beside and behind him. I took a photograph as he was arranging his sunglasses and positioning the pistol on the table. He laughed slightly angrily, as if he I had done wrong to capture him on film before he was ready.

'It will never be said of Charles Taylor that I'm wicked. But it will never be said that I'm weak,' he told me, as we sat under the tree. 'I won't be a candidate in a civilian election, but I may not feel comfortable leaving the job to somebody else.'

He talked about his history, and said he was chairman of the Union of Liberian Associations in the Americas, how he had eight children and a grandchild, despite his mere 42 years. Of the NPFL, he said the special forces had gone through two years of training and the special commandos through 14 months of training, and were now dispersed all over the country.

He went methodically through all the possible subjects I might like to talk about, and then explained the more substantial reasons behind the attack on the train.

'Doe is a principal shareholder in the holding company of the iron-ore mine, Nimbaco. He bought it for $15 million. Doe will lose money from the mine, and the train, we were told, was going to be used to carry troops to Nimba,' he said. He then rapidly moved on to attacking other would-be opponents of Doe, for reasons which only became clear after the events surrounding Taylor's own rise within the opposition movement became clear during the weeks and months which followed. He attacked the opportunist leader of the 1979 rice riots – the event which was supposed to have triggered Doe's coup – Gabriel Bacchus Matthews, as responsible for 'many Liberians losing their lives'. He attacked the Movement for Justice in Africa activist, Joe Wiley, whose accidental shooting of one of Thomas Quiwonkpa's fellow coup-makers in 1985 had shaken the confidence of the ill-fated dissidents, as a 'schizo Moja Marxist trained in Ethiopia and Cuba. It was because of Joe Wiley's lies that I was twice arrested in Ghana,' he said, referring to events and people which, at the time, meant nothing to me.

'And when we get to Monrovia, then we will break open the statue of the unknown soldier. Because in 1981 Doe sealed up an albino – alive – inside that statue,' he said, as Dokie approached to tell me it was time to leave.

We shook hands, not warmly. Alexander Kuilu, my fellow passenger on the train, approached as we talked. Taylor told me that Alexander had agreed to stay with the NPFL. I asked if I could speak with Alexander alone. We walked away from the crowd, and I asked him if this was true, and he said it was. He said he had not been forced, but that at the mine there would be no job for him anyway, because the rail link had been cut. Taylor returned to his house and I wondered if I would ever see him again.

Dokie walked with me into the forest behind Taylor's house. We passed a wired-off compound where several armoured cars lay, newly painted in black and green, with large red scorpions painted on the front and sides.

We walked along a newly scraped mud road, to a river where a small ferry, pulled across by hand, lay waiting for us. The morning sun dappled the water as we were dragged across the brown stream. On the other side an Ivorian soldier watched us, partially hidden by bushes which matched his camouflage uniform. On a small track which stopped at the water's edge stood an official from the British embassy in Abidjan, who introduced himself in stumbling French to Dokie.

'Je suis le premier secretaire de l'Ambassade de Grande Bretagne en Abidjan, Dermott Flanagan.' I told him he could speak in English. He thanked Dokie for bringing this British citizen safely back to the Ivory Coast, and Dokie spoke officially in the name of the Chairman and, without giving me any chance to reflect on what had happened, said goodbye, stepped back on to the ferry and was gone.

7   A City on the Ocean

'*C*'*EST LE Liberian*.'
        My telephone had been tapped.

Tom Woweiyu had just got through from New Jersey. The line echoed and the voice of the Ivorian security official listening in was loud and clear. Then I heard Woweiyu at the other end, introducing himself as a supporter of the National Patriotic Front of Liberia, calling from 'the States', and telling me, 'We wanna org'nise a press conference wi' the Chairman.'

His voice was deep and friendly. He called me by my first name. Over the telephone he seemed modest, even slightly embarrassed at calling – a second-hand car salesman talking about revolution. He gave the impression he was uncomfortable in the role of rebel. I told him I was sure it would be easy to organise a press conference. Where did he want to hold it?

'In Liberia,' he said.

Abidjan's morning rush-hour buses roared nine floors down below my apartment balcony. Hot fumes mingled with the rising wet heat trapped in the tunnel of trees lining Boulevard Clozel, where a million or more bats dangled from the branches and sang like hack-saws scratching through metal. Twenty storeys up, on a distant roof-top, a team of scaffolders languished like acrobats frozen on a metal frame they had assembled against the pale grey sky. The *bateaux-mouche* plied the water-front between Plateau, Treichville, Marcory and further up the lagoon of Ebrie. The Pont Houphouet-Boigny bore the 'Elephant de la Piste' – huge Mercedes trucks emblazoned with stickers bearing this title – as they roared in from the Sahelian towns of distant Burkina Faso, Mali and Niger, while groaning buses, from Ferkessedougou, Korhogo, Man and Aboisso, arrived and departed in smoky clouds billowing out under the weight of towering loads of goods, baggage and food piled high on their roofs.

Beneath this colourful and industrious surface, unrest was turning the streets of Abidjan into a battleground. Across the border Liberia lurched into war, and thousands of its people fled to the relative calm of the Ivory Coast. Meanwhile, Abidjan fell under the heavy guard of gendarmes who lingered at every crossroads. Soldiers patrolled the streets daily. Demonstrations – by students demanding better living conditions, and by professionals and civil servants demanding the abandonment of austerity measures, announced in March of that year, 1990, which had brought 40 per cent pay cuts – erupted until the riot squads arrived with tear-gas and batons to extinguish criticism of the regime.

My street was the channel to the heart of the protests.

Every other day, throughout April and into May, students poured along it down the hill from Abidjan cathedral, the singing and chanting growing louder, echoing between the tall buildings and beneath the soaring trees. The bats streamed across the sky in black clouds, shaken from their branches by the noise. The marchers drew closer to the gendarmes' road-block at the junction below my balcony, where the baker selling croissants and baguettes rapidly slid down his red shutters as tear-gas filled the air and the chanting stopped and the people fled.

In one week during April the marchers came down the boulevard every single morning, at the same time, 8.30am, and a fevered rush swept through the entire city. The poor districts of Marcory, Treichville and Adjame hummed with the new expression of grievances, repressed for so long amid the all-embracing pursuit of the myth of the common good, a goal now thrown to the wind, the reality of poverty having become too obvious beside the enormous wealth of the élite.

Through it all President Felix Houphouet-Boigny remained silent. The state-owned newspapers – the only newspapers then allowed to publish – criticised the protesters, the illegal opposition and foreign governments who demanded an end to the one-party system, by which Houphouet-Boigny had ruled with a mixture of benevolence and dictator-ship since 1960. The country had not been tested in this way before. The strong arm had not been shown and the old regime continued to resist. Houphouet-Boigny eventually spoke out to criticise foreign pressure on African governments. Just because the cold war was over, why did that mean that everybody in the world should adopt multiparty politics? That was the conservatives' question. In the end they clung on, until the government was forced to lift a ban on opposition politics, and five rival political parties were registered.

It was to this city that I returned from my journeys across West Africa, then and in the months and years to come. On the hot nights, nine floors up, overlooking the tree-tops below my balcony, I watched the flashing lights of the beer factory, the cars snaking over the long bridge into Treichville in the heat of the heavy, wet air, under clear skies with few stars visible, even after the sudden slipping away of the sun and the falling of the night after the ten-minute dusk. I would stand and watch from my balcony, and nobody would know I was there, the light from my hot room just another glow in the humming city of more than a million eager, anxious, colourful, cultured strong people from right across the region, caught between the desert and the forest and the ocean. I could feel the currents of what was swirling around me, the turbulence, the troubles, the dynamic which was setting the region ablaze in the hope of change. But I felt so distant from the source of the clamour, from understanding the character that it took, from knowing the place in which I lived, as my mind turned again and again from the city to the fleeting images of war I had seen. Images which had ended when Samuel Dokie turned and walked back onto the small ferry to cross the stream, deep in the forest of the border country between Liberia and the Ivory Coast. It was the day after I had left Dokie there that Tom Woweiyu called from New Jersey, saying he wanted to hold a press conference in Liberia.

Hot morning damp rose from the red-earth tracks off the main street through Danane, the north-western Ivory Coast town 20 minutes drive from the Liberian border-post at Logouatou. Woweiyu had told me, in one of our numerous bugged telephone calls following that first contact, that we should arrange to meet the NPFL fixer in Danane, Koulin Evarist, who would take us over the border.

'It's not going to be free,' Evarist had told me on a poor telephone line when I had managed to get through to him from Abidjan. 'Everything costs money. It won't be free, particularly for so many of you.'

There were ten reporters. Evarist gave no details over the telephone, but it became clear that it would not be straightforward getting into Liberia. We knew the Ivorian border authorities were antagonistic to reporters. Nobody had tried to cross into Liberia since my arrival back after the attack on the train a month previously.

It was night when we arrived at the Hotel des Lianes, on the edge of Danane. Next morning, 12 May, a convoy of pick-up trucks arrived in the forecourt. A young man with all the facial features of Charles Taylor but with ginger hair and an emaciated body, jumped down from the back of a pick-up and introduced himself.

'I'm Bartus. You should all come now,' he told us.

We rapidly threw our already-packed bags into the cars in which we had travelled from Abidjan the day before, and followed him through the streets thronging with Liberian refugees, army trucks and patrolling gendarmes who eyed us as we drove into the centre of the town. We turned just before a crossroads, headed down a muddy hill road, followed the road up another hill and then stopped alongside a low-walled compound. We walked inside, and Evarist introduced himself, offered us seats in a dark living-room, gave us Coke and Fanta to drink, and talked to us about the long time we would have to wait.

I wondered if he just wanted the money he had obliquely mentioned in our telephone calls. I was resistant to the idea of having to pay off a semi-official in a struggling rebel movement which needed free publicity. But he didn't ask for the money then, and I didn't offer.

Bartus drove away, then came back, and for the entire morning he repeated this routine. After two hours we drove back into the town and bought whisky for the rebels and wandered around the streets before returning to Evarist's house. A while later Bartus came back and told us to follow.

The reporters argued about which cars should go. Bartus said we should leave some of the cars behind, because we would not be taking them across the border. Suspicion mounted; those who were to leave their cars in Danane feared they would be deliberately deserted at the border on our return by the reporters with cars, who would drive back to Danane to send their stories before the competition was able to do so. The suspicion remained even after the decisions had been made and we drove to the edge of town, where Bartus and Evarist negotiated with Ivorian police at a security post who wanted to know where we were going. I don't know what they told them, but they let us through and I wondered how much money we would have to pay out to Evarist as compensation when we returned.

We drove fast along the damp red forest road. A goat trotted out in front of us and I thought we crushed it under the bumper. The driver did not stop. He didn't want to lose the convoy. Behind us I saw the goat roll in the road, then get up and trot off into the bush, apparently unharmed.

Less than a mile from the border we turned into a small enclave of thatched houses. Children watched the convoy of pick-ups, followed by the journalists' brand new Peugeots and Toyotas as they pulled up among the plantains in front of the neatly swept huts. Three boys from the village led the way, as we plunged into the thick forest, along a path which disappeared and had to be hacked with machetes, while the boys told us to be quiet as the border was close and the Ivorian military were always on the look-out for people crossing.

After an hour in the rising heat we reached the river. The same river which I had crossed downstream with Dokie. The sun dappled the weed-draped rocks on its bed as we slipped and slid across to the opposite bank where we waded through tall grass and emerged onto a track baking in the hot sun. From here we could see the metal bridge across the river and the Ivorian soldiers ambling around their border post, probably fully aware that we had crossed, aware also that their government favoured the NPFL but was still wary about the impact on relations with the Doe government in Monrovia if it was seen to be giving support to Taylor by allowing journalists to make the journey across the border to see him.

Deep in the forest I saw Dokie again. He sped past in a white ambulance. I saw his car approaching from behind us where we had stopped, and leaned out of the window when I saw him and waved. But neither he nor the driver, whom I also recognised, waved back. We had left the border and driven towards Kahnplay and then driven south towards Tapeta. We were bumping along the bad roads in a van. The pace was slower than when I had last sped through the silent forest. Then, the images had reached so far into me that every second of every day was constantly being relived in my mind, and is still being to this day. But there, stuck inside a van with familiar faces, friends from Abidjan, intruders had broken into the intense solitude of my recollections. Dokie's white ambulance disappeared into the forest and we bounced along for several more hours until the road was lined with people waving palm fronds and singing us into Tapeta. We stopped in the courtyard of the building where the old woman had fallen to her knees when she had seen Dokie, believing him to have been dead ever since she had attended his funeral in 1983.

The courtyard was filled with young fighters armed with Kalash-nikovs. A girl called out my name. She smiled as she held her gun. It was the girl Dokie had brought along with him the night that we had learned about the killing of the NPFL fighters in the next village and I had written a note to my family, thinking I might not see them again. I still have the note, and there was the girl who had stared out from the window with blue shutters, framed by the rambling bush. She was a fighter now, wearing an NPFL tee-shirt and a black beret. But still smiling.

Silk socks, well-polished brogues and a shiny six-shooter at his hip

gave my colleagues from Abidjan their first chance to see whether I had
been telling the truth about Charles Taylor.

He led Agnes and their daughter Amy into the recording studio at
Tapeta Baptist Mission radio studio, sat down on an easy chair and began
the task of creating a rebel leader before their eyes.

Just as I had wondered how the children of Liberia evolved into rebel
army fighters, I watched to see how a renegade from US justice, who
once had an overdraft of $16,000 and a penchant for betting at the dog
track, could perform the same metamorphosis, without losing control in
the process of portraying himself as the nation and the nation as himself.

He began by addressing what was then, in May 1990, the mere rumour that
he had somehow been connected with the Gadaffi regime in Libya, which,
it was being alleged, he had worked with in order to train his rebel force.

'We have never trained in Libya. We do not receive any assistance from
Libya. We have trained people from an original core group, trained in a
a certain place. But it was not Libya, nor Burkina Faso. Libya must not
be blamed.'

As if to further disprove these claims, he began speaking as if to the
entire world, and particularly to Washington's movers and shakers,
identifying his political heroes, in a bid to distance himself from the
revolutionaries with whom he had indeed mixed when in Libya.

'Nixon was one of the greatest presidents of the United States. He
messed up because he didn't come straight. I also like good old Ronny.
I just seem to like the guy, perhaps because there's a little bit of the
conservative in me,' Taylor said, with the vague hint that perhaps he was
once a guest of the Reagan White House.

For more than an hour he told the 'world' that he was a '42-year-old,
Aquarian, father of eight children, die-hard capitalist and teetotalling
Baptist who hadn't had a drink in 20 years', but who every six months
indulged in his only vice – smoking a fine cigar. At one point he addressed
claims by Doe that he had been shot, by pulling up his shirt and asking:
'Can you see any holes?' There were none. Then he calmly turned to
explaining the other side of the rebel leader, by approaching the thorny
issue of power, politics and Samuel Doe.

'It's so easy to make a dictator in Liberia. And I'm not going to let
myself be one,' he assured the press. Intrinsic to his assertion was the
possibility that it would be a struggle to subdue any dictatorial tendencies,
but that he would overcome. 'But I'm not going to turn government
over to someone to screw-up. We're going to build the kind of democracy
we want. We in the National Patriotic Front of Liberia have political

ambitions too, and there will be elections when the time is right. The NPFL will be the transition government.'

Having dealt with the issue of Libya, by lying, in the knowledge that none of the assembled journalists had any hard facts to question his denial of a link with Colonel Gadaffi, he returned to Liberia's relationship with the United States.

'The United States has permanent interests in Liberia, but not permanent friends. I would hope that we would have a real good marriage and a real good honeymoon. US foreign-policy advisors are going to go back to the drawing board.'

These were views, expressed by a would-be leader and politician, enshrined in the moment in which they were stated. They were views uttered at the turning-point of a period in the history of the twentieth century, when betrayal began to fill the world's most vulnerable regions with the real corpses of the cold war – not just the individual, murdered victims of dictatorship, but entire countries, which plunged into wars planned as a response to superpower-backed dictatorships, while those dictatorships were themselves being dropped by the superpowers which had sustained them.

Liberia was the first. Other countries followed. Old cold war conflicts lost their veneer of ideology and were exposed for what they had always been – power conflicts between tribal, class or regional rivals. In so doing, the ferocity of the conflicts was heightened, as they became fights to the death not between frail, imported ideologies which had never taken meaningful root in Africa, but between territorial rivals who had much more to lose than a debate over politics.

Taylor's belief that the Pentagon, the State Department and even the White House would rush to see how Liberia's new dawn would alter the position of what was, in May 1990, still to become the world's only superpower, was a reflection of that vulnerability. The United States, which had created Liberia, financed Doe, and effectively championed human rights' abuses in the belief that they were for the greater good, did not care what happened to Liberia. America was laughing at these pompous Africans with their antiquated ways who, in Chester Crocker's words, considered themselves 'honorary Americans'. Nobody on the other side of the Atlantic Ocean was going to lose sleep, even if Charles Taylor had been in Libya.

It was dark outside when he brought his presentation to a close. We all walked across an open area of grass, a group of journalists following a group of redeemers, who were leading a war which seemed big because it had enveloped the land, the roads and the town we were in, but which was a tiny detail beneath the stars. I saw Dokie again and gave him the whisky I had bought for him in Danane that morning. He accepted it grudgingly, because it was Johnny Walker Red Label and he said he wanted Black Label, which was more expensive. The silence of the night made everybody hopeful about tomorrow. There were none of the sounds of war, and the leader had just made his case with confidence, and one more tiny conflict had been made to move a few small steps further on.

The Baptist missionaries who had fled Tapeta left everything behind. We were shown to their rooms and slept on their bizarre array of water beds, which wallowed unnervingly beneath turning sleepers. Flying bullets would one day burst them and people would drown in their sleep, I was sure of it.

Next day the NPFL took us to the front line of Siathon, south of Tapeta and 33 miles north of the port of Buchanan. Behind a house there, the previous night's war of words faded into a distant part of the tapestry. Turning a sickening golden brown, bodies lay piled high in a haze of buzzing flies. It was the last thing the government troops had done before fleeing, our NPFL guides told us. After so much talk of war, it was real. The dying part had come. The scattered bodies I had seen before were not part of the same horror. At Siathon men, women and children lay hacked to pieces, deliberately dumped in a pile, perhaps forced there by soldiers, who then slaughtered them in a crowd which watched itself being killed. The smell was horrendous.

'They were made to strip and then they were killed.'

I had never seen a massacre before. I assumed that this was one.

We went to a hospital a few miles away in the well-tended grounds of the Liberian Agricultural Company rubber plantation, the largest American investment in Liberia since the sale of the Firestone rubber plantation to the Japanese.

Emmanuel Weh, a 12-year-old boy from Kpuetown close to Siathon, said that the shooting which forced him to flee was so intense that he was hit several times in the left arm. He arrived at the plantation hospital to find it barely attached to his body, and it was amputated. He stood surrounded by other people who had fled the slaughter which had swept through six neighbouring villages on 9 May.

There was an overpowering sense that no one knew whose hands they were in. They were frightened of the rebels, who sped around in pick-up trucks yelling orders, telling people to talk or not to talk as we asked them questions. There was enormous suspicion. Nobody said that they had seen the rebels commit atrocities, but there was fear of what might happen. These people who had lost everything stood along a wide verandah which skirted the hospital and waited and watched as the rebel troops, who had come to save them but who related to them as remotely as the people who had come to kill them, drove fast across the mile-wide area of grass which was the plantation golf course, set amid the calm, silent rows of rubber trees.

'I feel terrible. I get very angry. If I wasn't a physician I would be out there fighting,' said the doctor, Wilmott Harris, listing the 46 injured who came to the hospital, all but ten of whom were women and children, including a four-year-old girl who later died from a bullet which had passed right through her. 'But I'm imprisoned here,' he whispered. He didn't go any further or explain by whom he was imprisoned, but it was obvious that none of these people could move. He changed his tone and began analysing the war. 'The tribal element has become less important. It's not just Gio and Mano. It's the whole country which has been run very badly,' he said, as the NPFL fighters listened.

Stopped beside the dirt road in the thick forest on the way back to Tapeta we saw Elmer Johnson, the commander with the glass eye I had interviewed in the town in April. He smiled and laughed and said things were going well. Then we drove back to Tapeta, where Charles Taylor did an impromptu press conference as he wandered across the grounds of the Baptist mission, examining weaponry which it was unclear whether he knew how to use.

He wore a blue, short-sleeved suit, black brogues and his usual Ray-Ban aviator sunglasses, as he returned to condemnations of Doe, and again denied that Libya had trained the NPFL (which at one point he claimed had been trained in Liberia itself). Just before we climbed aboard the bus which was to return us to the border, he began a slight revision of the previous night's remarks about the United States, saying there was no friction between the NPFL and the US.

'The United States will always remember the relationship between our two countries,' he said, perhaps reflecting an awareness that Liberia was already being set adrift by the nation which had created it, but which was at odds with it in every aspect of culture and politics.

We left the leader and his rebels at their hill-top mission station. Next day, 16 May, we drove back though the Ivory Coast towards Abidjan.

Top left: President Samuel K. Doe. *Top right:* Brigadier-General Prince Y. Johnson.
Below: Charles Taylor, leader of the National Patriotic Party. *Source: West Africa Magazine*

Twenty miles from the city, groups of soldiers were lounging along the side of the motorway. It was uncharacteristic to see them out like that. As Abidjan's tower blocks appeared through the haze, more soldiers could be seen, running armed across the road, which was practically deserted of traffic.

It appeared there had been a coup.

The rest of the country was calm. I quickly learned that around 1,000 soldiers had mutinied, demanding an increase in their $16 per month salaries. They occupied and closed Abidjan-Port Bouet international airport and seized the radio station, which was now heavily guarded as I drove through the empty streets of Plateau. There was occasional sounds of shooting, but nobody to be seen except for the fleeting sight of a renegade army truck speeding across a distant crossroads.

The months of tension were reaching their climax. For hours the country, which had known such calm for most of the 30 years since its independence, was brought to a state of aching silence out of which anything could have burst.

President Houphouet-Boigny gathered his inner circle of political apparatchiks around him that night, after promises from the Defence Minister Jean Konan Banny that their grievances would be heard proved sufficient to convince the soldiers to return to barracks. The airport was reopened. The first incoming flight brought Lieutenant-Colonel Alain Le Caro, head of the French President's personal protection unit, sent by François Mitterrand to Houphouet-Boigny as a personal gesture to assure the Ivorian president of his personal security.

But within a few days the tension was diffused. The civil servants' salary cuts were scrapped, the soldiers were promised more, and France's interest in maintaining stability, in one of the few former African colonies where change had so far not led to widespread bloodshed, assured the provision of new funds from foreign donors to pay for the increases.

Meanwhile, as the financial agreement was being finalised in Abidjan and Paris, to maintain stability in the Ivory Coast, Charles Taylor's forces seized the port of Buchanan. Africa's oldest republic was split in two and Samuel Doe began to fight for his life.

Doe had only found one friend in the region during his ten-year rule, and in May he went to see him in Nigeria.

General Ibrahim Babangida, whose pretensions to being the leader of a regional superpower had led to his financing, equipping and staffing of military missions to several West African countries, openly sided with Doe throughout the late 1980s. Nigeria took over repayment of Liberia's

$50million debt to the African Development Bank in 1990, and Doe returned the compliment by opening the Ibrahim Babangida school of political science at Monrovia university. In May 1990 Doe sought further proof of these close ties when he asked Babangida to furnish him with arms and 2,000 troops with which to counter Charles Taylor's progress through the country. But this time the Nigerians refused.

Nigeria's attention to the evolving situation in Liberia, and the active role played by the self-styled 'revolutionary' government in Burkina Faso in housing, equipping and facilitating the training of the NPFL, had laid the groundwork for a regional split. By May 1990 this encompassed African states from Libya to the Ivory Coast, and overseas powers, notably the US and France. The split evolved in a direction determined by the broader political movements underway in the states affected by the war.

The key element was the readiness of the United States – long regarded as the guardian of Liberia, into which other regional influences had consequently barely penetrated – to forgo its influence, if maintaining it meant becoming involved in the war. Even the role played by Libya in the creation of the NPFL as a fighting force barely appeared to matter to the Americans. Libyans had already established a business presence in Liberia during the 1980s, owning the Pan-African Plaza office block and Monrovia's bottling plant. Meanwhile US diplomatic pressure, and what amounted to a $5million bribe, had encouraged Samuel Doe to cancel his planned trip to Tripoli in 1984.

As a conflict which straddled the end of the cold war and quickly lost its strategic significance, the war had its genesis during Ronald Reagan's period of support for Doe, but became a conflict fought out during the era of the Bush White House.

'The Libyan angle bugged us. We would have like to have targeted the Libyans and gone for Taylor. But supporting Doe was impossible. If Taylor had been committing atrocities it would have been easier. But there was nobody in the State Department saying there was somebody they could support in Liberia,' said a former official in the American embassy in Monrovia. 'Most of the people in the Department of State senior levels didn't really care. Bush wasn't focusing much on Liberia, and by mid-1990 Taylor looked okay. We didn't feel that the Libyan foothold in West Africa would be Charles Taylor's Liberia. He had no ideological link to Libya,' the official said, confirming, however, that the US had contingency plans which could include sending in troops to 'split the factions'.

American officials meanwhile took to watching from the Ivory Coast, as the regional balance of power responded to the clear sign that Liberia's closest ally was going to take no military steps to halt the rebel advance.

Family connections were seen as one cause of President Houphouet-Boigny's acceptance of Taylor's cause. The death of his friend President Tolbert in Doe's 1980 coup had been followed by the killing of the late Liberian leader's son, A. B. Tolbert, whose Ivorian wife Desiree 'Daisy' Delafosse was treated as an adopted daughter by Houphouet-Boigny. She returned to the Ivory Coast when Thomas Weh Seyn, the fellow coupmaker whom Doe eventually executed, ignored Doe's orders and killed A. B. Tolbert in Monrovia.

Houphouet-Boigny never publicly identified his personal motives as a reason for treating Doe with disdain, and they did not influence his policy towards Liberia as a country, until Taylor appeared on the scene and proved himself determined to overthrow Doe.

The Burkinabe leader Blaise Compaore was also a significant element in the regional political puzzle. Also married to an Ivorian, Chantale Terrasson, Compaore's relationship with both Taylor and Houphouet-Boigny was central to the NPFL's ability to mount a campaign from the Ivory Coast. Compaore was part of the generally conservative Francophone camp within the region, as well as viewing himself as a leader of the revolutionary left. He was grateful to Houphouet-Boigny, the elder statesman of the region, for having welcomed the coup which had brought him to power in 1987. He was able to pursue his revolutionary path by giving support to Taylor's insurrection, which was aimed at overthrowing a dictator. But it also suited his Francophone fellow-presidents – who were as keen as France itself to confront the Anglo-Saxon presence in the region – to promote a rebellion which would, it seemed, dilute American influence, by overthrowing Doe.

Houphouet-Boigny did not meet Taylor until November 1990, but Ivorian officials allowed the flow of arms through the country's northern regions into Liberia, amid official Ivorian denials that this was taking place. Houphouet-Boigny did not become directly involved until it was time for him to step into the breach and attempt to broker peace. This was only after Doe was dead and Taylor was confronted by the attempts of Houphouet-Boigny's traditional rivals, the Nigerians, to stop him seizing power.

Chester Crocker, the outspoken former US Assistant Secretary of State for African affairs, was clear about the impact of the regional and international relationships: 'None of this would have happened if the French had not had their hands in it. The Ivory Coast was a threat to Doe, but throughout the 1980s it wasn't apparent. It would have been useful [to the United States] if Houphouet-Boigny had been helpful to Doe. Doe needed Houphouet-Boigny,' he told me.

8 Warriors and Wild Fruit

> We captured ten AFL soldiers in Old Road. They put their hands up and we killed them. We cut their heads off. I don't feel good killing. I have knife-proof. But he is my enemy. I wear my charms – they are Sonkaley Goa. I have my medicine. It is Seke. I'm not sure what's in it. It was given to me by a medicine man in Saklepie. If you take the medicine then you can't have sex or eat raw cassava or palm oil. If you do, the medicine will spoil. I keep the medicine because everybody know I'm a rebel. I wear a ring and two fetishes on rope around my neck. If you are my enemy the ring will burn me. If somebody is my enemy at the checkpoint then I will know because my ring will tell me. If somebody is my enemy I will take him on one side. People beg. They say: 'Please don't kill me.' But I don't trust them. They are in my territory. I have killed fifty people. I cut off their heads or shot them. They begged for their lives, but I didn't trust them. My people in my area like me. I did things for them. If I think about the war I feel bad, because here's my own country and we have damaged our country. Now everybody has an enemy.
>
> ELIJAH MCCARTHEY, *NPFL soldier, Monrovia.*

GOD APPOINTED Moses to redeem the people of Egypt. The NPFL are here as redeemers and I know it. So I gave myself up, and that's why I wasn't killed. But if I have taken blood then I shouldn't see blessing in my lifetime. But I have never taken blood from anybody. It was hatred which led people to say it was me that killed people like that. I never lay down pregnant women on the ground and cut them and tore out their unborn children. It was somebody else using my name.'

Staff Sergeant Harrison S. Barjebo of the Armed Forces of Liberia knelt beneath one of the tall trees of the NPFL base at Gborplay and denied the accusations against him. Three deep gashes on the top of his head bore testimony to the beating meted out to him when he was captured. He was tied with rope but defiant, as Taylor's troops accused him of being the famous 'One-Foot Devil' of Tapeta, whose reputation had spread throughout the war zone.

'Of course he won't admit to being One-Foot. But he's that devil. Everybody knows him,' said Charles Taylor, as he wandered through the camp, followed by the camera of a CNN television crew which had arrived in Liberia one morning in early June.

107

'I watched him, I watched him,' said an old man, who yelled at the prisoner. 'I watched him as he picked up my three children by their feet and cut them right down, right from the throat down. Each of my children. I would know that man. I can see him. His teeth are rotting inside his head. I can see him. He used to use a crutch. That's why they call him One-Foot, even though he's got two feet,' the old man said.

But for Taylor and the NPFL troops questioning the cowering captive, the issue of importance seemed to be that Barjebo was denying that he was who they said he was. The horror of his crimes appeared less significant than the fact that he was lying to his captors. It was a question of honesty.

'And on one occasion, when Doe was in the Executive Mansion, he had one of his critics brought up to him on the fourth floor,' Taylor was telling CNN beneath another tree. 'Doe's people brought the man and left him with the president, who appeared in front of the man dressed in a devil's costume. Then the man began pleading for his life, and Doe chopped at him with a sword and cut off one of the man's arms. Doe was yelling at him all this time, and as the man lay on the floor of the office he chopped off the man's other arm. Then, accusing the man of betraying him, Doe chopped off both the man's legs. And all the while Doe was doing these things dressed in a devil's costume. This is a president I'm talking about.'

The CNN crew filmed Taylor's tale of Doe's brutality, one of the tales emerging out of ten years of tyranny, tales which had seeped into the popular imagination and may well have been true. Perhaps they were true. The war meant that it hardly mattered what was true and what was not. People knew what had happened to them. They had heard what had happened to other people, and the myths and realities melded together to form the morality of the uprising.

Taylor was in full flow on camera, recounting the trying times which had preceded his arrival as the leader of the NPFL, saying how he enjoyed the 'good things in life. I would rather buy a pair of shoes for $100 that will last for a few years, than a few pairs that will last for less time,' he told the camera crew.

'I want my name to be littered over the pages of history as being the man who started out the way it should be started out,' he went on. 'If I had some chances I would really start some trouble in this region. I'm not going to go down in history as a man who brought this country to war and then screwed-up. I want people to know that freedom is no threat to anybody. Nobody has been willing to risk fighting. So, we're trying.

All these things start as a dream, but now we have made it into a reality.'
   Reality. Reality.

Big white clouds rose up over the swamp and forest surrounding
Buchanan. A scatter of rain swept across the red-earth wasteground on
the edge of the port town. The familiar shape of the dead stood out on a
small rise of earth against the white clouds, blue sky, grey light. The rain-
soaked colours of clothes spilt from an open suitcase beside the body. A
shoe lay torn from a foot whose flesh had been chewed down to the bone.
The earth around the body had darkened as the fluid had seeped out.
Overhead, the clouds darkened to grey as the white cumulus were swept
inland from the sea. Dogs roamed among the shacks of the town, tearing
at the muddy flesh dumped among the roadside weeds of the main street.
Blood trails oozed across the road, up the kerbstones, down the mud
paths between tin-roof huts and into yards dappled with sunlight and
blood, beneath great trees shadowing the empty homes of the town.
   An old woman waved from an open window. She smiled where she
sat on a chair watching the rebels come through.
   'My family left me because I couldn't run. Perhaps they're dead, and
old age saved my life,' she said, peering out onto the main street, where
the sun drifted in light and shadow across the glitter of bottles looted,
emptied and shattered into splinters as they were dashed onto the ground,
amid bright red beer-crates, bright green bedsheets and bright yellow
taxis. She watched as the young men of Liberia poured into the town,
the army that was there to save her, patrolling the streets like packs of
wolves, the victors hidden behind their disguises – pink silk dresses, wigs
drooping over their eyes, white paint, masks, ski goggles, sunglasses –
costumes of war aimed at hiding the fighters from the reality of what
they were doing, so that after the war they could say it was somebody
else who did those things. Just like Harrison Barjebo, the child-killer of
Tapeta.
   'It's ours. Buchanan is ours. We're the rebels, and we're doing all right,'
the invaders chanted, as they smashed their way into shops. They were
not the same people as in peacetime, but they had it in the backs of their
minds that one day they would no longer be soldiers. So they hid behind
their disguises, and when it was all over, they would smoke the last of
their marijuana, remove their wigs and return to civilian life. Or so they
thought.
   A group of Lebanese shopkeepers stood smoking on the veranda of
their house in the Limco iron-ore company compound. They watched

the corner of their driveway, around which NPFL fighters occasionally sped in pick-up trucks, bursting into the yard, pushing their way into the house, demanding, asserting, yelling nothing in particular, but yelling as a sign that Buchanan was now theirs and the Lebanese were their subjects and the conquest was moving on. The Lebanese smoked furiously, brushed spilt ash from the dress shirts they thought they should wear as a sign of respect and welcome to the invaders, and occasionally turned to console a brightly coloured parrot which was perched precariously in a rusting cage on the veranda.

That afternoon Samuel Dokie drove in to the Lebanese compound.

'You are our brothers. You have been here many years,' he told them. 'We are almost at the end of the war, and you will have many problems if you go now and want to come back. We are now needing to think about reconstruction. Not just clearing up, but rebuilding our country. And you Lebanese are part of that. It's like building a house. It's easy to put up the walls and put on the roof. It's when you have to put in the finishing touches that you need money. And the Lebanese are part of that.'

The men listened to the threat. If they left now, when the NPFL needed them, they would be blacklisted. After Dokie left the house they talked about how desperate they were to leave and rejoin their families who had been evacuated two weeks before.

Dust draped the cushions in the clubhouse of the Limco compound, where the NPFL gave us a smart family house whose inhabitants had fled with barely anything at all. Grass was growing up through the cracks in the tennis courts. On that first afternoon, shooting broke out for a few seconds and a light aircraft gently edged its way across a stormy sky. There was more shooting, then night fell.

The cook who had worked at the house for the previous occupants appeared at the back door saying that he would like to prepare us meals and that he had lots of imagination, if few ingredients. The CNN cameraman stipulated that as he was vegetarian he would only be requiring fresh vegetables. The cook nodded uncertainly. When dinner came it was tinned luncheon-meat and spaghetti rings. The cameraman repeated his order for fresh vegetables. The cook offered tomato soup. When it came it was from a tin, and the cameraman calmly mocked the reality of Liberia by repeating his ludicrous order for food that had long since disappeared from Buchanan. The cook was embarrassed that he could not provide what was being asked of him, when instead he should just have laughed at the cameraman. But Liberians do not laugh at

Americans, and he said he would try hard to find something to please his bossman, who went to sleep and rocked the entire house with thunderous snoring.

Shooting started at first light. It was a wet, cold morning. A shirtless rebel turned up the radio, which was playing hymns. 'Let Jesus Into Your Heart' was being sung by a Monrovia choir. I walked across to the company telex-room to send a message to London. The building was empty so I walked to the house of the Lebanese. They were gathered around the parrot cage, smoking. They invited me inside their sitting-room, which was crammed full of new televisions, record players, videos. Dokie had written an official note for them, barring anybody from entering their house uninvited. They had stapled it on to the front door. As we sat there a car screeched to a halt outside and a group of heavily armed fighters burst in. One of the Lebanese pointed to the note on the door, which the leader of the NPFL group immediately tore from its staples and threw to the floor. The fighters, sweating, with blood-shot eyes, bullet-belts strapped across their shoulders, scorpion tee-shirts, black berets, yelled and paraded and disputed with each other. They had come for nothing. They demanded cigarettes, which the Lebanese handed over enthusiastically. But they didn't really know what the purpose of their visit was, other than to look inside houses that, in peacetime, would have been barred to them. Wartime was their freedom. They could go where they liked, and left as suddenly as they had arrived, sweeping across the veranda, shaking the cage, where the parrot fell in a squawking rage from its perch and landed in the pile of droppings which had collected beneath it.

Dokie arrived at our house in the compound. The morning's shooting was explained, as was that of the previous night. The rebel advance into Buchanan had been resisted by the AFL, who took back part of the town. Then they had been driven out by the NPFL, which had pushed well beyond the town, along the road towards Harbel and the Firestone rubber plantation.

But a pocket of AFL troops had hidden just outside Buchanan and, while the NPFL was looting the shops, had launched a new offensive. This had happened after NPFL troops, led by Elmer Johnson, had moved beyond Buchanan. Now, Elmer, whose presence may have prevented the looting of Buchanan had he been there instead of on the front-line, had disappeared. Dokie, who had joined Taylor in January along with Elmer, had arrived in Buchanan to look for his friend.

Two days later, on 6 June, Elmer was found lying face down in a

111

roadside swamp beside his bullet-riddled blue pick-up truck two miles outside Buchanan. Dokie had not thought to look there earlier. The government in Monrovia rejoiced. One of its soldiers claimed to have been in the ambush which trapped Elmer. The soldier made his way back to Monrovia with one of the dead commander's identity cards, which was displayed on national television.

Elmer had been shot in the back of the head. Two others lying beside him had been executed in the same way. Seven other bodies lay around the pick-up truck.

'Elmer Johnson, whose body we have just discovered, was a hero,' said Dokie, standing on the road beside the body the afternoon we found the ambush site. 'He was very important, in that this is a man who, upon hearing that Charles Taylor had already attacked Liberia, left a job for which he was paid $45,000 a year, to make sure that the war against Doe was a just war.'

Dokie did not explain why it had taken him so long to find Elmer's body, even though it was lying so close to Buchanan, beside the car which was easily recognisable as being his. Nor did he explain how the government in Monrovia managed to get hold of Elmer's identity card. To have done so would have meant the lone AFL soldier who reached the capital had quickly and easily passed through numerous NPFL checkpoints along the road to Robertsfield airport. Nor did Dokie explain why the government claimed the ambush took place on the dirt road north of Buchanan, towards the Lac rubber plantation, when in fact it took place on the tarmac road between Buchanan and Firestone.

These unexplained elements in the death of Elmer Johnson raised the suspicion that Elmer was the victim of an internal feud within the NPFL, in which Elmer's military successes had begun to overshadow the stature of the political leadership of Taylor. The government claimed its forces were active in the Lac plantation, where it said Elmer had been killed. In fact, the plantation was firmly under NPFL control at that time, as we had driven through it. Even the site of the ambush was so close to Buchanan itself that the AFL would have been in uncharacteristically brave mood to have launched an ambush so close to a town from which it had been ousted the day before.

Later that day Taylor drove into Buchanan. He was heavily guarded and said nothing as he went into the Limco office which had become the NPFL headquarters in the town. He left without saying a word.

In the evening Dokie told us we had to go to the Lac plantation to see Taylor. There was a red sky as we left Buchanan, driving in silence across the red wasteground where the body of the man lay with his open suitcase beside him.

'Move soldier, move,' the commander of the first checkpoint outside the town yelled to one of his subordinates. A month before the guards would have been alert, high-spirited, purposeful. Now they stared blankly at the passengers, ambled exhausted to the string of rubber strips tied together to form the barrier, which dropped into the mud, and we drove on into the forest and the night. Rain poured across the shaft of the headlights' beams. The darkness engulfed us until the next checkpoint, where the fighters yelled and fired into the air, demanding that the windows be opened, that we get out of the car, show passes and identity cards, explain ourselves there in the middle of the black forest, looking into the bloodshot eyes of the troops who had themselves been engulfed by the war and hunger and the loneliness of being far from home and far from the fighting that was raging miles away on the other side of Buchanan and creeping up the coast. They yelled and threatened and postured with their Kalashnikovs; high-voiced boys smoking marijuana ordered bearded men to search us; power seemed to be in the hands of whoever yelled loudest and strode most assertively around the car. Then, as aggressively, they told us to drive on, back into the darkness, till we emerged from the trees and skirted around the lawns of the Lac plantation and were shown into a dimly lit company house and told to wait in a room filled with silent people who lounged on chairs and said nothing.

'Elmer Johnson was a fine young man. But he was not my personal military adviser, though he did play an important role as an adviser to a battalion,' said Taylor, when asked about the death of the commander. He was playing down the significance of the loss to the NPFL. He sat on a settee in a one-piece khaki jump-suit. Dokie sat beside him on a chair. On the other side was a bearded man in military uniform, a peaked army cap pulled low over his eyes, awkwardly fumbling with a Kalashnikov which sat propped up between his legs. Taylor introduced the man as Tom Woweiyu, the NPFL representative in New Jersey with whom I had organised the press conference during May, but whom I had never met.

Taylor said the NPFL had pushed the government out of Harbel, the town close to the Firestone plantation, but was unclear about who controlled Robertsfield airport.

'You're lucky there's a free press here,' he said, criticising the reports of his troops looting Buchanan. 'But we're not stopping now, because there's been a lot of bloodshed. This war has not been the cleanest you can find, but we have done much better than the enemy. We are still in a very brutal war, and the enemy is the enemy, so we shoot him,' said Taylor. But he acknowledged that foreign pressure had led him to agree to send a delegation to peace talks which were to be held in the Sierra Leonean capital, Freetown. He said that it was only to try to secure the departure of the people living in Monrovia that he had agreed to send a delegation not to negotiate an end to the war.

'We as an organisation must listen to nations. If a country like the United States says that it would like to see us talk, we can't be so pompous as to say that we aren't going to talk. The US is playing a peaceful role, but we have had no formal contacts with the US on these matters,' he said.

By then the US had stationed 2,500 marines on ships off the coast of Liberia a few miles from Monrovia. According to a senior American source, there was no intention of involving the marines in combat.

'The marines were there because the American military was looking for a role, because there were no conflicts going on in the world,' the official said.

Herman Cohen, then US Assistant Secretary of State for African affairs, met Taylor in early June and told him that the US would try to convince Doe to leave before there was a battle for Monrovia. Throughout 1990 Cohen never once spoke directly to President George Bush about the Liberian crisis, a sign of how unimportant it was to the US. Cohen ran the policy on his own, and arranged with the Togolese dictator, General Gnassingbe Eyadema, to grant Doe asylum in Togo. In return, the Togolese, who had initially been reluctant to become involved in an essentially 'Anglophone' problem, had demanded American assistance in developing the Togolese capital, Lomé, as West Africa's regional freeport.

Doe agreed in principle to leave Monrovia if Taylor left Liberia as well, which Taylor refused to do, demanding that only Doe be removed. Cohen advanced these initiatives personally, speaking directly with Doe, who insisted on taking one of his favourite cars with him into exile and demanding that he be allowed safe passage to his native Grand Gedeh county to see his father *en route* to Togo, from where he insisted that he be accepted onto a graduate study course either at Oxford or in the United States.

Meanwhile, Taylor slowed his advance after seizing Firestone on 5 June, to await the outcome of the American discussions with Doe and to give the US the impression that he was not intransigent.

It was the mistake which cost him the war.

'Eat the wild fruits and come to the city,' Doe yelled down the radio which had crackled into life early on the morning of 14 May. The man listening on the other end smiled and chuckled, before hurling insults back at the president. Doe assumed he was talking to one of Taylor's commanders, though he knew it wasn't Taylor himself. In fact, the rebel yelling at Doe was Prince Johnson, who had led the split with Taylor in January 1990, a few days after the invasion.

'Taylor had promised Prince that weapons would be available in Butuo as soon as he crossed the border in December 1989. But there were no weapons there. So, Prince attacked the Butuo army-post with a shotgun and some machetes and captured a field radio and some M-16 rifles,' said one of the early recruits to Prince Johnson's force, who later became a key commander in Prince's Independent National Patriotic Front of Liberia (INPFL).

'Prince used the AFL radio to call for reinforcements, which were sent and ambushed by the INPFL. In January, at Zayeglay in Nimba, 37 of Taylor's people were killed by Prince's forces, just after the split. The villagers called in the "country devil" to try and resolve the split between the factions, but some of the fighters even shot at the country devil. The country devil is supposed to be an arbiter, who is believed to have supreme powers, and consequently supremacy over ordinary human beings. You cannot appeal against the country devil's decision in the settling of disputes, and the refusal of the two sides to reach a compromise was a reflection of how serious the split between Taylor and Prince was,' the INPFL commander told me.

Taylor had acknowledged the split with Prince Johnson during the press conference at Tapeta in May. But as Prince had no way of communicating to the outside world, only Taylor's version of the split had been broadcast. It was only in April that Doe realised he was fighting two rebel movements, and this was confirmed when he talked to Prince over the radio in May. After the battery on the radio he had captured in Butuo had gone dead, Prince captured a second radio after ambushing AFL troops at Dutah-Palala on 14 May. The AFL commander, Colonel John Krekue, was killed in the ambush, and Prince's troops moved towards Gbarnga, which was under the control of AFL troops under the command of Colonel Hezekiah Bowen.

In April the Liberian Senate had allowed Doe to withdraw $5 million from the Treasury – the entire budget of the electoral commission, which had intended to use the money for voter registration for forthcoming elections – to buy weapons and ammunition, including new rifles which arrived from North Korea in May. As a result, Doe's forces were well equipped, and each time they fell into INPFL ambushes substantial amounts of weapons were captured by the rebel group. On 28 May Prince's forces attacked Gbarnga and drove out the AFL, quickly capturing over 300 heavy weapons, Kalashnikovs, mortars and shotguns. Loading their armoury onto their heads, the INPFL deserted the town just as Taylor's forces attacked it. By then Prince was in the bush and Taylor's men occupied a town which was again under siege – from AFL reinforcements sent to recapture it. From there Prince advanced south towards Monrovia. By June 5, when Taylor called a temporary halt to his advance from Robertsfield, while the Americans tried to convince Doe to leave, Prince had gathered a force of 3,000 men, many joining because they were surrounded by fighting in all directions and had nowhere else to go.

'Fear of Prince among Taylor's troops meant that the NPFL often fled when the INPFL arrived. In Ballamah, Prince was meeting with the staff of Cuttington College when one of his soldiers ran up to him and said that some INPFL soldiers were raping a woman. Prince ordered that the woman, who had been stripped of all her clothes, be brought in front of him and the college staff. She was nude, and Prince told her to identify the people who had raped her, and then he shot all five of the men in front of everybody,' said the former INPFL commander. 'Prince was his own law. He even married couples. He would order the two people to come together and would have a general muster. He would say to the man: "Do you want this woman? Then kiss her. She is your wife." Then he would say to the gathering: "This woman is this man's wife and nobody's allowed to touch her".'

'Sometime in 1987 the Krahn and the Gio ate a sacrificial cat as a way of agreeing that they wouldn't fight against each other. This is called eating "kafu", and the invasion of 1989 was seen as breaking this agreement,' Hezekiah Bowen explained to me, as he looked out across the shanty town which formed the barracks in Monrovia over which he had jurisdiction. He only talked to me much later in the war, when his disillusionment with the AFL was deeply embedded but which, even as we spoke, he continued to lead as chief of staff.

'When I arrived [in Nimba] the thing was already going on. When you are fighting rebels you have to get on with the people, because the rebels can mix with the people. I tried to get the people on my side, but then the army discipline fell apart and people just started accusing everybody of being a rebel,' Bowen said.

Though one of Doe's Krahn tribe, Bowen was not part of the inner circle of military men the president preferred to have around him. Bowen was sent as AFL commander in Nimba in response to the NPFL invasion, but distrust rapidly brought an end to his tenure. At one point he asked Doe for money to buy an earth-mover to clear the border area in order to make it more difficult for the NPFL to cross from the Ivory Coast, and Doe accused him of planning to keep the money for himself. The accusation stemmed from a growing crisis within the army leadership.

'I didn't believe that the army was fighting. I believed that the army was lying,' said Doe's former vice-president Harry Moniba, when I met him later in 1990. 'If the AFL had been killing the rebels then they would have been taking their guns. But they didn't bring any guns back to Monrovia – so they must have been killing civilians. Soldiers would come back to the mansion and say they had killed some rebels dead. Doe would give money to ministers to give to the soldiers who had killed the rebels. The ministers would give a small amount to the soldiers and keep the rest for themselves,' he said.

Moniba, who was the most senior non-Krahn to survive the early months of the war in his government position, said Doe would give $20,000–$25,000 to Generals Smith, Craig and Nimley when they came back from missions.

'They were supposed to pay their men. But the generals were not paying the troops. Instead they would keep the money for themselves. This seriously weakened the army. The army was 6,000-strong, with 2,500 at the mansion, 3,000 at BTC [the Barclay Training Centre], and new people were being brought in to train, most of them rogues from Monrovia,' Moniba said.

According to Moniba, such was the decay within the leadership that on one occasion when Doe (who routinely wore hand grenades strapped to his fatigues and a revolver at his hip even inside the Executive Mansion) sent General Nimely out to buy rice for his entourage, Nimley returned with rice and sold it to Doe at a profit, demanding payment from Doe of $500 per bag. The AFL's routine failure to do anything other than attack unarmed civilians and make money out of the war meant that most people in the Executive Mansion were either lying about the military situation, or simply did not know the truth, said Moniba:

One day I saw Nimely at the mansion and I said to him: I hear the rebels have reached Buchanan. And Nimely said: 'No, I'm there. I'm there. We will keep it,' when in fact Buchanan had already fallen to the NPFL. Meanwhile the US was encouraging all of Doe's people to leave – the chief of staff Henry Dubar, Jonathan Taylor, Doe's speechwriter, Charles Julu, William Glay. Glay had been approached by the CIA in order to have somebody placed in the mansion who could arrange Doe's demise. All got visas very easily, to undermine Doe by removing his advisers. But Doe seemed quite convinced that he would overcome. Up to 9 September he felt that he would overcome. I'm certain he felt he could wade the stream. The army kept telling the government that they were doing well and that they were mopping up. I felt sad to see the place besieged. I did not like to see such an atmosphere in the mansion. It was a sorrowful experience to sit and see the place that had been bustling with life and people, come down to this kind of condition.

At mid-morning a note arrived at our house on the Limco compound in Buchanan:

> June 7, 1990. Dear Mark, You and all of the journalists are invited to witness the burial ceremony of our brother and friend Elmer Johnson at LAC. The funeral is at 10:00am. Yours, Samuel S. Dokie, Adviser and Special Assistant to the President, Chairman and CIC–NPFL.

It was too late for us to be at Lac by the appointed time. Dokie ordered that a volley be fired over the coffin as it was lowered into the ground at the small Catholic mission church on the hill above the plantation. There was a violent dispute among the fighters ordered to fire the shots. Why, they demanded, should Elmer Johnson be given a hero's burial when thousands of other people had been left to rot on Liberia's roadsides? Eventually shots were fired, though more out of anger than as a salute, according to the people who were there.

The radio news was full of stories about preparations for the talks in Sierra Leone. The CNN crew felt the war would soon be over and made plans to leave. We drove to Lac in the hope of finding Dokie. We went to the house where we had seen Taylor, but it was deserted. We drove across the golf course to the company houses. At one we found a woman wearing an army jacket with the name 'Johnson' on the breast pocket. She was Elmer Johnson's girlfriend. She said nothing as we offered condolences. Another woman said she had not spoken since Elmer died. She had not had the chance to tell her dead lover that she was pregnant.

In a nearby house the representatives of Keene Industries which owned Lac, Vincent Tan and Glenn Christian, were sitting as they always did, at their dining-room table, behind net curtains, drinking tea and discussing quietly how they could prevent the NPFL from ransacking their house. They had not seen Dokie, but thought that he was in Tapeta. We left them in their house, and drove through the plantation. Silence betrayed the war. The golf-course greens, rain drops clinging to the blades of grass, were growing in tufts. In peacetime they would have been cut. But now there was silence and emptiness and the threat of more rain.

The other journalist left for the border as soon as we arrived in Tapeta. We found Dokie at a house in a clearing in the forest. I said I would stay a few more days. Dokie was about to leave the town and said I could travel with him. I had no idea where we were going. I asked about the peace talks, and he was vague. He walked over to a dark blue Cadillac parked beneath a tree and told me to get in. The engine purred into life, Dokie in the front, me and an armed guard in the back. We left the clearing behind and glided along the dirt roads of Liberia, past overgrown plantations, through empty villages, through the endless darkness of the forests. At a village we stopped and Dokie brought back a girl who sat between me and the guard in the back. Then we continued. All was silent, the car windows keeping out the noise. Dokie and I had rarely travelled in such silence before, our usual transport being noisy and hot, with windows open to the clatter of the road. But now we sat in silence, watching the war through smoked-glass windows, as we drove through the late afternoon until darkness fell.

Dokie directed the driver to a half-finished house on the edge of a village, which gleamed with white paint in the moonlight. The Cadillac halted beneath a portico. The driver and guard walked through the entrance hall and lit petrol lamps to illuminate elaborately carved chairs which stood covered by transparent plastic sheets awaiting guests in the tiled living-room.

'It was the house of the deputy superintendent of the county. But he had to flee before he had a chance to live in it,' Dokie said, before disappearing into a room with the girl.

I lay beneath the canopy of a four-poster bed, in a room without light, and wondered where I was.

We left the house just after dawn. After 30 minutes we stopped near some huts between two villages and the girl got out and left without saying a word. The Cadillac seemed to glide over the holes in the road and I began to recognise the route as being the one which took us to

Gborplay, where we arrived an hour later, pulling up beneath the tall trees beside the small house where Taylor had shared his porridge with me in April.

'Is your name Huband?' said a white man with a broad American accent, who approached me where I was leaning proprietorially against the Cadillac. I said it was.

'You got my car,' he said.

'Nice car,' I said, confused as to how he could know me.

'My name's Bronson Fargo,' he said. 'Boy, we were worried about you.'

'How do you know my name?' I asked him, more defensively than I had intended to be.

'Well, who else would be driving around Liberia with Dokie in my Cadillac?' he asked. He told me he worked for the Limco iron-ore company, and that when the NPFL had attacked the train in April he had been in touch with my parents, my editor, the British embassy in Abidjan and just about everybody else. 'Boy, we were worried about you,' he said again. I was embarrassed. He made me feel as though I'd gone looking for trouble and that people I had never met before had been left to sort out the problems I had created for them.

'Well, that was kind of you to be so helpful. I'm sure my parents appreciated it.'

Dokie came out of the small house.

'Get in the car,' he said. I said goodbye to Bronson Fargo.

'We'll try and look after your car.'

'The Chairman was expecting us last night. Now we have to hurry,' Dokie said.

We drove quickly out of Gborplay and along roads which at first I recognised but which then became a mystery. We went for miles through unknown land.

'My land starts here,' said Dokie pointing to a large tree beside the road. 'One day I'll grow coffee there. Doe took it off me when I left the country.'

We drove on.

'And my land ends here,' he said, waving his hand across a swathe of bush on the edge of a town. The town was Saniquellie. We drove past a path on the left. At the bottom there was a pond, I remembered. I knew that path. We drove past the mission where I had stayed. It was deserted now. The priests had gone, the doors stood closed, and the fact of revisiting a place I been to before, on a different side of the conflict, cemented the past in my mind. I had moved on with the war, now that

Saniquellie belonged to somebody else. Its ruins belonged to the victors. The town was destroyed. The main street lay strewn with the rubble of fighting which had seen Saniquellie change hands three times, until the NPFL finally took it when the AFL fled Nimba in mid-May. The gas stations were rubble, the tin roofs had melted and twisted as fire had spread; the town had burned and black scars coated the fading paint of the small houses. Not even a dog could be seen prowling among the ruins. The victors had moved on. There was nobody there to walk beneath the ceremonial arch which, once again, bade us farewell.

At the barrier, where six months beforehand the immigration official had told me to 'tell the world', haunting me with his insistence that Liberia was about to be engulfed by a kind of horror I could not imagine but which he could already see clearly in his mind, there were a few young NPFL fighters. They raised the barrier and saluted Dokie, and were clearly intrigued by the Cadillac.

An hour later the front-line fighters yelled and screamed and sweated as they peered through the Cadillac's blackened windows, their bloodshot eyes set deep into dark faces covered by beards and wigs and strings of cowrie shells. Dokie announced himself, and the fighters saluted and ended their sentences with a US marine-style: 'Sir'. Then we left the main road and drove in among the mountains of slag from the Bong iron-ore mine and stopped among the neat gardens of the apparently deserted company houses.

'You see the trouble we are in. Our Jerusalem lies in ruins with its gates burned. Come, let us build the walls of our Jerusalem, that we may no longer suffer disgrace,' said Canon Burgess Carr. Whatever the emotions Liberia's warring leaders expressed about the damage they had wrought, they never appeared sincere beside the real emotion of the church leaders, whose trembling voices and calls for peace as the streets filled with bodies and the rivers ran with blood, sent shivers down the spines of congregations who were seeing what hell was like as they aspired to build their Jerusalem.

The peace talks opened in Freetown on 11 June.

At exactly 9am the day before, a German Air Force Hercules landed among the slag heaps of the Bong mine to evacuate to Freetown the remaining expatriate workers. It was also to take the six-member NPFL delegation to the peace talks, in which I had been included in order to secure me a seat on the plane to Freetown's Lunghi airport.

'You know, Mark, you owe the NPFL a lot of money,' said Dokie, as

121

the helicopter shuttle linking Lunghi with the Sierra Leonean capital clattered a few hundred feet above the wide bay. I was confused. He went on to tell me how lucky I had been that the NPFL had arranged for my transport to Freetown, and that generally the favours which he saw the NPFL as having accorded me had given me the chance to enhance my reputation as a reporter. I was stunned by what he said. I thought he had appreciated my effort, but instead he felt I was exploiting him and the NPFL.

'Well, now, I think the NPFL is one that owes Mark a great deal,' said Tom Woweiyu.

From then on I felt alienated from them, as we drove through Freetown in two Sierra Leonean government cars to the Cape Sierra Hotel, where they were shown to their rooms and I went a different way. I found the reporters from Abidjan whom I knew and had not seen for weeks and who made me feel that I had been away for many months.

We went together to the American embassy in the centre of the city, where the talks were to be held in the embassy library, and which opened with Canon Carr's heart-rending appeal.

'Do you know why there are so many journalists here? I don't,' Dokie asked Kenneth Best, owner of the Liberian *Daily Observer*, who had made his way to Freetown for the talks and was standing on the embassy steps as the delegations arrived.

'Because the world likes to see Africans killing each other. People get a kick out of it,' Best replied.

The churchmen prayed for a peaceful solution, and the NPFL delegation demanded that as a precondition for any ceasefire Doe had to leave Liberia immediately. They talked for five days. The government delegation had no power to agree to the NPFL precondition, the fighting in Liberia continued and Bong mine fell to Prince Johnson's advancing army. On 16 June the talks ended without agreement. The government delegates, who had tried to pressure Doe to leave the country in order to meet the NPFL demand, all deserted him by remaining in Freetown.

The day after the talks collapsed I flew back to Abidjan. Dokie and some others were on the same Ghana Airways flight, but they sat apart and we did not speak. When we reached Abidjan they were shown quickly through the airport by Ivorian officials, and I was back in the normality of my home, feeling relieved to be away from the Liberian war and the people fighting it.

9   The Eye of the Storm

PETER DE VOS, the new American ambassador to Liberia, was eating pancakes with strawberry jam on the terrace of the Lunghi airport hotel, across the bay from Freetown. It was early morning, the sky was mostly grey and big clouds smothered the sun. De Vos, veteran of superpower diplomacy in Africa after service in Mozambique and Guinea and later Somalia and Tanzania, with his neatly cut college haircut, pale grey double-breasted suit, red silk bow-tie, big glasses, round chubby face, half smiled that 'I can't talk in public, but maybe later' smile of diplomats who are not sure if they have met you before, so do not know if you can be trusted. I sat at another table.

The day before, 27 June, 20,000 people had marched through Monrovia demanding Samuel Doe's resignation. Troops had opened fire on the demonstrators. Witnesses said they had seen people fall when the shots were fired and some people had been crushed in the panic. Fourteen people were later admitted to hospital suffering from gunshot and, in a chilling sign of what would happen later, bayonet wounds. One man later died.

I had begged the woman on the check-in desk at Abidjan airport not to let the plane leave without me, while I scrounged US dollars from anyone I could contact, threw a heap of unwashed clothes into a bag and got to the airport, without a visa for Sierra Leone, just in time to catch the UTA–French Airlines evening flight to Freetown *en route* to Paris.

The flight took off, and suddenly I was scared about what lay ahead. The flight attendants brought sandwiches, but I had no appetite. I could not sleep, and the flight was less than two hours so what was the point? What was I doing? It was nearly midnight. The Paris-bound travellers lounged in their seats listening to soft music on the in-flight headphones, discreetly murmuring requests to the airline staff.

For days I had been in Abidjan, waiting for my newspaper to tell me to get to Liberia, not knowing if they, who were so far away, had any idea of what was going on there. I knew this was going to be a different trip from the previous ones I had made. Now the real battle was about to be fought. Taylor's radio statements were becoming more sinister. He made no attempt to salvage his former reputation as the good guy. He had become obstinate, making excuses for the revenge his fighters were now exacting, as the government troops fled, leaving the country open to rebel atrocities.

I walked down the steps with Gerald Bourke of *The Independent*, and out of the first-class compartment appeared Ken Noble from the *New York Times* with an enormous bag of luggage. We wandered to the airport hotel where there was only one empty room – all the others had been taken by American servicemen on breaks from the US Navy vessels which were patrolling the coast off Monrovia, just over the horizon so they could not be seen from the city. We went to our room, then hung around in the lobby where Charles Gurney, the political officer from the US embassy in Monrovia, said there were flights going in the morning to Monrovia from Lunghi.

We listened to music in our room, then slept for what seemed like no time at all before we were up and sitting on the hotel terrace, where Ambassador De Vos wiped his mouth, stood and said: 'Well, gentlemen, good luck and take care. Sorry I can't offer you a ride,' before walking to his waiting embassy Chevrolet Suburban which would take him to the airport.

We followed on foot, weighed down by our bags, treading the soft red-earth path, and then walking out on to the tarmac, intent on getting to Monrovia, oblivious to the airport officials demanding to see our papers. Gurney, habitually blowing from the corner of his mouth to clear his neatly parted hair from his forehead, tapped his tennis shoe on the ground nervously. A chubby secret-service agent in dark glasses hung around the ambassador like a cloak, as he mumbled into a crackling walkie-talkie. A small six-seater plane landed. The ambassador had too much luggage and the pilot, after examining the enormous pile of business suits in their carrying covers heaped on trunks and suitcases, said he would not take him.

'Well, gentlemen. It's all yours,' De Vos said, pointing to the plane. 'We'll just have to wait for another one. See you in Liberia.'

The pilot said we could pay the fare when we arrived in Monrovia. We sat and watched as De Vos, Gurney, the security man with his walkie-talkie and the airport officials disappeared into a small room, leaving only the pile of business suits out on the runway. After we left, De Vos, who was to take up the Monrovia ambassadorial post, which had lain vacant since James Bishop had fallen out with Doe and departed in January, was sworn in as ambassador by the consular officer at the American embassy in Freetown. Such was the rush to get De Vos in place, and so keen now was the US government to encourage Doe to leave, that the Freetown consular officer read De Vos the oath of allegiance over a walkie-talkie, while the new ambassador stood on the Lunghi tarmac with his hand on a bible repeating his oath into a crackling Motorola.

Rain swept across the tarmac as the engines started and the plane shook from side to side as it taxied along the runway. Over the sound of the engines, I heard thunder rumbling across the sky. As we reached the end of the runway I saw two women carrying loads wrapped on their heads carefully lay down their bundles and turn to watch us. We flew up towards a gathering storm. Through holes in the clouds we could see the mangrove swamps and rivers which twist down to the border. For almost an hour nobody spoke, then the pilot broke the silence. He nodded his head towards the circuitous line of a river: 'That's the border. Now we're in Liberia.' Thunder shook the airplane. Then the sky began to clear and we started to circle. I could see the froth of surf as we curved downwards, and in the distance, breaking the green sweep of the swamps, was Monrovia, the city I had not seen since I drove out of it to Buchanan in the back of Chauncey Cooper's Datsun, on that hot afternoon in early April.

The pilot pointed to the airline charter office inside a large hangar at the edge of the airfield. Since Taylor's forces had seized Robertsfield airport weeks before, small planes had used James Spriggs Payne airfield, the city-centre airstrip named after a Liberian president who would otherwise have been forgotten and whose runway had been carved out between the zoo and the swamps. The rain had flooded the runway and our landing sent spray flying. Near the gate were soldiers in dark brown uniforms and white helmets, carrying guns watching us. We paid our fare in US dollars at the airline office and walked towards the customs house as the rain started to pour. I was worried that everybody would know about the reporter who had been caught on the train and then spent time with the rebels. Worried that I would be accused of helping the rebel cause by giving them publicity.

The soldiers stared and stared and stared. Noble, a black American, who people said resembled Taylor, thought he knew somebody in the security office and disappeared inside with his passport. A grey military plane with Russian markings sat on the runway. Women and children lined up in the departure area of the cramped, cold, single-storey building. They had wrapped big cooking-pans and suitcases inside the cloths they must sometimes have worn. They were small people. Frightened people.

Nobody talked. They looked at no one but the soldiers, waiting to be told when they could walk through the flood to the waiting airplane. These were the Krahn, Doe's tribe, running away to Grand Gedeh from where they had come ten years before when their man became president. Later, I was told that each day more and more of them fled the city as the rebels moved closer. The airplane, an Antenov leased from the Soviet Air Force to Air Cargo of Liberia and its British operator, Howard Meredith, made daily flights to Freetown and Zwedru, Grand Gedeh's main town. Doe packed the flight with arms, ammunition and supplies in preparation for the defence of his tribal domain. Every day Meredith increased the fare for the Krahn, and for the Gio fleeing in the other direction to Freetown. In July the fare doubled then tripled until the one-way flight cost 600 US dollars.

Noble reappeared a few minutes later saying that he was all done and ready to go to the house of a friend of his outside the city centre, where he would be safer if trouble broke out. Bourke and I handed in our passports. A soldier told me that my visa was about to expire. It had two weeks to run. He asked how long I was planning on staying. I said maybe a week or two. He told me to go to immigration in the city for further authorisation. I asked him where the people on the Antenov were going: 'Thaa' goin' home,' he said. He looked as though he was about to cry. His eyes shone and he stared hard at me, then handed back my passport, and we walked out into the rain which was pouring so hard it was impossible to see clearly more than a few feet ahead.

I had no idea where I was. The taxi pulled out onto an empty road. We could have been anywhere in the world, as we passed houses where there were no signs of life. We left Noble at a house behind a large gate, somewhere in the suburbs, then drove along a wide street, our visibility obscured behind the steam and raindrops which covered the windows. There was no music on the radio. We turned off the main road and drove between the houses down a street suddenly lined with people hurrying through the rain, their heads piled high with baskets and pans wrapped in shawls, all of them walking toward us, away from the city. We stopped to ask where they were going, but they stared back, speechless. Nobody would talk. They rushed by. Women, young men, children, all carrying goods on their heads. But no one would say where they were going.

Up ahead some soldiers saw us. One came towards us. The others yelled through the pouring rain which was now falling so heavily I felt that any moment I would start drowning. The taxi-driver eased the car towards them slowly, his mouth slightly open, his eyes glaring ahead through the windscreen which was barely cleared by the wipers. The soldiers strode across the road, encircling the car, yelling more: 'Ge' down. E'erybaadi ge' dow',' they yelled, directing their guns at the car. 'Ge' down, Ge' down. I' tellin' you white man. Ge' down. Everybaadi ge' dow'.'

The driver stopped the engine and told us we should get out of the car. We opened the doors slowly. The soldiers continued to yell their orders: 'Ope' up the trunk. Open it. Open it.' The driver opened the boot of the car. 'Who are you white man, press man, you be press man?' one asked. I nodded.

'BBC. BBC. You' the damn fuckin' BBC,' he said, using his rifle to gesticulate, but avoiding pointing it in my direction. I told him I worked for a newspaper. 'Wha' yo' go' faa mi. Gi' mi J. J. Rober'.'

The taxi-driver gave three of them five Liberian dollars each, the notes depicting that long-gone founding president Joseph Jenkins Roberts, and we slowly got back inside the car. The driver started the engine and we left the soldiers behind. We drove in silence. Stunned. Frightened, driving deeper into uncertainty, but without thinking to look back. For the first time since April, when I had been caught on the ambushed train, I felt totally powerless.

Since January, when the soldiers at the checkpoint on the way to Nimba county had hinted that they knew something terrible was going to happen, it was the siege of Monrovia that everybody had been waiting for. Taylor had given warnings as early as May. People should leave the city. He was going to attack it, because there was no other way of getting Doe out. Doe would not leave, because he had been told that, if he tried to leave on the helicopter the Americans had promised him, the power of the juju working against him would make the helicopter crash. He had been told that in March. Taylor, the Western-educated Baptist, as the Associated Press always felt the need to describe him, knew that juju was keeping Doe on the ground in Monrovia. Taylor knew the war was irreversible, that the pressures at work which would inevitably lead to Doe's overthrow were the secret powers of superstition which drove the Gio on. For most of them it was not the lust to kill, it was the symbolic gesture, the belief that the slaughter was an act of devotion to power, and power was the force which bound society together – by bringing the death of the enemy. Taylor's fighters said they had drunk blood and sworn allegiance to him during the ritual in Zouen Hounien on the night before the invasion. Six months later they were still devoted to him. He had given them what they wanted. They had nearly wiped out the Krahn. Now they were moving in on the prize, the seat of the oppressor's power – Monrovia.

Outside the supermarkets, queues stretched along the wet streets. Hundreds of people waiting their turn. Soldiers guarded the shops, paid by the Lebanese and Indian shopkeepers to keep the crowds under control as people amassed stores for the siege they knew was about to happen. A few taxis plied up and down Broad Street, Randall Street, Camp Johnson Road. The Rally-Time market, opposite the army's Barclay Training Centre ('BTC'), was piled high with goods. Soldiers wandered among the stalls. The sentries at the gate to BTC were armed. They were rarely armed before – they could never be trusted with their weapons. They had proved that they could not be trusted when they were sent to do the killing in Nimba. But now they had been given their guns they would keep them. They watched through the rain as cars passed.

We watched through the steamed-up car windows at the people too afraid to stop walking, talking, carrying, leading their children, too afraid to stop anywhere on the street, determined to reach the place they could hide what they had bought. They splashed through the rain in flip-flops and tee-shirts. I saw a woman soldier striding along the street with a rifle slung over her back. She was short and had the pronounced jaw and sunken cheeks that people said was typical of the Krahn. She swaggered like a man. Her gaze was cast down, but she glanced at our car as we passed, then looked down again, adjusting the rifle on her back as she made her way quickly along the street beside the concrete patterned wall, through which one could see the barrack's parade-ground from where Samuel Doe launched his coup in 1980.

Moses Washington, acting Minister of Information since his boss, Emmanuel Bouwier, had stayed in Freetown following the failed May peace talks (he and others of the delegation had earned themselves a death penalty by appealing to the President to resign), sat behind his desk and pretended that everything was normal. Unlike Emmanuel Bouwier, whose arrogance had contributed to the bad press Doe's government had received, Washington felt he had to make foreign journalists understand Liberia. He hunched over a big desk on the upper floor of the Information Ministry without really trying to defend the government. I asked him if it was true that Doe had been forced to run inside the mansion to escape the bullets the previous day, when soldiers opened fire on the demonstrators and then rampaged through the city shooting at random.

'There was an incident yesterday and shots were fired. The march was not authorised by the government. The Ministry of Justice issued a statement saying that "the march was liable to be dispersed". I can give you a copy.'

'But isn't it clear that people are so frightened of the rebels moving in that their demand that Doe should go is a reasonable one?' I asked.

'The President has to make up his own mind. The troops are his people,' he replied, fiddling nervously with a silver paper-knife on his desk, rearranging two small poles on the desk carrying the Liberian flag and the flag of his native county. 'I read your piece after you had been on the train. Everybody read it. They sold photocopies of it on the streets of Monrovia for five dollars a-piece. The *Daily Observer* reprinted it, so everybody saw it. It proved that Taylor is not a democrat, don't you think?' he asked, looking up at me for the first time.

'Who are the democrats here?'

'Well, the election of 1985 was declared democratic by the government of the United States, so ...' but he didn't believe any of what he was saying. That was obvious when his deputy left the room: 'Everybody's leaving,' he said. 'All the ministers are leaving Doe behind. So now the Krahn are taking over, in the Executive Mansion, BTC, in the city. Everywhere,' he said quietly. Then the deputy came back into the room with my completed press accreditation card. Washington was silent. He signed the card and handed it to me. It said the Ministry of Information, Culture and Tourism would 'kindly accord all courtesies and assistance in the discharge' of my duties. More normality.

We shook hands.

In processing the card, the deputy had seen my name and realised that I had spent time with Taylor: 'Ah, the train. You. So what really is this Taylor man up to?' he asked. Washington, seated behind his desk fiddling with the silver paper knife, interrupted: 'You shouldn't ask a journalist his opinions, then he might appear to be biased.' The last gasp of normality perhaps.

It was the last time I saw Washington. He disappeared a few weeks later, escaping across the front line to Taylor's side with some minor government officials when life in Monrovia became too unbearable. He was executed almost immediately by the NPFL for having been in the government.

I walked out of the ministry, which was at the end of the approach road to the Executive Mansion and therefore surrounded by troops. They were silent. Some of them were young girls, heavily armed with US-made M-16 rifles, and dressed in crisp new uniforms. They stood guard beside the two battered plaster lions which crouched on either side of the entrance. One of the girls said they would stand guard there 'all day, all night'.

After thieves had climbed onto the eighth-floor balcony of Monrovia's once quite smart Ducor Palace Hotel, broken into a room where a foreign journalist had been sleeping, and stolen whatever they could lay their hands on before he woke up, the Associated Press correspondent had insisted the American embassy open up one of their staff houses in the embassy district of Mamba Point and allow journalists to stay there. The US rented most of the houses surrounding its large compound, which was perched on top of a sheer rock face at the western end of Mamba Point.

During June the Americans evacuated most of their staff as the rebels approached the city, leaving the houses empty. The journalists had moved in a few days before I arrived. The day after the move, Monrovia's water supply had stopped. As the number of reporters increased, the Americans agreed to open up another nearby apartment, which looked out over the golden beach and the Atlantic Ocean. The apartment was connected to the American domestic telephone system AT&T, from which we could ring the United States by reversing the charge of the call. I telephoned my newspaper's office in Washington to say I had arrived and described what the city was like. A few minutes later a call came through from the foreign desk in London. It was the last time I would speak to them for two months. On 2 July the city's telephone and telex links were cut, leaving journalists with no alternative but to rely on embassies who had their own communications and were prepared to break their rules to let us send our stories. We were limited to sending one pool story a day, to which five reporters contributed. This created ideal conditions for clashes between journalists, at a time when the government troops' anger at the foreign press grew more intense every time they turned on the BBC to hear Taylor being given air time during which he could abuse Doe and promote the NPFL cause. The pool system meant that Reuters, Associated Press, the BBC, as well as *The Guardian* (for whom I had started working in May) and *The Independent* were in the frustrating position of all receiving exactly the same text for editors in London or New York to play around with. Only the *New York Times* had secured personal use of US embassy facilities, allowing an individual effort on the part of its reporter.

By early afternoon on that first day the rain had stopped and the sun quickly dried the roads. The sounds of the city, obscured by the storm, returned. There were birds in the trees of Mamba Point. The waves crashed on the shore. People walked quietly under the hot sun which turned the water to steam. Water gushed from a stream which appeared from under the road opposite the apartment. The city hummed, even though there was no power. It hummed with the sound of generators, with the sound of taxis, dogs barking. Normal sounds. The birds never left the city.

I drove out towards the eastern suburbs we had been through to get in from the airfield.

There is a crossroads just after Crown Hill from where you can look over the city. By travelling straight on you pass the National Police Headquarters, the Temple of Justice and the Executive Mansion. But the soldiers directed all traffic to the left, down Sinkor Old Road, where the gauntlet of the army checkpoints was run, the number of barriers increasing every day. Michelle Faul of Associated Press, a keen smoker, handed out cigarettes to the soldiers on the checkpoints we had been through earlier. She told them that AP company rules forbade her from giving the money they automatically demanded when they stopped a car. Along the complete stretch of road there was the loud yelling of orders, the pretence of officialdom, of training, of some obscure qualification which entitled them to the authority which permitted their theft from every car, pedestrian and taxi-driver who passed by. I had never seen anything like this before my journey from Spriggs Payne that morning. I asked myself how it would evolve. Would the bribes get bigger as prices in the city increased? Or would the soldiers start preventing people getting through? What was the purpose of the checkpoints anyway? Was there any point in telling them we would possibly be passing every day until they disappeared into the mud of the battlefield, so why not wave us through and allow us to do our jobs as reporters? It was futile to say anything. There was no authority, nor any reason for it. Why were they collecting money when they would all be dead once the rebels reached the city? What were they going to spend it on?

A sound, like the hum of the city, which had returned once the rain had stopped, filled the mortuary at the John Fitzgerald Kennedy memorial hospital. But there the sound was from thousands of flies feeding on the bodies which nobody knew what to do with. We went to see if any more people had died from wounds received when the soldiers opened fire on the peace march. But there were only dead people in the large building. No doctors would go there as the smell had got too bad, a man outside told us, refusing to tell us his name or what his job was. He said an emergency committee had been set up to pay for the disposal of bodies because the hospital had overspent its mortuary budget. Inside, there was no light, except in the distance, where a broken door let the sun into the seemingly endless corridor which gave off onto rooms where the dead were rotting under plastic sheets.

Where had the dead come from?

'We're coming close to a catastrophe,' the duty nurse said quietly, sitting at a desk in his second-floor office in the hospital's main building. He ran his finger down the list of newly arrived government troops who had been injured the previous day, when the NPFL tried to retake Robertsfield airport after losing control of it for the second time earlier in the week. 'The army take most of their injured to the barracks clinic,' he said. He wondered why, clinging to the belief that JFK was still the country's best hospital, even though there had been no operations for five days and the doctors had gradually disappeared, leaving patients to the mercy of whichever army got there first.

We drove further out of the city, towards Paynesville. At the Red Light Junction soldiers were darting across the road and yelled at us to go back. We drove closer and they said the rebels were in the area. If this was true, it would have meant that the NPFL had advanced five miles in less than a day, which seemed unlikely. The soldiers were too frightened about what might happen to themselves to prevent us driving on further towards Mount Barclay and the last AFL checkpoint, five miles from the centre of the city.

The road was deserted. The sun disappeared behind grey clouds and a light rain began to fall. The wipers scraped the windscreen and the driver slowed until the car was crawling at around 20mph. Nobody spoke. The driver wanted to go back but I told him to go on. The slower he went the quieter the engine became and the more eerie the silence. Through trees and behind thick bushes bungalows stood empty. After ten minutes we saw some people hurrying towards us. Two women and a small child, all balancing suitcases on their heads. They pointed down the road towards where the army checkpoint was supposed to be, though nothing could be seen from where we were. They said there had been shooting the previous night. The earth around Mount Barclay was red with blood. But no bodies had been found. Nobody knew who had died. Now the area was deserted, the women said, fear in their eyes, speaking quickly, looking behind them to see who might be following. A car came round the corner: 'It's the soldiers,' they said, turning and hurrying on with their big loads, trying to run under the weight.

A yellow Monrovia taxi pulled up. The men inside wore no uniforms but said they were soldiers. We asked them about the shooting the women had heard: 'We were shooting to defend ourselves, because the rebels are close by all around here,' said one of the soldiers, keeping his foot hard down on the accelerator and pulling away as shots rang out from further down the road. We drove towards the checkpoint, failing to see it until we were face to face with three AFL soldiers cowering in the bushes beside the road. We got out of the car, and as we did so more shooting broke out and the soldiers uncovered a mounted machine-gun hidden in the bushes and began firing it down the empty road.

By now the taxi-driver was terrified, by the shooting, by the thought of being captured by the rebels, by being asked his tribe by the government troops – whatever it was, he started the engine, only letting us into the car when we promised to go back to the city. On our return, we learned that the government had cloaked itself in the last act of the dying animal – closing its eyes to blind itself from its fate – and imposed a nightime curfew, thus giving itself the cover of darkness necessary to obscure the crimes it was planning to perpetrate. For those imprisoned in their homes, who waited for the midnight knock at the door before being driven away to their deaths through the lonely streets, the law now barred any witnesses.

10 Moonlight and Murder

Colonel Manyea was left in charge of BTC in late June. Then massive killing started. The killing of AFL soldiers from the other tribes. The Loma and the Gio had a strong presence in the AFL. They became the main victims. From late June. These killings took place every day and every night. Michael Tilly ordered these killings. I worked with Tilly at the freeport. Tilly was brave. Tilly always wanted to be the first in the battle. He was a captain. But he was more powerful than the generals. He was a warrior. He would drink blood from a skull. He would say: 'Mo Koo. Mo Koo. I am a devil. I am a devil.' This would happen at night. At the port. He would say: 'The only way to be a strong warrior is to taste the blood of whom you kill.' Other brave fighters could see fire in Tilly's eyes. At the port he would kill soldiers who wouldn't fight. The skull he drank from was a very old skull. I saw him drinking blood.

ISAAC ROBERTS, *AFL soldier, Monrovia.*

BUDU KAISA always arrived early at the apartment, always in impeccably ironed shirts, usually pale pink or white. Before the war he had been a reporter on one of Monrovia's daily newspapers, *The News*. He listened hard to people in the streets. His tone of voice rarely changed. When he described terrible things he would say they were terrible in the same way he would ask for a can of Coke. I grew used to his way of describing things, though his coolness was sometimes exasperating; it seemed to reflect acceptance of what happened at times when I was despairing. Budu was from the Grebo tribe, which was not closely allied to either side in the conflict. For three months his home town of Harper in the far eastern county of Maryland had been cut off by the NPFL, so he was a prisoner in Monrovia. Unlike most other local journalists, many of whom had been forced into hiding or had left the country, he continued to work by scouring the city for news either on his own or with me. The morning after the curfew had been imposed we toured Monrovia on foot, with a video camera hidden inside a bag.

The previous night the long death of the city had begun. On 2 July the Defence Minister, Boima Barclay, fled on the first plane to fly directly from Spriggs Payne airfield to Guinea. On 4 July Doe's Minister for Presidential Affairs, G. Alvin Jones, regarded by the US as one of the most corrupt members of the government, fled on an unscheduled flight to the Ivory Coast. The army chief of staff, Lieutenant-General Henry Dubar, had resigned on 30 June. He had been replaced by General Charles Julu, head of the Executive Mansion Guard and former security chief at the Yekepa iron-ore mine, who had led the soldiers who avenged Thomas Quiwonkpa's failed 1985 coup.

For an hour preceding the first night of the curfew, troops sped through the city hanging on to the sides of their jeeps or the yellow taxis they had stolen. Their presence was enough to clear the streets. There was shooting well into the night, sometimes coming close to Mamba Point, sometimes in short bursts down the hill in the centre of the city. By next morning the troops had set up checkpoints in the city centre. Everybody who walked past was stopped, searched, interrogated, accused of lying, told to open their bags, left pleading beside the road as the soldiers accused them of rebel sympathies for no other reason than that they were trying to flee the city as the rebels approached.

Budu and I walked fast. I was frightened of the troops. At the junction of Newport and Gurley streets, opposite a petrol station where groups of soldiers hung out of the windows of taxis and jeeps, two soldiers strode over the crossroads demanding to look inside the bag in which I was carrying the camera. Budu smiled at them, intermittently talking seriously about the importance of the press, assuring them that I was not with BBC. They asked for cigarettes and I gave them a handful. They again demanded to see inside the bag. I gave them more cigarettes. More people passed and the soldiers yelled at them to stop and open all their bags on the road. We waited for them to start questioning the other people, then walked away, sure that they would shoot over our heads to stop us and resume their search. But no shots came.

Opposite Citibank a soldier was having his shoes shined while he smoked a cigarette. He shrugged when I asked him if I could film him. 'Why naat?' he drawled, then demanded a cigarette. His expressionless face looked directly into the camera from beneath the wide brim of his steel helmet. The shoeshine boy never looked up. People walked past without looking at us. I thanked the soldier, who said nothing, and we walked on down to Water Street market.

Between a stall selling small piles of bright red chillies and another selling tins of tuna, was the freshly killed body of a man lying awkwardly in the gutter, his face hidden by his arm which had been twisted around his head. People covered their noses and mouths. Nobody looked at the body. Business went on as usual at the surrounding market stalls. Budu had passed the body earlier that morning. He said the man had still been alive then and had asked the soldiers to take him to the hospital. He had bled for four hours. Now he was dead, and nobody would claim the body. So people walked past and tried not to look.

From the market hundreds of people streamed across the People's Bridge, the older of the two bridges linking the city centre with Bushrod Island, the freeport and the road to Sierra Leone. The bridge stretched across the grey water which lapped up against the scarred concrete of the quayside. The water throbbed with a slow pulse. A tee-shirt, two hands, the back of a head, trouser legs filled with water, bare feet, they moved slowly with the breeze which swept across the water. At the city-centre end of the bridge a soldier with 'Military Police' written on his helmet reassured us that he was there for our protection.

'If you ha' any praa'laam wi' the soldiers you co' an' tell mi', you hear?' he said. For a few seconds I felt reassured, embarrassed by what seemed like the prejudice which had created my fear of the army. Perhaps the soldiers' reputation was unfair? At the other end of the People's Bridge on Bushrod Island, the line of people skirted off the pavement and onto the road. In the grass lay two male bodies, killed the previous night. One of them had had his ears, lips and nose hacked off, leaving clean white stumps of flesh against his scarred and bloody skin.

At the end of the new bridge, a hundred yards away, lay another body. 'Take the picture. Make it real,' whispered a man, rushing past without looking at me or the body. As I was filming, an army jeep crossed the bridge and I dropped the camera to my side. A soldier watching us from across a stretch of wasteground saw me and began walking towards us. He demanded to know why I had hidden the camera when the jeep passed by. I said I hadn't seen the jeep.

'Whaa' you filming? Where' your pass?' I showed him the pass Moses Washington had given me the previous day. 'Whaa' you people doin' here? Whaa' you wanna' see this? You shou' lea' Monrovia. You should all lea' Monrovia. Damn press. You' all damn press. Whaa' you doin' here?'

I listened silently. He had no gun, having appeared from a small house on the edge of the wasteground just wearing a tee-shirt and his army trousers. He handed back my pass and demanded to see the camera, saying he was going to take it to the Barclay Training Centre. I told him the Information Ministry had given me permission to film, but he tried to grab the camera. Buda began talking to him, explaining quietly that we were just doing a job, that we had permission. All the time we were slowly walking away from the house from where the soldier had emerged, and eventually we left him standing beside the road which led to the port.

A convoy of army trucks sped past us, nine or ten of them, packed with heavily armed soldiers. The convoy of cars heading west to the border scattered as the trucks came through. Cars piled high with suitcases were making their way out of the city. It was the people who were rich enough to have cars who fled, packing the vehicles with passengers. The Lebanese in overloaded Mercedes, Europeans, Liberians in yellow taxis, trucks, buses, pick-ups, they all rolled slowly out of the city, refugees knowing that if they got through the AFL checkpoints this side of the border they would be safe.

The troops were being sent out towards Caldwell village, ten miles from the city centre. Rebel forces were advancing from White Plains where they had cut the water supply to Monrovia. More troops had set up checkpoints along the road from the bridge. They yelled and shouted at a woman escaping the city with her children. 'You're a damn fuckin' rebel. You're a damn rebel,' a tall young soldier yelled. The woman was carrying a suitcase on her head, a child wrapped in a shawl on her back and another child holding onto her hand who she dragged along behind her. The woman's face was screwed up into a knot of terror and despair as the soldier took his gun off his back and prepared it for firing, all the time yelling that she was a rebel. Other people in the queue backed away in fear, leaving the woman and her children standing alone on the street with the soldier. She pleaded, tears streaming down her face. The baby on her back and the boy holding her hand began to cry. The soldier grew agitated. He could not stop moving. He backed away from her as he levelled his accusations. He shook his gun. He flung his arms as he hurled abuse at her. He tried to kick her with his heavily booted foot, but missed and swung round on the pavement, while the queue of refugees watched silently. For no reason he let her go. She grabbed the boy and scurried off, still crying, while the soldier pointed fingers at her, still telling her she was a rebel.

We reached Monrovia Freeport, where merchants and shopkeepers were trying to get their goods out of the warehouses which had been taken over by the army. The port officials on the gate wanted to show us around, but they said the army had taken over so they no longer had any jurisdiction. 'You must remember that we are not in control here,' said the man in charge. We should go to the quayside where we would find the soldier in charge. 'His name is Tilly,' he said.

On the way to the quay we passed an American embassy car, the standard issue white Chevrolet Suburban, two-door, hatchback. I asked the officials inside the car where we could find Tilly: 'He's down at the ship. We just left him.' They drove off. Budu was nervous. His usual stride had slackened to a slow dragging of feet.

'Watch out for rogues,' Budu said. 'Doe brought Tilly from Grand Gedeh last week. He's a hunter from Tuzon. Doe's town. Everybody's afraid of him. He's an elephant hunter. That's how he lives,' he said.

We rounded the corner of the quay. There were soldiers overseeing the unloading of new jeeps like those we had seen earlier in the city centre. There were 40 or 50 Dacia jeeps being unloaded from a Romanian ship, the *Rupea*, which had been apprehended off the coast the day before on Doe's orders. The jeeps were being stolen in broad daylight. They were winched off by crane, while the crew leaned over the side of the ship helplessly watching their cargo disappear. I asked to speak to Tilly. He was in charge of the port, including food supplies to the city, which was our pretext for going to the port.

'That's Tilly,' said Budu, nodding at a short young man wearing a bandanna round his head and a collections of juju charms round his neck. He had a green bullet-proof jacket and two belts of cartridges slung in a cross over his shoulders. One of his soldiers said he would not talk to us. Tilly looked at us, knowing that few people would recognise him as yet. The soldier told us we should leave. What were we doing here? We told him we were reporters checking on the food situation. Reporters should not be here, so we should leave.

We learned later that soldiers at the port had shot four other soldiers for looting. The guards at the port, who had lost their authority to Tilly, then spread the story that the previous night Tilly had allowed all the Krahn soldiers into the rice warehouse to loot what they needed. Then non-Krahn were allowed in, thereby identifying themselves as being from other tribes, and the Krahn opened fire on them, killing 11.

We left. Back on the road the convoy of refugees had halted. People were hurrying back into the city. The rebels had advanced from Caldwell in the west. They had cut the road to Sierra Leone. There was panic as people ran dragging their children back towards the city, back towards the soldiers. They were trapped between two armies. Nobody knew what to do. Some just sat on the pavements and wept. They had nowhere to go. There was nowhere to go. Nothing to do but wait. Everybody with power was learning how to enjoy it before they lost it or were killed. More soldiers drove by in trucks towards Caldwell. Other rebel forces were approaching from the east. They had attacked and taken the 72nd

Army Reconnaissance base and occupied Paynesville where I had driven the previous afternoon. The city was cut off from the outside world. There was no longer any escape. People trying to return to their homes in Caldwell found the rebels there:

'It's terrible, terrible. There are so many of them. They are so armed and coming with vengeance written on their faces,' said one man who had fled back down the road to Monrovia when he had been confronted by the rebel forces. He didn't know why they had let him return to the city. Nor did he know who the rebels really were.

Back in the centre of the city the queues outside the supermarkets grew longer and more agitated. News of the rebel advance spread immediately. Troops stupidly opened fire over the heads of people in an effort to calm them down, but this only had the predictable effect of making them more frightened.

On 4 July De Vos held an hour-long meeting with Doe, who asked him about presenting his credentials as a new ambassador. Doe's evident lack of authority over most of the country meant he could hardly appear to be the head of state to whom diplomats should present themselves. Doe apparently told De Vos: 'Just give me an empty envelope and we can pretend.' De Vos repeated the US offer to take the president out of the country, if he requested it. The US Assistant Secretary of State for African Affairs, Herman Cohen, had by then arranged with the Togolese president General Gnassingbe Eyadema that Togo offer Doe asylum.

The repeated American offers to fly Doe out of the country, which were conditional on the security situation in Monrovia not declining so far that it would be impossible to do so, were backed up by a request, on 2 July, from three Liberian government officials – Vice President Harry Moniba, the Speaker Samuel Hill and Senator Archie Bernard – that Doe resign. The officials met with Doe in person, and he replied by saying that he would do so, if the safety of the Krahn who had stayed with him was assured. The request was futile, and Doe knew it. His ministers knew he never had any intention of resigning – the whole reason for his rule was to assure the supremacy of his tribe. Having courted the hatred of most other tribes during his ten years in power, Doe was fully aware that Taylor would only be satisfied with a battle to decide the victory. The battle would not end until one or other of the armies was defeated and its warlords were dead. After his meeting with Doe, Moniba went into hiding in a house on Mamba Point near the US embassy. That night, Doe sent troops to all three men's houses to kill them. The other two had also decided it was safer not to go home. Moniba hid on Mamba Point until his evacuation on a US helicopter on 9 September.

America, meanwhile, clung to diplomacy. It had to be seen to be able to talk to a president in whom it had invested over US$500 million and whose democratic credentials it had recognised after the rigged 1985 election. To about-turn would be undignified, so Ambassador De Vos continued to talk to the monster in the Executive Mansion, returning from his meeting with Doe in his convoy of Chevrolets on 4 July after repeating his offer of escape, through streets where, on that day alone, 18 civilian victims of AFL slaughter were found.

As Doe's ministers and senior military personnel fled, the Krahn soldiers took control. On the night of 4 July they blasted their way into shops and rampaged through the city yelling: 'No Doe, No Liberia', a chant they would repeat over and over. They stole tons of food from the supermarkets which they were able to break into. Some of the shop-keepers welded steel sheets onto their shopfronts to keep the soldiers out. Others slept inside their shops overnight, in the hope that their presence would deter the looters.

By the morning of 5 July another 16 bodies had appeared on the streets of the city. No ships were arriving at Monrovia port for fear of being pillaged by the troops, as had happened to a rice ship, the *Sea Star*, when it had moored the previous week, before leaving for the safety of the US fleet over the horizon. The soldiers took their stolen food into the Barclay Training Centre and the Executive Mansion, or sold it at the Rally Time market opposite BTC, where only the Krahn dared go. Other people, instead of suffering the army checkpoints and the risk of execution, took to staying inside their homes, their doors and shutters closed, avoiding giving any signs of life from inside their hiding-places. The grid of streets which formed the city emptied by mid-morning. People hid, expecting the terror to end soon. But the days became weeks and then months, and, after eating the dogs and cats which roamed the rubbish-tips, or sending their children to dig up the grass and weeds for soup or to eat raw, they began to starve to death.

We watched the rebels advancing across Bushrod Island from the roof of the Ducor Palace Hotel. We could see the entire city from there, the Executive Mansion behind its film of Atlantic spray, the crane which stood beside a half-completed office block on Broad Street and which dominated the city skyline, the swamps, the mouth of the Mesurado

River, the two bridges to Bushrod Island, the port and, out to sea, the US ships when they ventured over the horizon.

On 6 July Taylor's troops captured the national radio station. Doe used a makeshift radio to declare a unilateral ceasefire after the US refused to transport him and 100 of his troops out of the city and back to Grand Gedeh. Within hours fighting broke out, with heavy artillery being fired at the port. From the Ducor roof, 12 storeys up, we watched as government troops sped across the new bridge in jeeps and up the road across the island towards the port. Troops at the port surrendered quickly, abandoning the checkpoints. More troops were sent out from BTC and gunfire crackled throughout the morning of 7 July. In the afternoon three car-loads of soldiers, who had stripped off their uniforms, were identified by civilians when they drove back into the city centre. Doe toured the city in an open jeep, waving his army cap enthusiastically at people who fled as he approached. Soldiers saluted by firing into the air, forcing people in the street to flee in panic. At BTC soldiers fought each other over who should have the guns which had been stored in the barracks chapel.

But it was when night fell that the real war was fought.

In the morning it was always gunfire that woke me. Sometimes it seemed nearby, behind the apartment or on the road at the front. I would look out from the balcony at the sunrise and the white surf would be the same, the sky still turquoise, the usual queue would be forming silently around the water gushing from the pipe on the other side of the road, as people with buckets collected rainwater to drink. There would be silence and then gunfire and then more silence. Then the guns would clatter again, in the distance this time. Finally, silence would mark the beginning of another day. It was easier to explain the night-time gunfire as simply sporadic, than to say it had a purpose. The rebels were too far away for it to be a battle. Neither side fought at night, but the shooting continued into the darkness. In the morning I lay in bed confused about where to go to find out what was happening, not knowing whether the reality was what I was actually seeing by day –a city under siege, no water or power, hungry people, dead people – or what was happening at night. Why were the people so frightened of the soldiers? Something was happening which nobody would talk about, which outsiders could not see, to which people were reacting with a terror. We could not explain it because we could not see the cause.

Then slowly, people began to report what they had seen. On 8 July a man said he saw 16 civilians, including two small children, shot by soldiers near the port. The same day soldiers were seen burying 20 bodies on the beach below the Executive Mansion. I began to realise how far it was necessary to go to comprehend the truth. How it was necessary to see without watching, touch without feeling, listen without breaking down in horror. Only then could the war in the city be understood. It was a war about killing, and the soldiers knew that unarmed civilians were easy to kill. I was being numbed, and I wanted to be numb. I wanted not to think, even when I was alone and my sleep was broken by gunfire, and the world inside my mind became as desolate as the city in which I was living.

Archie Bernard, the senator who along with two other government officials had called on Doe to resign, still drove around the city centre, despite the threat to his life. He was rich, being the owner of the YES transport company. Being rich in Monrovia still meant you could expect people to think twice before they shot you. He had even retained his car, a big black Datsun with darkened windows. On the hot morning of 9 July he pulled up outside the apartment. Two senators had just stopped me as I was walking out, saying they wanted to speak with the BBC correspondent, Elizabeth Blunt. She had already gone out. The senators were nervous. They said they were keeping out of the way of the army. Why?

'It's not safe if you're not Krahn,' one said. They were not sleeping at home. Nobody was sleeping at home. Not even Doe. 'He slept last night just round the corner from here, opposite the American embassy,' one senator claimed, as Bernard drew-up on the other side of the road.

'You got a body on the beach. Behind the Ambassador Hotel,' he called over to them. 'No head.' Then, as an afterthought, he added with a grin which let the sun catch the gold arrows implanted in his front teeth, 'Can you identify it?'

He pulled away in his car and the senators left for their homes near the port: 'But we won't be sleeping there. We'll be sleeping somewhere else,' they assured me.

Opposite the apartment, on the other side of a stretch of grass and rubbish, was a large decaying house with a balcony on two sides where soldiers' families lived. There was a path winding through the grass past the house which led to the Ambassador Hotel and there was a pizzeria next to the hotel where we often ate lunch. As I drew close to the house I heard machine-gun fire from just round the corner. People ran towards me along the path.

'Don't go there. There are soldiers,' they said, running past. I rounded the corner of the building. Three soldiers were getting into a yellow taxi without number plates. On a stretch of gravel beside the beach a man lay dead, bleeding from bullet wounds in his head, back, arms, legs. I walked towards the soldiers but they said nothing as they got into the car and drove off. The man was holding his identification papers in his hand. He had died instantly. One of his eyes had burst out of its socket. I got out the video camera and filmed the man, then filmed the house across the road from the execution. It was the house of the US embassy's deputy chief of mission Dennis Jett. A stars and stripes flag, six-feet long and four-feet wide, fluttered in the breeze where it hung from the tall white iron-railing which surrounded the house.

In the pizzeria, Blunt, Faul and the Reuters chief West Africa correspondent Robert Mahoney were sitting at a table. They had been walking past the soldiers when the man was taken out of the car. They had stopped. The soldiers had turned to them and said: 'This man is a rebel.' Then the soldiers had turned to the man. 'Go to the beach,' they had told him. The man turned, holding his identification papers in the air, pleading with the soldiers, denying he was a rebel, and was mowed down by machine-gun fire. Then the soldiers drove off. Mahoney wrote the story down. In the hotel courtyard a group of soldiers pulled up in a large American car. One walked over to the pizzeria. We watched him as he approached the glass door. He came in and looked at us. Mahoney hid the computer he was writing on and ignored the soldier, who said: 'Everything's okay. Ev'rything' gonna be okay,' before leaving.

The Lebanese owner of the pizzeria then asked if we had seen the body on the beach. 'Just behind here. Just over there,' he said, pointing vaguely out of the restaurant. I walked out past the wooden tables, where his clients used to sit before the war and watch the sea as they ate.

'You're going to see something horrible now,' said a woman who passed me behind the restaurant. At first the beach looked deserted. Just the spray and big white waves crashing down on the sand. A wave turned and crashed onto the beach near the palm trees behind the hotel. Then it slipped back into the ocean leaving behind it a bloated, naked corpse slipping as if on ice across the sand. The current lifted the body slightly, turning it to expose the gaping hole where its neck and head had once been, then pulled it back into the water.

In the pizzeria people were wondering whether the dead man was Lebanese, since his skin was pale. Then it was suggested that whatever colour his skin was, it would have been bleached by the salt. So there was no way of telling where he was from, of whether the army was going to start killing foreigners. Mahoney finished writing the report.

Early in the morning of 10 July the same three soldiers arrived outside the same US diplomat's house with a 19-year-old student in the yellow taxi. People watched as they cut the student's throat and left him beside the corpse of their first victim which was still lying on the gravel.

Next day the bayoneted body of a man was found lying on the beach behind the pizzeria, and the Lebanese owner began talking about leaving the country. 'I have a wife. She is Irish. She lives in Dublin,' he told Gerry Bourke, who is also Irish. 'When you leave would you contact her in Dublin. Just to say I'm okay, business is going well, that sort of thing.' Gerry said he would and asked who he should telephone. The restaurant owner looked at him, then said: 'Well, I can't remember her name. It's something like Mary. Is that an Irish name?' Gerry said it was, but that there were a lot of people called Mary. The restaurant owner said he would try to remember her name.

Meanwhile, in the corner of the room, two prostitutes were on the telephone, still working for local calls: 'Hello, Hassan, it's me,' said one. She paused as her customer remembered her. 'No, I'm the short one.' She paused again. 'No, I'm the one with the long hair.'

11 The Hand of a Child

O N 11 JULY a delegation from Taylor's NPFL arrived in Freetown, Sierra Leone, on board a captured fishing-boat flying the NPFL's red and black scorpion flag. Their intention was to give the impression that they were prepared to discuss a negotiated end to the war. Taylor was under pressure. The United States had assured him, through the twice daily radio contacts the Monrovia embassy had with the NPFL, that it was still trying to make Doe leave by persuading him that his departure would save lives. But the NPFL was beginning to feel the Americans had deceived them by saying that they could convince the president to leave. The rebels later claimed they had deliberately slowed their advance from Buchanan in May on the understanding that US pressure would force Doe to resign and leave the country.

The US intention was to avoid a battle for Monrovia, a policy not shared by other Western embassies. By the time the NPFL was in the suburbs, even close allies of the US, like the British, held the view that if Taylor's forces were allowed or encouraged to move into the city then a few days of chaos would be followed by a resolution, whereas a long siege would leave many dead and bring Monrovia to its knees. In the end, they were all proved wrong.

Taylor was also under pressure from another direction. He knew but refused to acknowledge publicly that it was Prince Johnson's rebel faction which was advancing towards Monrovia from the west. In Monrovia we did not know this until Johnson's troops burst into the city later in July, even though we could see them fighting the AFL on Bushrod Island. By acceding in May to the US request that he slow his advance from Buchanan while pressure was put on Doe to leave, Taylor had allowed Johnson's forces to move more quickly than his own, making them the first within reach of the prize the NPFL considered its due. But Johnson had to wait until he had reached Monrovia before he could finally prove to the world he existed.

The US had repeatedly refused to meet Doe's request for the mass evacuation of the Krahn from Monrovia, and it was clearly impossible to guarantee the safety of the Krahn who would be left behind in the city if Doe was taken out. By mid-July, stories of mass executions of the Krahn by the NPFL in Paynesville and other eastern suburbs had filtered into Monrovia, either by word of mouth or in radio reports by journalists covering the war from Taylor's territory. One report told of a river north of Paynesville being clogged up with bodies, describing how troops at an NPFL checkpoint carried out summary executions, one after the other, beside the road and then threw the bodies into the river.

The Krahn in Monrovia responded in kind, and now and again government officials would emerge to make statements which were intended as a way of testing how far the country had gone down the road to hell. One morning the acting information minister Paul Allen Wie, who had replaced Moses Washington after his disappearance and execution by Taylor's troops, came in through the front door of one of the press apartments. He sat down, smiling awkwardly, and began to relay an official complaint about the report on the three soldiers who had killed the man outside the US diplomat's house: 'It's gratuitous reporting. It's unfair and gratuitous. And from now on we will be requiring to see all your reports before they are sent.'

There was a stunned silence. Then Mahoney asked: 'How do you propose to do that, when we are prevented from even getting to the ministry or the mansion by the soldiers at the checkpoints?'

Wie smiled awkwardly and scratched his silver grey hair. Then somebody else asked whether the government was doubting the accuracy of the reports or whether they simply wanted to censor what the outside world was hearing.

'We just want to ensure accuracy,' said Wie. Joseph, the assistant with him, began to nod and repeated what Wie had said, word for word.

'So are you denying that the soldiers killed the man down near the Ambassador Hotel?' I asked.

'Well ...,' said Wie.

'Because if you are, perhaps you would like me to take you to see the body. It's still there. As is the second one, whose throat they cut. You can see that one too.'

Mahoney repeated his question regarding the practical side of the threatened censorship. Wie repeated that we would be expected to bring our reports to the ministry. Just before he left, he told us that he was going to hold a press conference the following day at the Ducor Hotel. He refused to say what he was going to talk about, but we assumed it would be a government response to the discussions then being held in Freetown, and duly mentioned it in that day's report which was broadcast on the BBC.

The next day Wie sent Joseph to the apartment: 'The press conference has been cancelled,' he told us. 'You journalists are so irresponsible. Why did you have to broadcast the location. Now it's not safe for the minister to go there. This is irresponsible reporting.'

If ministers were too afraid to travel through the parts of the city they still controlled, then we decided it was best to let them come to us if they wanted to censor our reports. This quickly appeared to have been the right decision, as nobody ever came back to look at our stories.

Later that day (14 July) we did go to the Executive Mansion. A Liberian journalist, James Youbouty, came to tell us that Doe had agreed to meet our ongoing request for an interview, as long as we went immediately.

I felt then, as we drove to the meeting, that perhaps we had reached a point where it might be possible to emerge out of the growing horror of what we were seeing around us. Doe, who I had never met or even seen, would give us an explanation, I thought. He would reassure us that this was not the reality of the war, that all these things – the stench of decaying flesh filling the markets, lingering in the streets, being blown in by the wind from bodies on the beach – were somehow an aberration. He would reassure us that people were not really doing all this, that somehow it was not really happening.

We drove in two cars down United Nations Drive, along Sekou Toure Avenue, and past BTC. I saw the same Krahn woman soldier I had seen on the day I arrived. She was walking fast along the pavement past the market where a few people wandered among the remaining stalls. Later, somebody said that BTC had run out of fuel and that the soldiers had begun burning the market stalls as firewood.

The road was littered with rocks, glass, sand, mud, old clothes, signs of all the stages of panic felt by the people who had used it. The rocks and sand were for roadblocks, which had disappeared when the soldiers retreated behind the wall of the barracks. The glass was broken from looted goods, from stolen taxis driven to the barracks during the first few days, when the soldiers realised they had better steal while they could, before it was too late. As we passed the barracks, I saw machine-gun barrels sticking out of the ornamental holes in the wall. I looked back and realised that there were barrels directed at the street for the entire length of the long wall. Up to 100, held by silent soldiers, barely visible, watching, waiting.

We turned up the road towards the Executive Mansion. There, 20 or 30 soldiers with the brown uniforms of the Executive Mansion Guard stalked towards the car telling us to get out. The journalist accompanying us told the soldiers we were here to see the president. They checked the cars, demanded to look in our bags, and let us through.

We were taken through the large metal doors at the front of the mansion. A pond where there had once been a fountain had become clogged with leaves and the blue paint had peeled. We were hurried to an upper floor and led along a dimly lit wood-panelled corridor with a thick crimson carpet cushioning our footsteps. Large oil-paintings had been leaned up against the wall of the corridor – paintings of Doe. In gaudy colours, an unsmiling Doe stood on a carpet bearing the national emblem, with his hand resting on a large globe. In another his head and shoulders were surrounded by the heads of ministers from one of his cabinets, with their names written underneath each portrait. Another painting depicted a scroll on which was written 'The Soldier's Creed', giving guidelines for the correct behaviour of troops.

It was horrifyingly sad.

Doe, assuming the posture of a statesman, the portraits of ministers who had fled, while a few minutes' walk away the troops who had not read 'The Soldier's Creed' were cutting the throats of the defenceless. I wondered how it was going to be possible for Doe to bring all these things together once we started asking him questions. How could he explain which of the realities we could see was the true one. Was it the reality of the soldiers on the street, or of the man in the dark suit, captured in oils and leaning against the wall of the corridor outside his office? What, if any, was the relationship between the two?

I wondered why the paintings had been left leaning against the wall instead of being hung. It seemed impossible, as we sank back in leather armchairs in a glass-walled waiting-room, that anybody involved in the war could face scrutiny. Every explanation of the violence would have to lead to acceptance of the fact that Liberia had pretended for too long that American influence and its existence as Africa's oldest republic meant its social fabric was stronger than other countries. For years it had imitated the US, pretended it had a special relationship which would save it from itself. In fact, the only thing it had inherited from its spiritual godfather was a belief in the virtue of money and a free market philosophy which was misinterpreted as a promotion of theft. When the war started the US quickly realised that the tribalism which lay at Liberia's heart was beyond American comprehension and, rightly, stopped short of playing a role, thus leaving Liberia orphaned.

Doe exemplified the country's identity crisis by his adoption of statesmanlike airs, by his pretence of leadership and nationhood, when it was becoming clear that the people he was most relying on to protect him had become monsters. Chief among them was the elephant hunter from Tuzon, Michael Tilly.

It was no surprise that my questions for Doe never got answered. After a two-hour wait we were told the president no longer had time to see us and that it was not, at that point, possible to arrange another meeting.

We left, and the following day the government, or what was left of it, withdrew press accreditation from the BBC correspondent Elizabeth Blunt, accusing her of biased reporting, though telling her she could remain in Monrovia as a tourist if she wanted to. We drove out to Spriggs Payne airfield, through the AFL checkpoints which had become more intimidating than ever, with shots being fired over the heads of the endless line of people passing into and out of the city in the search for food. Blunt gave the soldiers biscuits instead of meeting their demands for cigarettes, which she told them were bad for their health. It was the only time we ever laughed while going through the checkpoints, though we were perhaps laughing at ourselves and our failure to remember that this was somebody else's war and that we didn't have to think like them, didn't have to feel trapped. But as the Antenov airplane took off, with Blunt, and also Faul and Mahoney on board, I did feel trapped, in a state of mind which was telling me that seeing this war was all I had to live for.

For a few days the city centre was relatively calm, while fighting continued in the suburbs. The AP had replaced Faul with its North Africa correspondent Michael Goldsmith and Reuters sent in Mike Roddy from Abidjan to replace Mahoney. I intended to report for the BBC, but as there was no radio communication the BBC would continue to use the pool reports and attribute them to the agencies.

The departing correspondents took my video film which was then sent on to Channel Four in London and CNN in the United States. Channel Four complained about the quality of the pictures and CNN only paid after more than a year. I came to realise, months later, that neither of them were actually interested in Liberia, and that the dangers involved in taking the film in the first place seemed to have been pointless. It was always surprising, given the deep involvement of the US in Liberia, that no American film crews set foot in Monrovia after US citizens had been evacuated in early June. After Ken Noble of the *New York Times* fled in fear of his life in early July, his Taylor-like looks having nearly got him arrested by the AFL, no American newspaper reporters were there to see the city fall apart. CNN's Africa team, based in Nairobi, filmed a few contrived scenes of Taylor's rebels interrogating their enemies and drew heavily on homespun social anthropology to explain what was going on. Most of their pictures were suitable for schools television, as was their commentary. Not once did they analyse the situation in any depth, by looking at the US role and the activities of neighbouring countries.

I was able to see my own film on CNN in the apartment, which was wired up to the network via the US embassy. A naïve commentary had been added, in which the listener was told yet again that Liberia had been founded in 1847 by freed American slaves. It was not really made clear that Doe's ten years of tyranny had been financed by American money and assured by Israeli security advisers, or that he was a fraudulent kleptomaniac responsible for mass murder throughout his years in power, to which the US had turned a blind eye, just as it had to so many of its other dictator friends in Africa, until they were no longer needed.

Day after day government troops were sent out to halt the rebel advance. On 16 July, a Taylor spokesman broadcast a message from one of the captured radio stations calling on the AFL to surrender to the rebels. In the same broadcast, the NPFL said it had captured AFL troops in the north of the country, around Voinjama. Next day heavy fighting was reported around Paynesville, and General Julu began training a volunteer force in the grounds of the Executive Mansion. Some of them as young as 14, the volunteers were given a few days' training and a gun and then sent out to the battlefront.

Wanting to see how far the NPFL had advanced I hitched a ride with an American priest and an Irish layman who took me out to St Joseph's Catholic hospital in Sinkor, where the French branch of Medecins Sans Frontières had maintained the only working clinic in the city. JFK was still inhabited, but there had been no operations carried out there since before my visit to the mortuary.

'Please let us through. I beg you. We are taking food for your people,' the American priest said to a soldier at the first checkpoint on Sinkor Old Road. He offered the soldier a cigarette from a packet which he said he had bought specially to offer to soldiers on the checkpoints.

'Open up,' the soldier yelled. The priest got out and opened the boot of the car where he had boxes of food which he had forced a supermarket owner to open his doors to sell him. 'Give me more cigarettes. I wa' mo'.

Gi' mi money. Gi' mi faa dollar,' the soldier yelled louder. It began to rain. We sat in the long line of traffic. People streamed along each side of the road.

'We're taking food for your people at the hospital. I beg you to let us through,' the priest pleaded. Money changed hands. The soldier yelled at him to drive on. 'Ten more checkpoints to go,' the priest murmured to himself. 'This is why we haven't been out for two weeks.'

The man from Ireland, who was fat, red-faced and wore a shiny green short-sleeved shirt, said he had lived in Liberia for years, had then retired to Ireland but had come back to Liberia to have a look around. The priest said he could not understand why his friend had come back, but the Irishman tried to be nonchalant:

'Well, I just like to look around at things, you see. I'm interested. I'm very interested in things. So, that's why I like to look around. So, I thought I'd just come back and have a look around, you see,' he said, turning his head to make his point to those on the back seat of the car. We reached another checkpoint.

'Give me five dollars and I won't make you get out,' said a smiling young soldier. We all reached for our money.

We turned onto a road across a swamp which took us to the hospital. People walking towards us covered their mouths and noses as they walked along the causeway which crossed the swamp. There was nothing there, except the nauseating smell of bodies rotting somewhere in the water, a smell which clung to our nostrils and filled the car even with the windows closed.

A sign leaning against a pillar at the hospital entrance said: 'ABSOLUTELY NO GUNS ALLOWED IN THE HOSPITAL.' Wounded soldiers lay on mattresses spread out across the floor, under soft lights powered by the hospital's generator.

'The rebels caught me in Paynesville,' a thin man lying in bed with a bandage wrapped round his neck whispered. 'They kicked me to the ground and cut my throat. They thought I was dead, so they left. I didn't die. They hadn't cut my throat deep enough, and I came to the hospital.' He refused to say who brought him to the hospital, and denied that he had ever been in the army. Beside him was an AFL soldier who had been on the roadblocks in the city centre before being sent out to the battlefront. A bullet had passed right through him.

In the next bed was a 15-year-old boy: 'The army found me in the bush. They beat me then shot me. The doctors had to cut off my toes, but I don't know why,' said the boy, looking without blinking at the two soldiers he was sharing his room with, wondering if it may have been them who shot him.

The priests who ran the hospital talked incessantly. One from Ireland gave me details of where the Order they belonged to had its office in London and said I would always be welcome there and that I 'must come round some time. Just tell the brothers you saw us here in Liberia.' Liberia's chief medical officer, Dr Robert Kpoto, was working there after the collapse of services at JFK.

'It's no problem putting people together in the same wards who have been attacked by each other's sides. Nobody says who they are when they are in hospital. Some may have wounded each other and then arrived here for treatment. After all, there are no other hospitals to go to,' he said.

Two days later the NPFL ambushed government troops sent to recapture the area around the Red Light Junction, and the hospital overflowed with 60 more wounded soldiers. I tried to drive to Red Light with Roddy and Goldsmith, but we were turned back by the government troops who had retreated to the Nigerian embassy, which they had decided to loot. At the request of the diplomats, the troops had been sent to guard the embassies in the area, including the West German one, which was next to the Nigerian embassy. Instead of guarding them they had tried to loot the West German embassy by jumping over the wall, but the European Community countries, all of whom were in radio contact with each other, had lodged a complaint at the Executive Mansion and the troops were withdrawn. At the West German embassy, staff were still working. A few days before they had had a party in the grounds when they had eaten the last of their German delicacies. Unfortunately, there had been no swimming, because the water shortage meant that embassy staff were now drinking the pool.

By the next day, 19 July, wounded government troops were being rushed through the near deserted city from Logantown in the east. From the roof of the Ducor Hotel, we watched as the AFL launched attacks from one of its two remaining Romanian-made 40-barrel rocket launchers. A third rocket launcher, commonly called a Stalin Organ, had been captured by Taylor early in the war and was being stored at the NPFL base in Gborplay.

That morning we drove out to the western surburbs to see how far the rebels had advanced from Red Light Junction. In Sinkor we talked to the Gio who had taken refuge in churches where the Red Cross had draped large flags over the walls in an effort to make them *bona fide* refugee camps.

'We have everything here,' said a man at St Peter's Lutheran church, showing us his small clinic where he had tins with used syringes and boxes of cotton wool which had begun to turn brown. A small boy held my hand as I walked across the churchyard where they had set up rows of chairs for lessons. The boy held my hand tight without saying anything. He was joined by another boy who took my notebook from me in order to hold on to my other hand. The man from the clinic walked alongside us, talking quickly.

'The soldiers have come round here every night for the past few days. Just before the curfew, they drive round here to make sure nobody can go out on the street. They drive round, and sometimes they shoot in the air and rattle the gate and yell things at us. It frightens the children,' he said.

We drove towards JFK. We stopped outside so a photographer with us, Jean-Marie de Craine, could take a photograph of a cigarette-smoking soldier with his gun slung over his shoulder riding a bicycle. The soldier was angry at having his picture taken, and De Craine captured him while he was in the process of yelling at him not to take the picture. We were immediately surrounded by angry soldiers yelling at us about their hatred of the press and how it was illegal to take photographs. De Craine was unmoved. Two soldiers said they would take us to the Executive Mansion for questioning. They squeezed into the car with us, then directed us to an army post in the centre of the city. Goldsmith, whose quiet manner was made more disarming by the fact that, at 68-years-old, his mere presence as a reporter in Monrovia left people bemused, smiled at the commanding officer and said that De Craine, a Belgian whose English was not good, had not understood that the soldier was reluctant to be photographed. Within a few minutes we were liberated. The soldier asked if we could give him a ride back to JFK because he had left his bicycle there. As we left the army post, Roddy cracked his head on an air-conditioning machine which protruded from the side of the building, and with blood seeping through his white handkerchief we drove back to JFK to see if there was anybody left there who could patch him up.

A doctor skilfully anaesthetised and stitched up the wound. I wandered up to the wards where I had talked to the proud duty-nurse two weeks before. But there were no patients there. The duty-nurse had gone. I asked an old nurse why the hospital was empty:

'The soldiers came here every day last week. They have been finding all the Gio and taking them out of their beds and killing them down on the beach. Down past the Catholic hospital, and down behind here too.

Just the Gio. They have taken them all. Killed them. Killed them. There's nobody left. All gone.'

She left me standing at the crossroads of the hospital's dim corridors, and disappeared with shuffling feet into the darkness.

Goldsmith, who had last been in Liberia in 1980 to watch the Tolbert government being stripped and machine-gunned to death on the beach, offered us lunch at El Meson. Soldiers wandered through the city-centre streets, looking at us without the urge to stop and search our car. Big four-wheel-drive Land Cruisers were parked haphazardly outside El Meson. Old men pretended they would guard the car. Dwarfs and cripples, who sped around Monrovia in smart wheel-chairs which had been donated by the British government, appeared at the windows asking for money. Who would look after them, I thought? Who on earth would look after them? The centre for handicapped people was on the edge of the city centre in Newport Street, which became the front line when the rebels arrived. They were targets for anybody who wanted to kill them. They stayed together, five, six, seven of them all moving round the city centre in a group, asking for money.

On a second-floor balcony, a group of south-east Asian prostitutes waved at us as we got out of the car:

'Here are the lovely ladies,' they shouted down to us. Roddy, amazed that there was still any business to be had, called up to them: 'What are you doing here still?'

'We make love,' they called back, laughing, waving. Inside El Meson, a bar, restaurant and hotel, the shelves of the bar were glittering with bottles of every spirit and liquor imaginable. Expatriates slouched on bar stools. They were middle-aged men who looked much older, from Britain, the Netherlands, Ireland, Lebanon, Israel, Spain. Few of the expatriates could deny that the attraction of Liberia was that business could be conducted in ways which were not always openly accepted in Europe, at least not by the heads of state. They were reluctant to talk, aware that we were journalists. They talked as if wanting to show that they were ready for whatever was about to happen. They only ever went as far as remembering that they preferred my newspaper when it was the *Manchester Guardian*, to which I would reply that I was too young to remember it in those days. They could barely raise nostalgia for Liberia, even though most had been there for years after drifting from Nigeria or Ghana or as far afield as the Middle East. After a few drinks, some acknowledged that they were there basically because, as rich whites, they could have as much sex as they wanted. Some of them had fathered two or three entire families in different parts of the country. Most said they would have preferred to go to South Africa, though it was no longer an easy life down there because the whites had lost their nerve. I allowed myself momentarily to feel a bond of nationality with the English people there. But it evaporated instantly. No affinity could save us now. There was nothing we could say to rescue each other. We were all entirely alone.

The Spanish owner sat babbling in a corner. His mixture of Spanish and Liberian English was totally incomprehensible to everybody, so he rarely found himself in conversation. A smartly dressed waiter wearing a black bow-tie showed us the menu. Goldsmith asked what the special was:

'I shall just enquire,' said the waiter. He disappeared into the kitchen, returning less than a minute later: 'Lobster,' he replied, licking his pencil and preparing to take our order. We all ordered lobster. Lobster! It was cheap too, because they were taking Liberian dollars whose black-market rate had been devalued one thousand per cent in six days against the US dollar.

12 The Face of a Man

I dream about the people I killed. Those who I saw face to face. I can see them. When I see them, I see them all sitting round a table. But we're not talking to each other. Nothing happens. They don't talk to me. The only thing is that they're wearing white gowns and white hats and white gloves. I don't see their bodies at all. I can't see their faces even. But I know it's them. There are forty-three of them. They don't even talk to each other. But I know it's them. Forty-three of them. All the people I killed.

BOIMA BROWN, *AFL soldier, Monrovia.*

THE CITY fire-engine swerved through the abandoned remains of an oil-drum checkpoint and roared through the empty streets between the dark, empty, rain-soaked buildings of central Monrovia. At the crossroads of Johnson Street and Broad Street the AFL's 40-barrelled Romanian rocket launcher limped back towards the Executive Mansion with a flat back tyre. The fire-engine sped down the hill towards a plume of smoke billowing grey with tongues of red fire against the black rain clouds of the early morning sky.

The Mermaid Bar, the Gold Dollar shop and the Azzam supermarket did not open. The weeks of waiting seemed to be coming to an end. It was 20 July. A body lay at the top of some wet, blackened, moss-covered steps at a crossroads near the supermarket. A rusting, pale green gate swung open at the base of the steps. Blood had been seeping down onto the street for a few hours, gathering in a crack in the pavement, where the rain diluted the thick redness and washed it down into the roadside gutter.

The beggars of Randall Street had nobody to beg from. Instead they cleaned the gutters of paper, keeping the city tidy, while the firemen rushed to put out the flames. Tyres lay across the road at every junction, but for the first time the menacing soldiers had nobody to check and threaten. Instead, they were breaking into buildings, burning the offices they could find nothing to steal from. Families ran past the closed doors of the shops, out of the criss-cross of city-centre streets where the soldiers had threatened and stolen from them, up to the gates of the American embassy, which remained firmly closed.

156

We drove, Goldsmith, Roddy and I, past El Meson. The prostitutes watched from behind the grille which enclosed their balcony. They didn't wave, as they had done before. Instead, they sat and smoked and watched a Lebanese couple on a balcony opposite argue loudly about who should make the breakfast. We drove on towards the bright green Ministry of Defence building. Goldsmith regarded it as a landmark. If it fell, the war was over. That was his view.

We slowed our dark blue Peugeot at the crossroads where the body lay at the top of the steps. Twenty yards away AFL troops directed their M-16s at the car and yelled at us to stop.

'Go on,' Goldsmith told Abdullai Bah, the Guinean driver who never let us down. 'Go on. Don't be frightened of them.'

But Bah stopped. Goldsmith raised his voice, and Bah slowly edged forward, as the soldiers fired over the roof of the car and Goldsmith forced him to go a little further, as the soldiers fired again and yelled at us to stop. Still Goldsmith insisted that he go on. The soldiers slowly edged their way towards the car, their rifles trained at the windscreen, their shots directed just above it.

Goldsmith's experience, after 45 years with the Associated Press, made me look like nobody at all. He had weathered more storms than this one, and he was still alive. I asked myself whether his age and experience perhaps meant that he no longer had anything to look forward to. He was prepared to take the risk that the AFL troops might actually hit us. Perhaps they were aiming for us but couldn't hit the bull's-eye. Goldsmith didn't know. I wanted to tell him that I thought he was mad. Instead, I told him that I wouldn't be driving in the car with them anymore. Roddy thought that was fine, because, as he reminded me, AP and Reuters were paying for the car-hire anyway. It was true that I had hardly any money to finance myself there. Roddy was resentful that I didn't even have money to buy food. After my dollars ran out I ate what they bought. I could feel our relationship deteriorating, they thinking I was just an amateur working for a cheap newspaper which sent me out with nothing, in the hope – which proved correct – that it would get the story for free, as we drove past the yelling soldiers and up to the Defence Ministry to see who controlled it.

It was no surprise to find it was in government hands.

The cold, empty streets were shining with rain. Rainbows of spilt petrol arced across the tarmac. We turned onto Camp Johnson Road, beneath shattered traffic lights hung on wires, which swung in the wind and hadn't flashed on or off since the power was cut. There was a chemist, the Itter Pharmacy, open at the end of the road. The owner unlocked an enormous padlock and we went inside and bought bottled water and talked with the pharmacist who said that there were people living in apartments the length of Camp Johnson Road, but you wouldn't think it because they stayed inside and hid and hoped the war would end before they died of hunger.

We went outside to look, and occasionally saw shutters or curtains opening a crack, and then close immediately.

As we watched, a line of cars passed the junction at the end of the road and halted a little further up. The convoy was led by the blue Cadillac police car used by Doe's State Security Service (SSS). It was followed by two white US embassy Chevrolet Suburbans.

A moustachioed American security agent sitting in the front car talked into the ear of a Liberian soldier standing nearby. The soldier strode towards us flinging his arms around.

'Move on,' he said. 'Orders from the president.' We moved around the car, wondering which president he was taking his orders from, but didn't get back inside. The door of the second American car opened and Ambassador De Vos stepped out onto the rain-soaked street, dressed in the smartest of his grey business suits and the largest and brightest of his selection of bow-ties. He did not acknowledge us, though he knew us all. The blue Cadillac SSS car, which had driven up the hill to the army checkpoint just before the entrance to the Executive Mansion, returned and placed itself, siren blaring, lights flashing, at the front of the convoy. De Vos got back inside the embassy vehicle, and the convoy sped quickly up the hill and disappeared through the mansion gates, while the Liberian soldiers yelled at us to move, this time with nobody to stop them enforcing what they said. As they yelled, another group of soldiers ran towards us and ordered us into the car and then crammed inside themselves. They ordered Bah to drive back along Camp Johnson Road, through the city centre, along Broad Street. We were being arrested, they said. We were being taken to see a commander, they told us. We were spies, we were intruders, what were we doing here if we weren't spies?

They yelled at Bah to drive up the hill to the Ducor Palace Hotel, at the highest point of the city. We drove up the hill and reached the parking circle at the entrance and the soldiers leapt out, telling us to do the same. We stood at the entrance, waiting to see what they had planned for us. As we waited, gunfire burst out nearby. It was unclear where it came from. The rebels were still on the other side of the bridges. But it was enough to scare the soldiers. They demanded that Bah give them the key, jumped inside and drove away, leaving us standing in the hotel entrance, discussing whether the entire incident had been a rather elaborate plan to steal the car.

'That day we had mashed potatoes and hot dogs, cooked by the bishops and minister who were attending an international Lutheran conference,' said James Kpabeh, the acting manager of the Ducor Palace.

When I wanted to sit somewhere that was too far from the army barracks to be infested with soldiers, I would go to the Ducor and wander around the empty swimming-pool, where orange lizards darted across faded, sun-baked blue tiles, and look out over the thick smoke rising from cooking fires on the seaward side of the Ducor hill. From there, in the afternoons, after the morning fight, everything could appear calm. There were no bodies, no blood. The poolside barbecue had been closed down, and its decorative wood surround torn away and used as firewood. In the entrance driveway, cars had been parked. I liked seeing the cars parked, waiting to be driven away. Their owners would hopefully reappear one day, when the war was over, and their families would get in and, with a turn of the key, tomorrow would come and they would drive off down the hill and life would return to the city.

The sweep of the stairs rising from the hotel lobby, the closed shops that sold West African memorabilia on the mezzanine floor, the warm breeze blowing net curtains in the lobby, like the sails of the canoes which occasionally ventured out onto the sea below the hotel in search of fish, would instil calm, which was only occasionally broken by the sound of thunder, or was it gunfire?

'James Brown stayed here, and Mohammed Ali. And the former American vice-president Hubert Humphrey took a room when he came for the inauguration of the late president,' Mr Kpabeh reminisced. 'And when the coup happened in 1980 and President Doe seized power, and we ate the mashed potato and hot dogs that the churchmen cooked for us, Doe's soldiers began to search the hotel for members of the old government. They were running up the stairs, but when they got to the third floor they got tired out and didn't search any further, because there was no electricity to power the elevators to take them to the top,' he remembered, half smiling, wondering, without saying it, how many lives were saved by the soldiers' lack of energy.

The pitch-black corridors smelled of rotting cheese. Occasionally, the door of a hotel room would open and bright sunlight would pour onto the moulding brown carpet, then be quickly closed, the voices of the hiding people dying down into silence. From the Ducor rooftop the changing battle-lines were clear. AFL troops in jeeps or army trucks sped across the Johnson Street bridge to the port side, and disappeared from view behind the warehouses which lined the road through Viatown. Barriers of metal pipes, oil drums and the carcasses of scrapped vehicles had been dragged across the ends of the bridges. Now nobody could escape across to the other side from the city centre, where smoke belched from the building the firemen had sped towards earlier in the day.

Freddie from the Lebanese embassy arrived at the apartment. He had been waiting for us. He was with Tahseen, a Palestinian who survived the checkpoints, the harassment and the food shortages, by talking with everybody, being a fixer, turning up at lunchtime, and being a mine of information about everything that was happening on all sides – his stories always appearing credible even though it was never clear how he was able to find out what he did.

'I have a nice piece of meat,' said Freddie, producing an enormous side of cooked ham from a plastic bag. It was fresh and had been in a refrigerator until he somehow got his hands on it. 'And I have milk, prunes, Ritz Crackers, Frankfurters ...' He laid the food out on the dining-room table, tins of milk, dried fruit and 'to drink, I have Amaretto and Cinzano, and some cigars.'

He had been to the apartment several times and used to take orders in advance. Now he just brought the food. We (or rather Roddy and Goldsmith) were the only people who could buy it. We all knew it was stolen from the shops that had been abandoned. Freddie would only tell us the prices after showing us the produce, then mutter for a while about the sliding exchange-rate, knowing that Roddy and Goldsmith had enough dollars to buy several months' supply. They bought the entire hoard, not asking where it came from.

We referred to De Vos' visit to the Executive Mansion in the story we wrote while eating Freddie's piece of ham:

> The US ambassador, Peter De Vos, went in a well-guarded convoy to the President's mansion in the morning. A spokesman said he was received by the acting foreign minister, George Wallace, but did not see Mr Doe himself.

This was how the story was transmitted to the outside world. To avoid antagonising the people in the city who had communications, we alternated between two different embassies to send our stories. The De Vos visit was transmitted through the American embassy. David Krecke, the embassy information officer called us in the afternoon to say that he had not transmitted exactly what we had written, and that he had changed the text. Our original story had said that De Vos met with a 'minor official'. George Wallace was a nobody. But the US embassy, still determined to deal with the ally in which it had invested so much money, portrayed him as the representative of a government, even though that government no longer existed.

Outside the American embassy, where marigolds were blossoming in the perfect flower-beds, hundreds of people who had fled the city centre that morning were waiting beneath the trees on the opposite side of the road.

Krecke met the three of us in the embassy lobby where Goldsmith, before a word had been spoken in protest at the censorship, punched him, then condemned him for changing the story. Liking neither of these grey-haired pugilists, I stepped in between them, while the armed US Marine guard watched with amusement from behind three-inches of bullet-proof glass.

For Goldsmith and Roddy the American censorship was particularly awkward. As another aspect of their attempt to isolate what they viewed as my amateurish efforts at reporting, they had opted to use the American embassy as a two-man pool. They had only told me this after sending a story from the embassy the previous day, without including my name on it. I had gone elsewhere and sent my own story, upset by their attitude but determined not to let it get me down. Now, when they realised the Americans could not be trusted, they enthusiastically demanded that the three-man pool be revitalised, since I had arranged to file on the only alternative communication system in the city, which they now had no choice but to use.

Outside the embassy the frightened people waited for the United States to save them.

'We haven't asked them yet if we can go inside. All we can do is ask,' said a man who had run there with his wife and three children. All they had left to protect them was the embassy wall – inside it they would live, outside they would be at the mercy of whoever got to them first.

Roddy and Goldsmith drove away and I walked back to the apartment. Close to the large house where soldiers' families lived, Tahseen appeared and said he knew where the AFL had been taking people for execution. We walked along the road beside the sea, past the Ambassador Pizzeria, which only opened occasionally now, and continued in the direction of the Barclay Training Centre. There were large, walled compounds on both sides of the road, mostly housing construction companies, filled with bricks and machinery. At the end of the road, on the right, was a small cluster of palm trees. Before the war it had been the Coconut Grove Amusement Park. Now it was overgrown. The palm trees swayed in the breeze and spray coming off the sea. We left the road and walked through the long grass which grew among the palm trees, until we reached an area where the land dipped slightly and saw, among the tall blades of pale grass, arms, skulls, clothes, legs bent and twisted, hacked faces, hands frozen with fingers splayed as the bodies had become bloated. It was impossible to say how many people were lying there. As the wind rushed through the grass, we could see more bodies closer to the beach and towards the wall which reached along the length of the beach to the BTC. Suddenly, around the corner of the wall, a group of soldiers appeared. They immediately saw us and started to run towards us. We fled back along the road. Two shots were fired. We jumped over the wall of a compound and ran into a deserted workshop whose floor lay covered in a soft bed of wood shavings. Feeling we had not run far enough away from the soldiers, we leapt over another wall which adjoined a second compound. Here, in a house, some Lebanese were drinking tea. As soon as we appeared they told us to get out. Their guards forced us out of the gate. We ran beside the wall which continued for the length of the road. We could see the soldiers as they rounded the corner of the road we had fled along. The yelled at us to stop. Another shot was fired. We did not look back. We reached the pizzeria, skirted round it onto the beach, ran behind the Foreign Ministry building, then crossed the road, walked quickly past the military families' house and onto the road close to the apartment.

Just before reaching it, on a road leading to the walled Greystone compound, formerly occupied by the Firestone rubber company but later a US embassy residence, I heard shouting. Tahseen walked away down the road towards town. I turned the corner and saw four AFL soldiers, faces dark beneath the brims of their helmets, their olive-green uniforms crumpled, their boots soiled, their M-16 rifle butts edging a lone man in a neatly ironed white shirt into a yellow Monrovia taxi.

Standing at the corner I could see the terror on the man's face. The soldiers were not even waiting for the protection of the night-time curfew to pick people up. They spoke with the man. They didn't shout. They didn't really use any force. They were just edging the man into the taxi.

His pleading grew to panic. He begged loudly. His face was screwed into wrinkles and knots of cold terror, tears falling, his voice breaking.

'Please. Please. I beg you.' The soldiers seemed almost moved. They were quite gentle with him, though the movement of their rifle butts was always edging him into the taxi.

'Let's go. Let's go,' they said, just as a group of friends would say to each other. The man eventually sat down inside the taxi on the back seat, begging with his hands, his voice. The soldiers closed the doors of the taxi, turned, drove past the house of the US embassy political officer on the corner of the street, went left down UN Drive, and headed into town. I saw the man from behind as they drove away, his head turning desperately from one soldier to another.

I walked among the rubble outside the tenement building from which the man had been taken. In the doorway of a ground-floor apartment some people were gathered silently. I nodded. They nodded back. I walked inside. There, an entire family was screaming hysterically, their fear uncontrollable, their pain and terror and grief filling the room with the most intense despair and horror. There were four children, three women and several men, all in tears, crying, screaming, tearing at their hair. There was nothing they could do. They had watched as their father, brother and husband had been taken away to his death.

'No, no, no, no, no, no, no, no, no,' one of the women kept screaming. Her children were inconsolable, sitting in a line on the settee, helplessly crying for the father they knew they would never see again. This was what the people of Monrovia were hiding from. This was the war only they knew was being fought. The war Doe's army, having already lost the country, was waging against the people of the city, who sat in their houses and waited for the knock at the door, whether at night or in the early afternoon.

Heavy shooting broke out on the far side of Mamba Point as I was leaving the family's apartment. I was outraged by what the army was doing in the city while it still had the run of the streets. Outraged that the world was doing nothing to stop this. The shooting on the other side of Mamba point grew more intense, not just small arms and machine-guns but heavier weapons. I walked back up the hill past the American embassy, where the people were still waiting outside, past the iron gates of the French embassy, and onto a mud path which led up to the Ducor Hotel. From the hilltop I could see the fire in town still burning. I walked up through the darkness of the hotel and from the roof could see government troops fighting just beyond the two bridges linking the city centre with Bushrod Island and the freeport. Bodies littered both bridges, alive or dead it was difficult to tell, and plumes of smoke rose above Bushrod Island, close to the freeport which by then, I learned later, was firmly in rebel hands.

Control of Bushrod Island had alternated between Taylor and Johnson's troops throughout July. On 6 July, Taylor's 'navy' had used fishing boats captured in Buchanan to travel along the coast to attack and seize the port and the nearby national coast-guard base. However, Taylor's forces were not able to push further from the freeport, which was recaptured by the AFL.

Meanwhile, Prince Johnson's troops arrived in the north-western suburb of Caldwell in early July, having walked from Nimba through the bush, gathering weapons and troops *en route* via the Bong mine, which they had seized during the Freetown peace talks on 18 June. Prince seized the Monrovia water-treatment plant at White Plains, 20 miles outside the city, where his troops had crushed the AFL, captured three Romanian-built anti-aircraft guns and cut Monrovia's water supply. The INPFL then moved to Caldwell, where it established its base in the Bong mine's Monrovia residential compound. In response to the INPFL advance, the AFL had mounted weapons on the railway bridge between Caldwell and the city centre, which carried iron-ore from Bong mine to the port. But the AFL fled as Prince advanced down the main road through Duala and towards the port, which he secured on 25 July. On the afternoon of 20 July, the rearguard of the AFL had been forced to defend the bridges, whose loss would see Prince's troops at the gates of the city centre from the north-west. At the same time, Taylor's forces had reached Spriggs Payne airfield on the eastern side, by wading through the swamp at the end of the runway, and were bombarding the Executive Mansion with long-range rockets.

'We can't have him staying here,' said Roddy, when I said that because the bridges had been cut Budu Kaisa, the correspondent for *The News*, with whom I had been walking the city for almost a month, could no longer reach his house in Claratown. 'He's a spy. Look, you can tell,' Roddy went on. 'He's obviously spying for the government. Otherwise why does he hang around here all the time? We gotta be really careful. I really don't want him staying here if he's gonna be informing on everything we're doing. It's obvious Huband. We gotta be careful.'

He had no reason to think that Budu was a spy, and the accusation was a sign that the last semblance of reason had finally evaporated among we three correspondents. I left the house with Budu, who said he didn't 'appreciate' my colleagues, but that he would be back before the official 7pm curfew, which had been unofficially extended to become a 24-hour curfew.

'I'm not sure about your colleagues, particularly that Goldsmith fellow,' said the British ambassador, Michael Gore, as we sat on his balcony looking out over the beautiful, sparkling Atlantic Ocean later that day. It was another golden late afternoon. Hot, steamy, but with a breeze which cooled the balcony where Joseph, the ambassador's butler, dressed in an impeccable white uniform with the gold buttons of the British foreign service staff, brought gin and tonic. Gore had sent the five British soldiers dispatched to guard him and provide communications, down onto the beach earlier in the day to bury bodies which had been gathering on the rocky headland below the embassy.

'They had started to smell,' he said. We talked about the Liberia of nightclubs and diplomatic cocktails during Doe's heyday. He told a story about the day he had once sacked a member of the embassy staff. The following day the embassy Union Jack had gone missing from the flagpole. The day after that he was sitting on the balcony and saw a canoe with a sail speeding past just off the coast. He looked through his binoculars to see that the sail being used was the embassy flag, which he photographed and had mounted in the lobby of his residence with the caption: 'It could only happen in Liberia'.

We watched the sun go down, then I walked back to the apartment. The sun-baked city was quiet.

A woman sat crouched on the kerbstone opposite the apartment, slowly swaying back and forth, holding her baby loosely in her shawl. It was past 7pm. The soldiers would find her if she stayed there, but she no longer cared. She had given up. Her bare feet splashed in a rainwater puddle, stirring the sand. She was young. She was lost. The war had killed her spirit, but she wasn't weak enough to die. I offered her money.

'I can't, I can't. There's nothing. I don't want your money. Nothing to buy. Nothing to buy. I don't want your money,' she said, putting my dollars on the pavement beside her, as Budu arrived from the apartment, and gave her some food he had taken for her.

For two more days we watched the rebels advancing towards the two bridges. Then, on the morning of 23 July, Budu, who had found another place to stay, arrived to say the rebels had reached the city centre overnight.

13 Death of a City

> The Krahn would say, referring to all other tribes, 'It's nothing but a snake. If it's a snake it's a snake. If it's a small snake, chop it. If it's a big snake, chop it.'
>
> GENERAL HEZEKIAH BOWEN, *AFL Commanding General, Monrovia.*

> When non-Krahn soldiers come to the freeport, Tilly would ask them: 'Ma Bleh You? Are you my countryman?', then he could kill them. Tilly killed hundreds of non-Krahn AFL soldiers.
>
> J. BARCEE COOPER, *former AFL soldier who later joined the INPFL, Monrovia.*

> I am a warrior now. I have made myself real.
>
> MICHAEL TILLY, *AFL death squad commander, to General Bowen, Monrovia.*

GOVERNMENT TROOPS crouched behind a tank on Centre Street, just beyond the last checkpoint at the Defence Ministry. A lone soldier scuttled across the mirror-like wet street, went up the hill and then disappeared into a building. Rain and smoke swept the skyline. Gun barrels protruded from the wall of the Barclay Training Centre, where another tank was stationed at the entrance. There was silence. I could hear the birds.

On the hillside, dominated by Monrovia's masonic temple, fires burned. People pulled leaves from among the grass to eat. They waited in hidden compounds and yards, deep within the maze of shanties. Budu and I walked along a dirt road beneath the masonic temple, its grey columns streaked with the accumulated grime of ten years of neglect. It was looted after Doe's 1980 coup and the masonic élite was ousted at the same time as the government, who were all freemasons. The dirt road ended at a house.

We trod slowly along a moss-coated alley which zigzagged between the high walls of two tenements. A drain-pipe had overflowed and water poured in a stream, turning the moss of the alley to slime. A ten-feet high iron gate between the houses was usually open, allowing anybody who knew the path to cross from one side of the city centre to the other, without passing through any AFL checkpoints. This morning, 23 July, it was locked. We stopped and listened for any sound of life. There was nobody. Only the sound of water dripping from a cracked drain pipe. We waited for a few more minutes, then called out softly to see if anybody was there. A child looked around the dark corner ahead, the light behind him falling onto the shining path. I smiled. He disappeared. A tall thin woman appeared and recognised me from the previous times I had passed this way. She had the key to the gate wrapped in the folds of her shawl, and opened it for us quickly then locked it behind us without saying a word. We walked into the light at the end of the alley, thanked her, and said we would be coming back this way; she nodded. A dirt road led to Broad Street, and we turned right half-way up the hill, looking down towards the city. Smoke rose from a fire somewhere close to the City Hall on the other side. Occasionally, somebody ran across the road far up ahead; it was impossible to know from which side. There was no fighting.

We walked beside the wall on the far side of Broad Street, passed Salvatore's looted Italian restaurant, which the government troops had ransacked one night in early July, telling the owner that he was being punished because Elizabeth Blunt, of what the AFL viewed as the biased BBC, often ate there. The day after the looting a civilian official from the Defence Ministry had arrived to request that Salvatore hand over an M-16 rifle which one of the looting soldiers had left behind the previous night – a request with which Salvatore readily complied, producing the forgotten gun from beneath the bar.

We walked past Joseph, deputy to the acting information minister Paul Allen Wie. Joseph was walking quickly away from the city centre, up the hill towards the Ducor Hotel. The previous evening he had come to our apartment with Wie, the official who had said to us:

> I don't want to be quoted on dead bodies in town. I'm not speaking on the dead bodies issue. It's not the government policy to kill civilians. The government has given concessions in the hope of a peaceful solution. But there is only a military solution. Doe's concern is for an orderly transfer of power, and to avoid further bloodshed. But these options have been turned down. Now there's only a military alternative. This is a tribal war. If 'the people' come they will kill all of us. The battle is not for Liberia. The moment Charles Taylor entered Nimba the battle was for the mansion … People get killed in all revolutions. Ours [i.e., Doe's 1980 coup] was not the worst.

There on Broad Street, Joseph, who had stood beside Wie, nodding throughout the previous evening's meeting, waved a finger at us, as if to say that we should not recognise him. We walked on, left Broad Street and passed Monrovia Catholic Cathedral, and went down towards Front Street and Waterside, which the AFL had chosen as a favourite spot to leave the bodies of their overnight victims. But the AFL had gone. We reached Front Street, where dilapidated shanties stood between areas of earth and boulders.

At a café on a corner which overlooked the two bridges to Bushrod Island, as well as giving a view down the street towards the centre of the city on the northern side, a group of soldiers had mounted a machine-gun. They were talking with some civilians, who smiled and chatted and appeared at ease. We approached the soldiers, said 'good morning', told them we were reporters and asked them who they were. They wore smart military uniforms and black military boots, and had new weapons, mostly AK-47s, as well as boxes of bullets; an array of water bottles in webbing carriers hanging from their thick belts, and long knives in leather holders completed their attire.

'Our leader is Prince Johnson,' one said, carefully, clearly. I asked where Prince Johnson was, and was told he was on the other side of the bridge. We could cross whenever we liked, they told us confidently, it was all under their control. We said we would come back and walked down Front Street.

A tall, thin man pushed a wheelbarrow quickly uphill on the far side of the road. Two arms and two legs dangled onto the wet tarmac from the wheelbarrow. He stared at us and shouted:

'Don't look. Never seen it before?' he said, without stopping, his voice breaking slightly, his thin face sunk with the signs of hunger, his eyes big.

Up some steps, in front of a two-storey house, a group of men yelled at us.

'You. You. You can't come here. Not allowed. Where' your pass?' They were dressed in civilian clothes, but it was clear that they were AFL soldiers who had shed their uniforms. And still, after the house they were in had fallen into the hands of their enemy, they were asserting their ridiculous authority. I had my video camera and one of them walked down the steps and tried to take it from me. He grabbed the eye-piece and started to bend it. I asked him who he was and he said he was AFL. I told him to let go of the camera, and looked up the street at Prince Johnson's troops on the corner, and wondered where the front line was, if there was a front line. How were these people identifying with the invaders, if they still had the confidence to intimidate us as if they were still in control? I pulled the camera away from the man. The uncertainty of who was in control meant it was easy to just walk away. I wanted to find the right time to tell the AFL soldiers what I thought of their crimes, but there on the street was not the time. I would just watch them instead. We went further down Front Street, turned a corner and walked straight into a battle.

A barrage of 50-calibre machine-gun fire streaked overhead, echoing between the empty, shattered office-blocks we were walking among. But the street was deserted. Unless it was being fired from the top of one of the buildings, it was impossible to know where the shooting was coming from. I stood at a crossroads and the clatter and boom of gunfire filled the air in all directions. But still the streets remained completely deserted.

We walked back towards Front Street, past the house where the AFL soldiers were still standing on the steps, to where the INPFL troops had been at the corner café. But they had gone, as had the civilians they had been talking to. The echo of the battle resounded, but I could see nobody. We walked back to the apartment, where Roddy and Goldsmith were about to drive down to the People's Bridge to see who controlled it. Since they had bought another Peugeot, this time from the French embassy, to replace the one stolen by the AFL, I had felt even less inclined to travel with them, as I had been unable to contribute to the $2,000 they had spent on it. But now there was no choice but to drive with them. They reluctantly allowed Budu into the car, and we drove past the American and French embassies then turned left, away from the city centre, down a steep hill behind the Ducor Hotel to Waterside. We passed two women on the road. They were talking to two men inside a car. The men were dressed in AFL uniforms, and the women were handing them civilian clothes, telling them: 'Put them on. Change quickly.'

They looked at us, suddenly terrified, but we drove on down the hill to Waterside without stopping. Driving over the concrete slabs which constituted the road was like travelling on glass. Thousands of bullet cases coated the road, crunching beneath the tyres for the entire length of the street. At a crossroads up ahead, strewn with empty wooden market-stalls, the INPFL had built two sand-bag walls and mounted two heavy machine-guns, one facing in the direction from which we were coming, the other facing towards the market. On the other side of the road, among the shacks of Waterside, a large crowd had gathered to watch them. We walked among the crowd and down to the beach where fishermen were mending nets. They said the rebels had fought their way across in the early morning.

'They ha'n't be' troublin' us,' said an old man, whose face had become so thin that his cheekbones had barely enough flesh to cover them. He wore a knitted red pullover, which hung wet from his boney frame. These people were starving. They moved slowly as we walked among them. The way they watched the rebels, without fear or caring, showed they had no energy left to react. They had been trapped on a muddy corner of Monrovia, unable to put out to sea to fish with any regularity, for fear of being shot at by the AFL, who had banned all fishing when they realised Taylor was commandeering fishing boats and using them as a cover to attack the city from the Atlantic side.

We crossed the road back to where Prince's troops had set up their guns. They said they would take us across to the other side. As they spoke, heavy gunfire poured down from close to the Ducor Hotel. On this side, the hill at the top of which the hotel stood was a steep climb between massive boulders and small houses which clung to the rock. The rebels had only been in the town for a few hours, giving the AFL a chance to move its troops towards the Ducor, through the streets it still controlled. The barrage sent the hungry crowd fleeing back among the shacks of Waterside. The INPFL opened fire with deafening 50-calibre machine-guns, shooting along the street, deserted but for the market-stalls.

We were unable to cross the bridge for two more days. The INPFL remained in the positions they had taken on that first day. The AFL in the city centre cruised around in their stolen yellow taxis, still looking for people to 'carry' and kill. One afternoon some of Doe's remaining officials arrived at the American embassy to say that they planned to send troops into the Greystone compound, into which thousands of people had fled when the fighting intensified in the city centre.

'We're going to go in to see if there are rebels there,' one of Doe's officials told the American ambassador.

'Oh, no, you're not going in there,' De Vos replied.

The Americans were unsure whether the AFL, who had already encircled the compound, would burst in anyway. The ambassador tried to delay them as long as possible in order to warn the people inside the compound that if there were any rebels inside they should leave, along with anybody else who thought the AFL would accuse them of rebel sympathies. Which meant just about everybody who was not Krahn. But the evacuation proved unnecessary, as Doe's officials eventually backed down and the AFL withdrew.

After Waterside had been completely cleared of people and the fishermen had fled into town, we reached the crossroads early one morning.

'We go,' said an INPFL soldier, during a lull in the fighting.

He and five others jumped into a camouflage green pick-up. We crept back to the Peugeot. The shooting started again, but the soldiers screeched towards the People's Bridge, crunching across the bullet-strewn crossroads. We followed. They did not stop at the end of the bridge, just sped across it.

The dead lay clinging to the railings, among the blood, bullets, discarded ammunition boxes, torn uniforms and army boots which had been left as the battle for the bridge had raged during three days of fighting. As we reached the centre of the bridge a barrage of gunfire burst over our heads. The grey swell of the Mesurado River below us swayed with the motion of corpses. We reached the junction on the other side, where more INPFL troops lay in the grass, their guns trained on the Ducor hill opposite, drove left onto Bushrod Island and into the shelter of the warehouses which lined the road, and breathed again.

Scores of bodies lay draped over the kerbstones along the central reservation as far as the freeport, after which the road narrows, with shops on one side and open grassland on the other stretching down to the port perimeter wall. A convoy of pick-ups sped along the wet road towards us. Hundreds of people stood beside the road, aimlessly moving in one direction then the other, with no idea where to go. The convoy drew closer, slowed then stopped. A man was standing up in the back of a white Toyota. We got out of the car.

'I,' said the man with a rasping voice, 'am Prince Yormie Johnson.' He had a close-cropped beard, a peaked army-cap with a scorpion insignia, field-glasses on a leather strap around his neck, an AK-47 and was dressed in one-piece khaki fatigues. 'I,' he paused, 'spent one and a half years training in Libya, and Charles Taylor killed my family in Saklepie. He, Charles Taylor, is a senior security adviser to Blaise Compaore. But I,' he paused again, 'am not in favour of Gadaffi. We must protect democracy. I was Taylor's planning and training officer in Libya. And I led 167 troops from Libya. And he, Charles Taylor, took money from Libya. He is not going to come here and make himself president. While I,' he said, pausing for a sharp intake of breath, 'am not here to fight my brothers. I don't want power. I don't want to be president. It's the True Whig Party which is coming back [with Taylor]. I want fair elections. Taylor will manipulate the elections. But there should be no army government. I will get Doe. He is not going to get away. That's what I say, and I am Prince Yormie Johnson, and I was born on July 6, 1952.'

He smiled and chuckled and blew through his nose, as he yelled orders for his four-car convoy to reassemble. Then he ordered its advance in the direction of the city.

Prince sat down on a garden chair placed in but not attached to the back of the Toyota pick-up. As the car started it jerked forward and he, the chair and the young guards standing beside their leader all tumbled backwards and were left sprawled in the back of the car and on the road. Prince, the leader, laughed and chuckled and enjoyed his own humiliation. His guards picked themselves and their leader up, the driver was scolded mildly and asked if he had ever learned to drive, and they set off again, towards the group of more than a hundred people standing beside the road further up.

Prince ordered the convoy to stop. He leapt down from the pick-up and strode over to the people, yelling. It was too dangerous for them to stand on the road like that, he screamed at them. This was a war and they would get hurt if they stayed out on the road. The people mumbled, and Prince got angry. He pulled off the safety-catch of his AK-47 and opened fire less than a foot above the heads of the cold, wet hungry people. They winced and screamed and fled in between the warehouses lining the road.

'Move. Get o' tha' road. Stupi' people. Get o' the road,' he yelled, sending another volley of shots over their heads. The people scattered, Prince leapt back onto his garden chair in the pick-up, and looked over to us where we were standing beside the Peugeot.

'Bye-bye,' he said, in a childish voice, waving. 'Co' o'er an' see u' in Caldwell.' And in a flurry of roaring engines and orders, gripping his chair tightly as the car jerked into action, he returned the way he had come, leaving us to brave the People's Bridge without any of his troops to lead us back.

We drove back across the bridge to Bushrod Island that afternoon. The afternoons were usually quiet, the morning's fighting having exhausted the soldiers, the sun having grown hot, drowsiness having set in. There were no shots as we crossed the bridge, and drove between the deserted allies and streets of Viatown and on towards Duala and Caldwell. We found Prince swigging a bottle of Cinzano in a café at a junction on the main road, where a right turn leads to Caldwell and eventually reaches the White Plains waterworks. He assembled his convoy, and we drove along the dirt road towards Caldwell, crossing Stockton Creek and then stopping at a junction leading to the Monrovia residential compound of the Bong iron-ore company. Around 200 armed, uniformed men, women and children quickly assembled themselves into rows as Prince arrived. They chanted slogans, stood to attention, clapped their hands on their new guns, then were ordered to stand easy. We talked to the soldiers, some of whom had whitened their faces with chalk. They were cautious and would not say how they had got there, though Prince said that 40 per cent of what he claimed was a 7,000-strong army were AFL soldiers who had deserted during the past weeks of fighting on Bushrod Island. After an hour we returned along the road, whose long empty expanse felt good to drive along, after so many weeks of being enclosed in the ever-narrowing strip of land to which the fighting, the AFL and the fear had confined us.

'They killed hundreds. Hundreds. They're all fleeing from there.' Tahseen was out of breath. He had run all the way from Camp Johnson Road to the apartment, through the AFL checkpoints, around the INPFL checkpoints. We listened. It was early morning, 30 July. The AFL had done what everybody had been waiting for.

I could feel the children gripping my hands when we had walked across the churchyard less than two weeks before. I could hear the nurse telling me about all the facilities that he, in this time of adversity, was striving to provide, as he opened his tins to show the syringes he was using, displayed the rotting cotton wool, and showed us his lists of patients, their maladies, his cures. Then I heard him telling how the AFL came in the early evening just after curfew, rattling the gates, firing volleys into the air.

'They frighten the children,' he had said. 'They frighten the children. They frighten the children.'

At first it seemed that Doe's Executive Mansion Guard had murdered everybody in Saint Peter's Lutheran church that night of 29 July.

'Julu was in charge of the Executive Mansion Guard at the time of the Lutheran church attack,' General Bowen told me later.

'Earlier in July the AFL had planned to go to the church, but Bowen had stopped it. But there was no one person giving orders,' said Isaac Roberts, an AFL soldier who later told me how he had been with the death-squad commander Michael Tilly, leader of the attack on the church, but who denied that he was there that night.

'Some people said they saw Doe at the Lutheran church. Doe's cousin, Jackson E. Doe, was there, as was Colonel Goah of the Executive Mansion Guard,' the former vice-president, Harry Moniba, told me.

'Mike Adams, the administrative counsellor at the embassy, said that the US could not protect the church. We knew they were sitting ducks and that the AFL was going to get them. The US had a figure of 183 dead, but this didn't included bodies in the outlying buildings,' said an official who was at the American embassy in Monrovia that night.

Tahseen, advising us against trying to cross the front line and make our way to the church in Sinkor, said he would try and get there himself, and would come back to tell us what had happened. Two hours later he returned to the apartment.

'They made me strip off my clothes to let me inside. I saw women with their heads smashed to pieces, with babies still tied to their backs. I saw the bodies of people who had tried to escape hanging from the window frames. I saw people draped over the altar, who had been butchered with knives and shot with machine-guns. The floor was thick with blood, and there were bodies huddled together under the pews where people had tried to hide. The crucifix had been thrown to the ground and the ceiling was riddled with bullet-holes. And then outside, in the school buildings, where there had been people sleeping, everybody was dead. People had been killed where they lay on their mattresses. Everywhere dead people. There must have been hundreds. Six hundred I counted, around six hundred, or maybe more. And there were people who survived and jumped over the wall and went to houses across the road. And I talked to people who said they saw the soldiers going into the houses and finding these people and then taking them down the road to the beach. I don't know what happened to them then. Then they made me leave the area.'

General Bowen later told me he was having his day off when the church was attacked.

'There were more than 200 AFL who came that night. They came just before the curfew, just before 7pm. They had come before, at the same time, to shoot outside, and threaten us, but they didn't come in. You see, we had a Red Cross flag on the wall, and they wouldn't come in, because we had the flag on the wall,' said Johnny Teah, lying on a bed and holding the stump of his arm when I spoke with him, months later. He had survived.

> The soldiers shot the door open, and took all the food they could see inside, and they killed the woman who had the key to the warehouse, after raping her. And we saw the AFL soldiers argue over the food, about who should have it. They wanted the food, and they argued about the food, and then

they left, and they left guards on the gate and said that nobody could leave. And the guards stood on the gate and we stayed inside. Nobody could leave, and then it got dark, and then they came back again the same night. The soldiers came back. They broke in again, through the door on the side of the church. There were around 200 of them, they came in, all speaking Krahn. And they began cutting a boy, with a knife, and they cut and cut and came inside the church, and cut everybody with their knives and machetes. And then I heard one of them say: 'Boss, I'm tired. My arm is tired,' and he said to the soldier: 'Use your gun if you're tired,' so they shot. And one of my friends, Saye Dolo, he saw President Doe there. He saw Doe take off his mask. And then the next day the death squad came back at around 5am to see if anybody was alive. They killed one person then. But I lay there, with my eyes closed, and then I escaped.

He stopped, saying that he did not want to talk about it any more.

Doctors at St Joseph's Catholic hospital, on the eastern edge of the city, heard about the massacre as it was taking place. Next day, they sent convoys to the church from the hospital. They reckoned there were about 1,000 people inside the church, that 600 were killed, and 150 were wounded. The doctors from Medecins Sans Frontières, who were still working at the Catholic hospital, treated 80 injured people who were brought in vehicles from the church. Another 40 walked through AFL territory to the hospital to be treated.

'The day after the massacre, Tilly came to the Catholic hospital, with a white cross painted on his forehead,' said one of the doctors who treated those who managed to escape from the church.

Tilly and his men checked the identity cards of everybody in the hospital. They put all the Liberians on one side, and the remaining expatriate doctors on the other, and pretended to all the Liberians that they were going to shoot them. The same AFL people had burst into JFK hospital a week beforehand, where we had extended our facilities because there were so many injured people. At JFK the AFL had forced the gate and come inside, and they began looking for rebels, and they killed many of the patients in the wards. They killed about 20 people. But after the Lutheran church massacre they put Dr Bowman, the hospital director, in a car with a security person, and then they left. Then on 2 August, Charles Taylor's people moved into Sinkor.

The day after the massacre, we fell back into AFL hands.

The slaughter of the civilians at the church was the morale booster the AFL had been searching for. Fighting erupted in the early morning of 31 July, bullets whizzing through Mamba Point, forcing us to stay inside for most of the day and wonder whose territory we were in – the INPFL never having established a strong presence in the embassy district, the AFL having concentrated its troops in the city centre. Our uncertainty was strengthened by the presence of INPFL troops wandering around what appeared to be AFL territory on Mamba Point. INPFL troops we had seen at Prince Johnson's Caldwell base, dressed in military uniform and with their faces painted with chalk, stood in civilian clothes on the street corner close to the British embassy, apparently unmoved as AFL troops drove past.

By the next day, 1 August, the AFL had been driven back to the positions they had held before their offensive, and the city centre was once again cut in half.

14 Music in the Graveyard

To kill a man is not an easy thing.
PRINCE JOHNSON, *Commander of the INPFL, Monrovia.*

T HE RUSTING carcass of an abandoned black Cadillac lay beneath the colonnade around the base of the national bank's multi-storey headquarters. I heard music playing. I had heard the song many times without knowing who played it. It became, to me, the song of the war, but nobody could tell me who was singing, with the pain of a man who had suffered, who was looking for hope when everything around him seemed hopeless, and in a world where the rules he had been raised to abide by no longer seemed to apply. The song told of a boy who had been steered away from crime when he was young, told that if he attended school and pursued his education he would be rescued from poverty and desperation. But then the song goes on to tell how no amount of effort saved him in the end. The song he is singing is being sung from inside the prison to which life has brought him, in the midst of a country which has lost its way, where education has not brought anything, where the only buildings being constructed are prisons like the one in which he is sitting.

The song would shatter the silence of Monrovia, sometimes even seem to be a musical accompaniment to the desolation of the city and the desperation of the people trapped there, unable to flee, too late to get out, too afraid perhaps to leave the apparent security of their familiar homes. They were all prisoners, but trapped in their country by fear rather than the empty walls of a cell, imprisoned not by the waywardness of any particular one of them, but by their entire country having lost its way and plunged into crime. Years later I stopped beside the road for a rest in the heart of the Cameroonian rain forest. A truck drove by playing the song, and I chased after the driver and found him in a bar and asked him the name of the singer. He slowly wrote it down on a piece of paper for me, so I could buy a copy of it and play it, to remind myself of the afternoons spent in the city of the dead.

Prince Johnson's troops sat on deck-chairs in the shadow of the national bank. They all smiled and said hello as I walked up to them. Two men in civilian clothes, sitting on the ground nearby, smiled and said hello, too, but were then told by the soldiers to be quiet.

'Terrible. Terrible,' the soldiers said, shaking their heads, as we talked about the massacre at the church. 'That's Doe,' they said. Their lack of emotion made it as if they were not involved in what was going on. They did not appear to regret not having been able to save those people; they felt no sense of failure at having been unable to do so.

Moses, the soldier in charge of the group, instead reflected the relief of somebody who *had* been saved by Prince Johnson. Moses was not a redeemer. He was one of the redeemed.

'I have been waiting for Prince to come,' he cried out, tears welling up in his eyes and then falling down his quivering cheeks. 'Now I can rejoice. He is going to steer our ship. I would rather die than see him fail,' he half shouted, half moaned. Then he turned on the two men in civilian clothes sitting on the ground nearby. 'Meantime, all you can do is loot and steal from innocent people. And now we are going to kill you,' he yelled at the two cowering men, crouched on the pavement strewn with glass and bullet cases. As he spoke three other rebel soldiers began kicking the prisoners where they sat on the ground. They beat them with their rifle butts, and kicked and kicked, as the men writhed on the floor, thin, hungry, terrified.

Moses opened the boot of the wrecked black Cadillac. The sun was hot that afternoon.

'And this is what they stole,' he said, pointing inside at bottles of pink champagne and tins of beans and luncheon meat. 'Now we are going to kill them. Because we have suffered. My family has suffered so much because of Samuel Doe. They have suffered so much.' He began to cry again, uncontrollably, big tears rolling down his face. 'We have suffered so much,' he said, as his fellow soldiers put their arms on his shoulders to comfort him, embarrassed and smiling.

One of the rebels led me away from the looters, who remained crouched on the ground. Then one of the looters scuttled past me on all-fours. He ran out onto the road. They chased him, They opened fire. The shooting went on and on. Then the man lay on the road without moving. They turned to the other man. His face was cracked with tears.

'Don't be afraid. There's nothing you can do,' Moses said to me. 'Go on. Write it down. Prince's army kills looters.'

The second man prayed to his executioners, begged them. Then he scurried under the Cadillac. They forced him out from underneath by opening fire on him where he hid. He crawled out from beneath the car and lay on the ground wounded. Five of the soldiers pointed the barrels of their guns at where he lay. Blood pumped out from inside his pink tee-shirt as they shot and shot and shot. The man curled his left leg beneath him, slowly.

Then he was still.

They offered me rice.

We ate among the spent bullet cases. A man walked past on the road pushing in a wheelbarrow another man who had a bloody wound in his leg. The man pushing said the injured man was his brother. The rebels rounded on him.

'We saw you in uniform firing on us this morning. We're going to kill. you.' They prepared their guns. I moved in between them and the injured man, saying his injury meant he couldn't do much harm. Why doesn't he just disappear?

'The pressman thinks he should just disappear,' Moses said to the others. 'Where can he disappear to?'

I told his brother to push the wheelbarrow out of the city. But the injured man kept arguing, justifying, denying the rebels' accusations that he was who they said he was. I told him to get out before he was killed, and looked over to the bodies of the looters. He kept arguing. The rebels aimed their guns. I told the brother to get out of sight, and he wheeled the injured man away, and the rebels ate more rice and I said good-bye and walked further up Broad Street towards the Ducor Hotel. The injured man was lying further up the road, bleeding heavily. The wheelbarrow had tipped over. The brother was asking some people peering out of a house if they would help him. Some children were throwing sticks at a lime tree, trying to bring down the unripe fruit.

I walked back to the apartment, and drove with Budu down to the People's Bridge in a yellow pick-up of the Liberian Electricity Company, which Prince Johnson had given us – as a contribution to the freedom of the press, he said.

'Liberia's motherland is America. We don't want bloodshed. We want the United States to intervene,' Prince Johnson claimed. He was sitting at the same roadside bar, this time drinking Martini.

'What is America's role? I, Prince Johnson, the commander of the special forces, have decided to give an order to have all foreign nationals arrested on the ground and kept in my camp. British, Indian, American – I will arrest you all and cause a big regional conflict. Then the world will intervene. I give you two days. Then I'm going to begin arresting people,' he said.

The previous day Prince had personally executed a Liberian called Bashi, who had been carrying out a policy of selling relief food which Prince had agreed with the American embassy would be sold by the Liberian Red Cross. Prince had arrested him, after subsequently declaring that relief food should be free. On being arrested, the man was handcuffed to a Frenchman, who had also been selling the rice, and shot. The rice being sold had belonged to the Firestone rubber company and had been bought by the American government for distribution in Monrovia. Only after the American embassy had vouched for the identity of the Frenchman had Prince freed him. The killing had reasserted Prince's credentials as a player whom it was impossible to ignore – as he had the guns and the mentality to terrorise everybody in his territory.

'We will start with US citizens. Any Americans. We will be searching from house to house. They will be held hostage, if there's no response from Washington. I want the United Nations to send a peacekeeping force right away,' he said, though demanding that Nigeria be excluded from such a force due to Babangida's past support for Doe. 'I will arrest everybody, except the press and the church,' he said, then added, with a wry smile, 'Who is going to stop me?'

Prince refused to let us go to his camp at Caldwell, because he had actually already given his men the order to start arresting foreigners but did not know whether they had carried it out. In fact, his troops had gone to the Hotel Africa that day and arrested 48 foreigners. The Hotel Africa, the largest hotel in Liberia, had become the refuge of the expatriates who, for reasons that most of them preferred not to share, did not wish to return to their own countries, despite the danger of remaining in Liberia. Most had turned whatever assets they had in the country into cash and taken rooms at the hotel, which lies outside the city on the road to Sierra Leone. Their presence at the Hotel Africa, which had been the site of an Organisation of African Unity conference in 1979, had attracted Liberia's seedy underbell; anybody who ventured to the hotel was guaranteed a good time at discount rates. The fun only stopped on 4 August when Prince Johnson's men arrived to arrest them.

The next day there was a new sound. The American marines landed in Monrovia and, for an hour or so, it seemed that the world cared enough to stop the carnage.

For weeks there had only been the waves crashing on the shore, or the sound of guns. That morning, having given Doe a few minutes' notice, US navy helicopters clattered over the palm trees and rooftops bringing

235 marines, vehicles, razor wire and fresh vegetables for the embassy. Ambassador De Vos stood on the lawn behind the embassy's social-club, watching the close-cropped marines who had been waiting for action since their arrival offshore in May.

But it soon became clear that they were not going to do anything for Liberia. During the morning they blocked the roads approaching the embassy with coils of wire, built sand-bagged gun emplacements on the roofs of the two entrances to the embassy, and waited.

It was the perceived threat to take hostages that had led to De Vos requesting what amounted merely to a stepping-up of embassy security. Upon his arrival at Mamba Point, Prince Johnson had secured an American embassy radio and made regular contacts with embassy officials.

'Prince Johnson would come to the embassy unannounced and want to see De Vos, though sometimes he would call from Bushrod Island to say that he was on his way. But his visits to the embassy were almost never arranged by the US,' said a former embassy official. 'Johnson was often drunk when he arrived, and sometimes just seemed to want to have contact with us. He would walk through the embassy looking for De Vos, and would sometimes find him on the tennis court, and would give him big bear-hugs. There were up to 12 meetings in the embassy. But the US discouraged contact with him. He was a murderer, and we were very leary of him right from the beginning. We knew that Prince Johnson was not the kind of guy we were going to do business with.'

Among the 48 foreigners Prince Johnson arrested there was only one American. Johnson was least likely to provoke the US of all countries – it was the most awesome and therefore least likely target of rebel venom. It was always much more likely that the AFL would finally turn on the US, citing American betrayal of its ally which had done so much for the superpower as a reason for feeling aggrieved. But this never happened either. The fact that, as one embassy official put it, 'the US military was looking for a role, because there were no conflicts going on in the world', offers the best explanation for the marine landing of 5 August.

The landing was a faultless military exercise, but one which would barely alter the military situation on the ground, and it could be done without too much concern for the sensibilities of the Liberians, whose sovereignty had long ago been lost at their own hands.

We drove out to Caldwell the next day, and Prince took us to his hostages, lined up on the steps of the building where we had seen the INPFL assembled on the first day we saw Prince. We talked to the 48 men there, took their names and asked them where they came from and what they did. There were Chinese, Indians, Greeks, Argentinians, British, Lebanese and others, serious, tough-looking men, reluctant to talk, unnerved but not frightened, as they stood there in the holiday clothes, turbans, flip-flops and shorts in which they had been arrested. They had messages for various girlfriends, but most had nothing to say to anybody in the outside world, as if they had long ago severed links with life outside the one which only freewheeling Liberia allowed them to lead.

Prince took us to the Bong Mining Company compound he had made his headquarters. Neat bungalows stood among the trees where his soldiers ambled. Behind an iron gate, which glided on small wheels across a driveway, Prince's bungalow teemed with guards, camouflage-painted vehicles, guns mounted on the backs of pick-ups. We were invited inside, and shown into a living-room furnished only with settees around the walls and a low coffee-table in the centre. A small, chubby woman with a pony-tail and dressed in military fatigues offered round a plate with large chunks of luncheon meat, each pierced with a cocktail stick. Somebody else handed round cans of cold Budweiser beer.

Then Prince left us. We waited for a while, and then asked if he was going to come back.

'He's coming. He asks for you to wait,' we were told. So we waited. Thirty minutes later we were still there, and stood up to leave. We walked outside, and saw Prince walking across the gravel driveway with his deputy, Samuel Varney. Prince angrily approached a group of uniformed young soldiers who were standing near the bungalow garage. He began to abuse them.

'You're damn fuckin' looters,' he yelled at the nervous soldiers. He railed against them, knowing that some of them were defectors from the AFL whom he had recruited, he suggested, on trust. They had stolen food from the port, he said. He made them drop their trousers and lie on the ground. As they lay there he walked among them, kicking their heads while they screamed, not knowing whether they were going to be shot at the end of this first bout of punishment.

They were taken away, limping, bleeding, and Prince strode off. We drove back to the city, sick of his violence, passing the building at Caldwell road junction where the hostages were still waiting.

That night I lay on my bed and listened as the radio announced that at last our reports of what was going on in Liberia had been heeded, or so I liked to think at the time. At last, the people of the region had decided

182

to take steps to end the carnage their neighbour was inflicting upon itself. It had been decided that a peacekeeping force was to be sent to Liberia.

Details were not clear until the following day. What was clear was that Nigeria, keen to portray itself as a regional leader, had taken the lead and would send troops. Occasionally it appeared that there was a region-wide sense of humiliation at the reports emanating from Liberia, reports which tended to reinforce the outside world's prejudices about Africans. Nigeria, and all those involved in the peacekeeping force, hated to be portrayed in this way, and a regional initiative to stop the slaughter would show Africans in a more positive light.

'Although the conflict is an internal matter, the wanton killings now going on in Liberia have made that country a slaughterhouse,' the then Gambian president, Sir Dawda Jawara, said at a meeting in Banjul, at which the formation of the peacekeeping force had been agreed.

Prince Johnson appeared to have achieved what he wanted and released his foreign hostages two days later.

Unknown to him at the time, however, was a second motive behind the Economic Community Monitoring Group force (or Ecomog, as the force became known), which was regional opposition to Taylor, whose imprisonment in Ghana in 1987 and proximity to the Francophone rather than Anglophone zone within the region, raised the prospect of Liberia becoming a thorn in the flesh of Nigeria and its would-be role of regional superpower. Also unknown on 6 August, was the fact that Nigerian troops were on their way to Monrovia by sea, even before the meeting of the Economic Community of West African States (Ecowas) in The Gambia had approved the formation of the Ecomog force. Such was Nigeria's determination to halt the war, stamp on Taylor and rescue up to 3,000 Nigerians trapped in Liberia – most of them in Taylor's territory – that it would pursue its military plans even if it had to do so alone. Meanwhile, the declared aim of the force was to maintain a ceasefire – a ceasefire which had yet to exist, since the warring sides had not reached the climax of their campaigns.

We left the car on Crown Hill, in front of the burned-out offices of the *Daily Observer* newspaper. Prince's troops stood watching. They said they would look after the Peugeot. I had not been to this area of the city since early July, when we had driven that way to Spriggs Payne airfield and out into the eastern suburbs. Ash from burned buildings spiralled into a whirlwind. The city was quiet. It was early morning on 12 August. We had decided to cross the front line, to try to see Doe and talk to him about the peacekeeping force and, if we could, make our way to the Lutheran church.

We walked, Roddy, Goldsmith and I, up the hill to the corner which looks out over the mangrove swamps between which the grey Mesurado River curls, across a plain stretching into the hazy distance where Taylor's army was in control and smoke from fires spiralled up into the morning sky. We turned the sharp corner at the top of the hill. Corrugated-iron sheets lay ripped along the roadside. Huts lay burned. Bloated limbs lay in the grass. But the street was deserted. We listened to the sound of our own voices, our own footsteps, until a group of AFL soldiers outside a small house across some wasteland from the road opened fire at us with a roar of bullets. There were five or six of them, strutting and posturing with their heavy machine-guns. They yelled at us to stop, halt, stand where we were, don't move, don't move. They would not approach us, and just yelled from twenty yards away, ordering us to cross the wasteland of mud and grass to where they were standing.

We slowly made our way across to them. They shot into the air as we approached, yelling, ordering. I couldn't understand what they were saying, and barely knew what they wanted us to do.

I realised that I was now in exactly the same situation as the soldiers I had seen executed beneath the colonnade of the national bank. I was helpless. There is nothing you can do to a man with a gun, except wait.

We slowly walked up a slope to where they were standing. I tried to work out who was the most senior among them. One taller man with a beard said he was a major, and I addressed myself to him, told him very quietly who we were and what we were doing. Again and again, the other soldiers let off bursts of gunfire just beside us, deafening sounds turning the air around us to ice. The major tentatively asserted himself, but was completely unable to stop the shooting. They all hated us.

'American. American. Don' fuck wi' me man. Fuckin' America'. Don't fuck wi' me. Don' fu' wi' me. Do' you fu' wi' me,' the wildest of the soldiers, a man around five feet tall, yelled louder and louder, until he reached a furious crescendo and fired-off a burst of bullets. He grabbed my shirt and shouted into my face and ordered us to empty our pockets. He seized my pocket knife and my pen and notebook and handkerchief and then tore my glasses from my face, and those of Roddy and Goldsmith, and ordered us to follow him in among the small huts whose walls formed empty alleys winding down the slope to the mangrove swamps and the river.

184

I could not follow him.

Again and again he ordered us to follow. He could have only one intention if he took us down there. I think we all realised that how we behaved with these men was going to mean that we either lived or died. The soldier pushed us from behind with his gun, pushed us in the direction of the river, towards the empty alleys. But we lingered, and directed ourselves to the Major, hoping he would assert his authority. They talked, and finally one led us back the way we had come. They yelled at us to follow, and we filed across the wasteland back onto the tarmac road, and I saw the corner to the right around which we had come, and thought about Prince Johnson's troops just around the corner, and the car parked beside the road. But the soldiers led us the other way, along the pavement. They stopped us, demanded that we remove our shirts, our shoes and socks, then led us blind, our glasses twisted in one of their hands, into the heart of the land of the death squad, the massacres, the desperation of a defeated army gathered round the last bastion of its appalling power. They screamed at us, hurling insults, one of them at the front followed by Roddy, then me and Goldsmith behind, who argued cantankerously with his captors, refusing to take off his shirt, which they tore from him till it hung in shreds from his ageing body.

Through the blur of my useless eyes, I saw more soldiers ahead, then a yellow taxi turned on the road and came towards us. The soldiers we were with forced us inside the taxi as it pulled up. We crammed inside, seven or eight of us, as other soldiers ran up to us and began insulting us, then punching us through the open windows of the car. The engine whined but we did not move.

'Fuckin' Americans,' they yelled, threatening us with their rifle butts but refraining from using them. The taxi started. We drove up the sloping driveway of a government building. I could make out familiar buildings. But everything was deserted. We were completely alone with these monsters, and nobody knew we were there. We stopped and then drove off again, down a slope past the police headquarters which leads eventually to a junction with the road to the Executive Mansion.

These were the streets of a nightmare. Deserted alleys and houses, where killings had happened. Streets roamed by murderers who had lost contact with the outside world, killers who had become the horror which perhaps lies inside us all – a brooding savagery, suppressed only by the absence of a stage upon which it can burst out. I was in the hands of men from whose faces peered the squinting, bloodshot eyes of people who had committed evil and who would kill to hide what they had done. I could see Prince Johnson's wry smile, and heard him say: 'Who is going to stop me?'

There was nobody, no conscience at work, no law, just raw humanity, the mud of the alleys, the blue sky. There was nothing to stop them.

The soldiers stopped the taxi in a closed entrance beside the Ministry of Information. The building had been burned inside. The plaster lions sat, pock-marked, at the entrance. We stopped for no reason. I felt that they wanted us in their hands. We were their trophies, their assets. They could bargain with us, their captives, their hostages. They would not want to let us go, it would be like throwing away a valuable prize.

'We're going to stop here,' they said.

All around us there was emptiness. Tranquillity. This is where they were going to shoot us. There was no other reason to stop. We were out of sight of the soldiers at the top of the road. We were out of sight of the Executive Mansion, which the Information Ministry blocked from our view. We were quiet. They switched off the engine and asked us questions, but I could barely hear them. We stayed there for five minutes or more, then they started the engine again and gave us our glasses back so we could see. We drove to the bottom of the hill, turned left towards the Executive Mansion, and then continued past it, beneath a colonnade of trees, past two-storey houses, government buildings, and finally stopped on a parade-ground.

Soldiers stared at us. The ones who had brought us forced us to sit on the step of a building.

'Damn fuckin' spies. Damn fuckin' Americans,' said the small soldier who had been with us from the beginning.

He was told to be quiet by the other soldiers. Goldsmith, his shirt torn, refused to sit on the step, just to show them that he was not somebody who had got through life by obeying the orders of people he believed were his inferiors. He stood. We had been given our shirts back, and shoes and socks. A soldier came to us and said he wanted us to inter-view one of those injured in a rocket attack on the mansion. The AFL had claimed a few day's previously that an American submarine had launched an attack on the mansion, in a bid to kill Doe. The Americans had denied it, saying that if they had tried they would not have missed their target. It eventually became clear that what had been an attack from the sea had come from one of Taylor's fishing boats, armed either with a mortar or something bigger,

An old man sat in an upstairs room in the building. He showed us his injuries. We sympathised, said we would write a story about him, and realised that this was the way to turn the soldiers round. They became communicative and stopped threatening us. We left the old man, walked outside, and were confronted by the information minister, Paul Allen Wie. We had occasionally wondered where he might be. We had heard nothing from him for nearly two weeks and had assumed that he had fled. He smiled his friendly smile and led us into a building opposite, into the office of Lieutenant-Colonel Moses Thomas, head of Doe's Strategic Anti-Terrorist Unit (SATU).

Don Williams's songs oozed from an under-powered cassette-player on Thomas's desk. He sat on a chair beside a camp-bed, dressed in battle fatigues and a bullet-proof jacket, fiddling with a miniature Israeli flag on his desk, an Israeli calendar depicting an ageing rabbi was stuck on the wall behind him, beside a poster advertising efforts to restore parts of the Old City of Jerusalem. This memorabilia of his training in Israel, whose training of Liberians and provision of permanent military advisers had turned the SATU into the organ which protected Doe and denied his enemies the chance to mount a limited coup rather than a war to overthrow him, was proudly displayed. Thomas explained that what we had done by crossing the lines was very dangerous. He said it calmly, pointing out that it might have been unwise. His calm was infectious. Then, after a few minutes, a civilian in a flowery shirt appeared and introduced himself.

'I'm Sellie Thompson, spokesman for the President,' he said, out of breath, sweating slightly, smoking profusely.

We asked if we could see Doe, and he said he would transmit the request. He disappeared and came back ten minutes later to tell us that our request had been refused as the President was just too busy. Then Roddy asked why Doe had not contacted the American embassy, whose offer to take him out had not been withdrawn, though it would have been very difficult had the demand been made.

'The President is shy,' said Thompson.

Lieutenant-Colonel Thomas said he would like to show us the damage inflicted by the American submarine. We got into his car. He showed us a hole in the wall of a house on the other side of the Executive Mansion, then took us down towards the Barclay Training Centre. We drove through the entrance and saw Abdullai Bah's Peugeot sitting on the parade-ground. We were shown up some stairs and into a back room.

'If our men have treated you badly then I am sorry. I am very sorry. It's not right, and I am very sorry. And I would like to welcome you to the barracks.' General Hezekiah Bowen smiled and held out his hand for us to shake.

We sat on the pine furniture in his office and were introduced to his deputy, General Moses Wright, who laughed and commiserated with us, and smiled and smiled, until we were shown to the perimeter wall. We walked through the hellish normality of a sunny afternoon out of the barracks, where non-Krahn soldiers were being killed, where the beach at the back within sight of Bowen's office was a graveyard. We walked along outside the wall of the barracks, in the direction of Mamba Point. On the street corner, at the end of the wall, the most forward AFL position in that part of town, a manhole cover had been removed. An old man stood waist-high in the hole, staring through the sight of an ancient rifle. He grinned.

'We're gonna get 'em. Them damn rebels,' he said, a funny, clown-like old man, peering down an empty street, waving us good-bye from his hole, telling us that we could come back any time.

The American embassy had left a message at the apartment that we should call. The USS *Saipan*, the enormous, all-purpose amphibious assault helicopter-carrier, which was the flagship of the US Navy presence off the coast, was to sail down to Buchanan that night to evacuate foreigners. Roddy and Goldsmith, keen to have me out the way if a big story broke in Monrovia, were almost obscenely eager that I should take up the US Navy's offer of a place on board.

I flew out on a navy helicopter, as the afternoon sun was beginning to turn the sea gold. The three of us had been out to the *Saipan*, just after the marines had landed on 5 August. Then the Admiral had given us a box of fruit and vegetables and we had bought USS *Saipan* baseball hats. The horror of what we were seeing in the city set sharply against the mundanity of ship-board life, as marines and sailors drifted around the ship, going to the gymnasium or the canteen, saluting, chatting about work.

I was given a bed in the isolation ward of the ship's hospital, which was the only available space for guests staying overnight. A young crew-man from Idaho who wore denim bell-bottoms was put in charge of me.

Time passed quickly.

I had the same sense of not knowing where I was that I had experienced on the train roaring into Taylor's territory in April. I had stepped off the streets of a city in which I felt I knew every sound, in which every street corner haunted me, and had emerged among the steel corridors of institutional America, of rules, of order. I was between two, diametrically opposed worlds which were passing within a few miles of each other. My mind replayed again and again the sights of the city, as I queued for meatballs and coleslaw salad among the marines clamouring for food in the dining-hall.

I was up at 5am and was led through the maze of corridors until I eventually saw daylight, cold rain and the vast expanse of the *Saipan*'s landing-pad. Buchanan, where I had been two months before, lay out of sight, beyond the rain. The helicopter rose out of the ship's hold, and we boarded after a small boat had been sent to the port to prepare our arrival and returned to announce the all-clear. We clattered through the rain and my mind slowly got around to thinking about what it was that I might now see in Taylor's territory. The war was nine months old. My last impressions were old. So much had changed. Who would I see? Would it be the place that I had left behind, or once again would events have moved so far on that my memories would be mine alone?

We landed on the beach, among coarse grass close to a line of palm trees. Taylor's troops stood sentry as the helicopter blew up the wet sand. It poured with rain. I jumped down, hoping that perhaps I might see some of my friends from Abidjan, but instead, as I walked up a paved path, I was forced aside by two guards striding purposefully towards the American officers. Between them was Dokie.

I smiled, and he smiled back. But then he walked on, without saying a word, leaving me standing beside the path.

'Mark,' said a voice from nearby. I turned and looked into a face that had aged, which smiled with rotting teeth, the face of Alexander Kuilu, with whom I had been on that train in April. We embraced. It was good to see him, to feel that I was not an outsider. We talked, then he said good-bye; he had to leave with the senior NPFL officers who had arrived to meet the Americans from the ship.

I began to recognise faces among the NPFL soldiers, people whose names I didn't know. Worried faces. They, like the AFL soldiers who had menaced us the previous day, were suffering from their own isolation within a world geared for war.

'There are planes landing all the time at Robertsfield airport, coming with more weapons from Burkina Faso, and ammunition to keep the war going on and on. And now the peacemakers may come there are plans to bring in more and more weapons to fight them,' said one whom I had met in April. The few I talked with seemed uncertain about how they wanted the war to go, and I told them about Monrovia, and they listened

189

with dismay as I described the city and the brutality, and felt guilty at telling them that their efforts at liberation seemed only to have resulted in more suffering.

After an hour we flew back to the ship, with the Papal Nuncio, the Spanish ambassador and 50 other foreigners, who were being helicoptered on board after driving the 80 miles in convoy from eastern Monrovia down to Buchanan. None of them wanted to talk as we sailed back. Their journey through Taylor's territory had been hell, and many had been caught in fighting when the NPFL advanced through Sinkor towards the Executive Mansion in early August. They stayed on board as we arrived off the coast near Monrovia a few hours later, and a helicopter took me back to the city. I walked back along the deserted, sun-baked evening streets to the apartment.

In 24 hours nothing had changed. Two days previously Taylor had announced that he would launch a final assault on the Executive Mansion, and by 13 August had retaken streets in the eastern suburbs from which he had been driven a few days before. But a government counter-attack that day drove him back to Congotown, and he agreed to talk to President Jawara of The Gambia about peacemaking, though he would not compromise on his demand that Doe should leave immediately, before any ceasefire was discussed. Prince Johnson had meanwhile retained his positions in the city centre, and was increasingly preoccupied by attacks from Taylor's forces in the north-west of the city.

I woke the next morning, 14 August, more tired than I had been when I had gone to sleep. I packed my bag and walked to the American embassy with Roddy and filled out an 'Evacuation Documentation' form, upon which I was listed as a 'probable immediate alien'. I had to get out of there. I simply had to be somewhere else. I felt no need to stay in order to see what happened next.

Four days later Prince Johnson agreed a ceasefire with the AFL, and their soldiers formed joint bands to loot the remaining shops while their leaders agreed to fight Taylor together. Five days after that, on 23 August, the peacekeeping force of Ecomog arrived.

But I thought only of departure, as I walked out onto the embassy basketball court, and the blast from the blades of a helicopter tore at the palm trees as it lifted me out of there, above the curling surf along the coast and north to Freetown.

15 Death of a Dictator

The Krahn nation has done no wrong to anybody. If Doe is guilty, that's not because of the Krahn. The Krahn did not fight for Doe. They fought for themselves.

BAI GBALA, *former senior adviser to Samuel Doe, Freetown, November 1990.*

The Americans kept pressing Doe to be evacuated. Doe kept saying no. Doe's view was that Liberia was his home.

Former vice-president HARRY MONIBA, *Freetown, November 1990.*

The Armed Forces of Liberia is a body of professional soldiers who have taken oath to defend lives and property and the sovereignty of Liberia.

AFL press statement, Monrovia, October 1990.

RAIN SWEPT across the lush meadow stretching from the verandah behind Prince John's bungalow down to Stockton Creek. The soft notes of an electric organ drifted out from behind the net curtains hung across the French windows. A soldier sang as he splayed his hands across the keys of the organ: 'If you're a white man, you will be beaten. If you're a black man you will be beaten,' he moaned, eyes closed, voice lilting.

Prince sat behind a desk at the end of the sitting-room, which had become a cluttered operations' centre since I had last been there in August. It was now October. A kitsch, pastel portrait of Christ carrying a lamb on his shoulder had been nailed to the wall behind him, bearing the message: 'Look at me and be saved'. On another wall a small photograph of Yasser Arafat introduced an element of politics into the room. Prince's desk was a shrine to lofty aspiration, with a golden penholder, elaborate paper-knife, small flags, a Model-T Ford in shiny metal. Prince had become an executive, and now had the desk to prove it, while he mused over the issues of the day and yelled orders at a small secretariat at the other end of the room, who were furiously typing press releases and shuffling paperwork.

'Do you want to see my film?' Prince rasped. Refusing his offers was not easily done, and we were led out onto the verandah, expecting to see a visual account of Prince's adventures and exploits. A large colour television was wheeled out, and Prince's wife said that she would fast forward the video so we did not have to see ordinary shots of rebel troops. Behind the television the rain fell across the meadow. The organist played on in the sitting-room. We were given chairs in the front row. The rebels gathered in rows behind us. The singer became more passionate. The man in the next seat kept talking, as the screen burst into life. A group of children played in the meadow beyond the verandah, yelling to their friends gathered behind us watching the film.

Samuel Doe looked out of the television screen. His face was bruised and bloody. Rolls of flab oozed out over the blood-stained white underpants which were all that he was wearing. His arms were tied tightly behind his back. The organist's plunging notes grew to a crescendo in the room beside where we were sitting, the room in fact where Doe had been sitting when the film was taken.

'I want to say something, if you will just listen to me,' Doe tells his captors, half smiling, half sneering. Samuel Varney and another of Prince's men, John Yormie, stroke Doe's head, which has been shaved, we are told, with a broken bottle.

'You untie my hands and I will talk … I never ordered anybody's execution.'

The camera moves to Prince, who is sitting behind the desk, with the same pink and blue portrait of Christ watching impassively from above him on the wall.

'I'm a humanitarian,' Prince rasps. 'Cut off one ear,' he calmly tells his men.

The television audience sat gripped in total silence. Prince sat slightly slumped on a chair beside me, watching himself give the order to begin the torture, his hands clasped in semi-prayer. The camera swings to Doe, where he is sitting with his legs stretched out in front of him, his arms tightly tied behind him. A knife flashes in the bright light. The camera gets close. Doe is forced to lie down. The camera cannot catch the moment. An arm can be seen sawing, as a scream pierces the verandah, the meadow, the whole world. Suddenly the organist stopped, and there was silence.

Doe sits up, shaking his head violently, as the fighters grapple with him. Then he is seen to blow down on his own chest, and the rebels sitting beside us say that Doe is trying to use magic to make himself disappear.

'I beg you,' Doe says.

One grabs his head and forces him down onto the carpet, as the sheen of the knife catches the light, and the scream sends the birds flying away from Prince's verandah, as the action shows Prince chewing the sawn flesh of his prey, holding an ear high above his mouth and then lowering it down.

For a few seconds the audience sat in silence, then they clapped. A small fishing boat on Stockton Creek sent ripples across the brown water.

The action moves to the end of Prince's garden, where Doe sits bound and naked, barely recognisable, the stumps of ears bleeding.

'Varney, I'm dying.' Doe tells Prince's deputy.

'1985,' says Varney, the year of the rigged elections, the Quiwonkpa coup and the horror that followed it.

'We know you,' another rebel soldier tells Doe. Then Yormie says:

'We are asking you in a polite manner now: what did you do with the Liberian people's money?' But Doe refuses to say, and the knife comes out again.

'My penis. No, please, not my penis.'

Tahseen, the Palestinian who had been in the city throughout the war and eventually thrown in his lot with Prince in August, appears on the screen. It then becomes clear that during the torture he has been holding the camera. Tahseen tells Doe to repeat after him: 'I, Samuel Kanyon Doe declare that the government is overthrown. I'm therefore asking the armed forces to surrender to Field Marshall Prince Johnson.' Doe repeats the words. His tyranny is over. Somebody says: 'fuck' off-screen and is reprimanded:

'Don't abuse the man,' the rebel is told.

'I want to talk. I need pee,' says Doe. Then the screen went blank.

Prince Johnson and his men tortured Samuel Doe on 9 September, three weeks after Prince had signed a ceasefire agreement with the AFL, in which they agreed to fight together against Charles Taylor.

Prince's film, which has since been a best-selling video throughout West Africa, contains the best evidence that Doe was tricked by Prince right from the start. The ceasefire was simply a ploy to give Doe a false sense of security, so that he could be lured out of the Executive Mansion and done to death.

An earlier scene on the video shows Prince visiting the Island Clinic, formerly Monrovia's leading private hospital, where INPFL troops were taken for medical treatment. Prince is filmed arriving at the clinic with a large convoy of heavily armed troops, far more, it is said, than he usually took with him on such visits. Throughout the sequence, Prince does not enter the clinic to talk to his injured men. Instead, he is filmed outside, constantly in radio contact – with whom, the film does not make clear.

Several witnesses who were at the clinic that day said that Prince received a message over the radio, and that he immediately ordered his troops to follow him.

A group of Monrovians who had spent the entire summer listening to radio messages being sent between all sides in the conflict and the American embassy (which had given radios to Doe and Taylor and then found Prince already had one) were also listening that day.

'I heard an American say: "Your man is coming to the Freeport. Get ready",' one of the eavesdroppers said. 'He used the codename "Scorpion", to talk with Prince Johnson.'

Before the sequence on the video showing Doe's torture Prince is seen calling over the radio, giving his call-sign as 'Scorpion', but getting no response at the other end.

'I have Doe,' he keeps repeating, but the news leaves his correspondent cold.

American denials of any involvement in the events which led to Doe's death were swift. Not only was America not involved, but the embassy had no idea that Doe was even at the port until news of his capture filtered back into the city, so the embassy said.

Prince Johnson was incensed when he heard, on 10 September, that Doe was dead. After torturing him on that first day, he ordered that Doe be locked in the bathroom of the Caldwell bungalow and a guard be put on the door. Doe was still alive, but bleeding profusely from the torture and from the gun-shot wounds he had sustained when Prince's men captured him after a battle at Monrovia freeport, during which 68 of Doe's men were killed. After being dumped in the bath, Doe spent several hours banging his head against the side of the tub and the walls of the room, eventually bringing on the haemorrhage which killed him. Prince, on hearing this, was apparently disappointed because he had wanted to put Doe on trial. Given the savagery he had already meted out to Doe, however, a trial would have been difficult to stage, and it would appear that Prince had simply hoped to recommence the torture, with the added energy born of a good night's sleep.

Sellie Thompson, the former insurance salesman and Doe adviser whom I had seen in August at the barracks beside the Executive Mansion, went into hiding after Doe's death. On the morning of 9 September, Thompson went on one of his routine visits to the US embassy, and also paid two visits to Monrovia freeport. Since 24 August, the freeport had become the headquarters of the multinational peacekeeping force,

Ecomog, and had been filling up with troops from Nigeria, Ghana, The Gambia, Sierra Leone and Guinea. It was to visit Ecomog's commanding officer, Ghanaian Lieutenant-General Arnold Quainoo, that Doe went to the freeport on 9 September, driving himself in his favourite sport's car. Sellie Thompson apparently went to the port in the morning to alert the Ecomog commander that Doe planned to visit him that afternoon. General Quainoo, however, later denied that he had advance warning of Doe's visit.

'I heard you had been looking for me,' said a voice on the other end of the telephone. 'My name's Sellie Thompson.'

I was standing in the lobby of Freetown's Paramount Hotel, having almost given up hope of finding Thompson. I had gone to Freetown in late October, in the hope of learning what had really happened on the day of Doe's capture. For a week I had followed one clue after another in order to try to find him. An official at the Nigerian High Commission in Freetown had said Thompson had a girlfriend who worked at the Vista nightclub in the city, so I hung around outside until 11pm when she arrived. But she said she hadn't seen him. She thought he was staying at the Brookfield Hotel; the hotel told me he had left two weeks before. I went back to the Nigerians, and I was told that he kept in contact with the second secretary at the High Commission. Freetown is small and 'Yellow Man', my taxi-driver, knew where the official lived. We arrived, and the official was suspicious, but said that if he had any knowledge of where Thompson was he would pass the message on that I wanted to talk to him.

'My disclosures would explain the whole thing,' Thompson told me over the telephone when he called the following day. 'But I have refused to speak because I don't feel safe. The countries that are concerned would be frightened. I have sufficient information to come up in the final analysis to say who is responsible. If [George] Bush is involved I will say so. If it means that the repercussions will take my life, that's okay,' he said.

Two weeks previously, on 3 October, he had returned to Monrovia, he said, 'to speak with Ambassador De Vos in confidence. I didn't go with Ecomog, I went some other way,' he told me. The only other way at that time was with the US Navy.

'I didn't commit any crimes in Liberia. I haven't done anything that will scare me away from my own country. I'm protecting myself. I would never have set up Doe. I would never have sacrificed him. Not for $5 billion. To have sacrificed Doe would have been like sacrificing my country.'

Thompson has never fully explained what happened. But the accusations that he was involved in an elaborate plan, if not to hand Doe to Prince Johnson then at least to get him onto a ship and out of the country, remain.

The convoy of cars which left the Executive Mansion and drove to the freeport that afternoon was stopped at the port entrance, and all the presidential bodyguards were disarmed by Ecomog troops before being allowed to enter the port area and drive towards the Ecomog head-quarters. When Prince Johnson arrived from the Island Clinic a few minutes later, his troops were not disarmed even though the port was an Ecomog zone, in which everybody should have been disarmed.

Colonel Goah, former deputy-commander of Doe's Executive Mansion Guard and one of those said to have been at St Peter's Lutheran Church on the night of the July massacre, was waiting for me at the top of the steps of the Liberian ambassador's residence in Freetown. I looked up at him, at that time knowing nothing about him, only that the people in the house were those who had been with Doe at Monrovia freeport, but who had survived, been evacuated and put in this house by the Sierra Leoneans. Colonel Goah smiled and showed me to a terrace, where Paul Allen Wie, the former Information Minister, was nursing a leg wound he had received at the port when Doe was attacked. We had seen each other in all possible scenarios. Now we looked out over the trees of Freetown as dusk gathered, feeling that something had come to an end.

'During the battle, Sellie Thompson came down from inside the Ecomog headquarters with Quainoo, and then went into hiding. When they came out, Prince Johnson called for his men to stop firing so that they could hide,' said Sam Johnson, Doe's former head of security, who was also at the port with Doe and managed to escape with Wie. Even Johnson had no advance warning of Doe's visit to the port, until Doe was in his car and preparing to leave the Executive Mansion.

When Sellie Thompson arrived in Freetown, he was taken to Peekay Lodge, a Sierra Leonean government residence where other senior Doe advisers had been given rooms.

'Sellie Thompson was in a state of fear at Peekay Lodge,' said Gbai Bala, a member of the government delegation to the May peace talks, who had deserted Doe and remained in Freetown and been housed at Peekay. 'He was afraid that we might give him to the Doe people. He kept saying: "This thing is a set up and the US is involved". But he said he was afraid of the Americans, if he implicated the US in the set-up. Nobody in the Mansion knew about the visit to the port in advance, except Sellie Thompson, and Doe sent him to the port to make the arrangements. It could have been the case that Ecomog wanted Doe on a ship, on which he could then sail away. But the plan backfired.'

If the strategy was simply to remove Doe from the scene, on the grounds that this was the best way of securing peace between the warring sides, then such a plan was entirely consistent with the views of many of those involved, not least the United States. The US had felt all along that if Doe left there would be a chance for peace, and had earlier initiated the arrangements with Togo for Doe to go into exile there. However, it is unlikely that the US had wanted overtly to be involved in the kidnapping of Doe, so would have left it to Ecomog to carry out. As it is, the US embassy was the only institution in Monrovia which had radio communications with all sides at the same time, and would have been able to assist Ecomog in bringing Doe to the port, while the Nigerians kidnapped him. This, of course, does not explain from whom Prince Johnson received his tip-off. But given the ceasefire he had signed with the AFL and the reasonable intent it signified, perhaps he deceived his co-plotters by secretly aiming to capture Doe, rather than merely force him out of the country.

That early October day at Prince Johnson's base, before I made my trip to Freetown in an effort to piece the story together, we walked silently to the car waiting on Prince's gravel driveway. I had travelled back to Monrovia on a Nigerian cargo ship with Stephen Smith, Africa editor of the French daily *Libération*, and the photographer Patrick Robert of *Sygma*. We started the car, the sound of the engine intruding on the vision of the world into which Prince's film had just given us a glimpse. As we left, there were none of the fake pleasantries with which one usually engaged Prince, who had declared himself interim head of state following Doe's death. After that numbing film-show, there was nothing to say. We all wanted to get out of his compound. It was sickening being there, being pressured by the presence of his protocol team, the sound of typewriters in the secretariat, the desk laden with his executive toys – all these things forcing us to behave in a way which confirmed the myth about him being a liberator. In fact, more than any other figure, Prince Johnson confirmed the view that in Liberia there was an enormous gulf between the lofty ideal of liberation and the base reality of the country, in which savagery ruled and humanity was, like the Krahns' snake, being 'chopped'.

197

Stephen drove the car out of Prince's gate, which squeaked shut behind us. We were not supposed to understand his film, or sympathise with it. His film was for him and his people. I realised that it was an, albeit extreme, example of the gulf between myself and the people I had spent so much time with. Though my instinct was to try to understand, to empathise even, I still knew nothing about them. They knew more about me and the world I came from. They knew how to use Western technology – to capture events on video, just like anybody with a camera would.

Black rainclouds hung over the junction of the compound road and the muddy track which, to the left, went to White Plains and, to the right, back into the city. There, I had first seen the INPFL troops on parade. Now, on the right, two men in bright white underpants were being led by Johnson's troops into a small hut at the side of the road. On the left a group of INPFL in uniform were standing on a patch of grass. A naked man was before them on his knees, holding up his hands as he begged the soldiers not to harm him. From inside the car we could hear nothing; we could only see, as one of the soldiers brought a machete hard down from above his head onto the palms of the man's pleading hands.

The troops with whom we had sailed from Freetown were part of a 1,200-strong Nigerian contingent being sent to reinforce the 4,000 troops which had begun arriving in Monrovia as I was leaving in August. On 17 September Taylor had rejected a peace plan allowing the establishment of an interim government to administer a ceasefire. The government was to be led by the Liberian politician Dr Amos Sawyer, a vocal opponent of both Tolbert and Doe, who had been in exile in the US from the mid-1980s. Sawyer, who had been one of 24 intellectuals and lawyers drafted in by Doe to rewrite Liberia's constitution in 1981, had been appointed head of the interim government at a meeting of Liberian political parties, interest groups and religious leaders, convened by the Standing Mediation Committee of Ecowas, and held in Banjul, The Gambia between 27 August and 1 September. Among the politicians present were some of those who had been courted by Taylor in the run-up to the 1989 invasion, but who had realised that he was far from being the democrat with which they had been looking to replace Doe.

The Banjul conference, which brought together political forces largely exiled since the rigged election of 1985, gave itself the power to suspend parts of the Liberian constitution relating to the appointment of the legislature, executive and judiciary. Instead of giving Taylor any of the credit he claimed he was due, the conference correctly depicted Liberia as a country 'apportioned among the three warring factions which are holding the entire population hostage'. This effectively relegated the three self-styled heads of state – Taylor, Prince Johnson and Doe's successor, Brigadier General David Nimley – to the status of warlords. Meanwhile, the interim government envisaged at the Banjul conference allotted legislative seats to the NPFL, the INPFL, Liberia's 13 counties, and the political parties which were registered in 1985, thereby attempting to dilute the warlords' role in a post-Doe Liberia.

While Prince Johnson was apparently in accord with the decisions of the conference, which grouped together men like Sawyer and Boima Fahnbulleh who voiced substantial political views rather than the platitudinous hot air of the warring factions, it infuriated Taylor, who had declared himself president on 27 July, in expectation of seizing Doe, the Executive Mansion and Monrovia. But he had achieved none of these objectives, and had seen most of them slip into Prince Johnson's grasp. However, he remained in control of Robertsfield airport, into which military supplies from Burkina Faso continued to be flown. In early October, the Burkinabe president Blaise Compaore visited Togo and met with General Eyadema, the two issuing a statement stressing that all the Ecowas countries were signatories to the continent-wide treaty which forbade members of the Organisation of African Unity from becoming militarily involved in other members' internal conflicts. Meanwhile, the Ivorians, whose support for Taylor intensified as the Nigerian-led Ecomog initiative evolved into reality, continued to allow supplies to be ferried through northern Ivory Coast and across its border into NPFL territory. Having brought in extra weapons, Taylor, on 22 September, declared a unilateral ceasefire in order to relocate his troops. Six days later he was ready to break the ceasefire, and attacked Prince Johnson's troops in the north of Monrovia, while simultaneously launching attacks on Ecomog in the eastern suburbs.

Major-General Joshua Dogonyaro, the new commander forced on Ecomog by Nigeria as a replacement to Lieutenant General Quainoo, after the latter had been discredited by the events leading to Doe's capture, was the region's response to Taylor's onslaught. While the Guinean commander Colonel Magassouba was fleeing home in fear, pretending to be injured in order to avoid engaging in what, to him, was the mysterious prospect of war, Nigeria's Dogonyaro ordered Ecomog's Ghanaian Aeromachina fighters and Nigerian Alpha Jets to bomb targets in Taylor's territory, including a house near Robertsfield airport where

Taylor himself stayed. Heavy artillery fire forced Taylor's troops to retreat from within sight of the Executive Mansion, which Ecomog planned to evacuate. In response, Taylor said there were 1,500 Nigerians in his territory, and that he would kill one for every Liberian killed by Ecomog. Simultaneously, Taylor used rocket fire to attack Monrovia freeport, the Ecomog headquarters.

Meanwhile, the attempts to conceal the real character of regional support for the different sides quickly began to unravel. State radio in Burkina Faso condemned Ecomog's attacks on Taylor's NPFL, when it reported on 19 September that the 'war could have ended a few weeks ago, had the white-helmeted troops of the Economic Community of West African States not intervened'.

The same day Tom Wowieyu, who had become the NPFL's main spokesman, told the BBC: 'There is no doubt in my mind that some of these countries, some of whom we would have restrained from helping us, will have to come forward and help us.' To the end, the NPFL maintained the charade that they had received no outside support. Even now, Taylor will not admit that he spent time Libya.

Early on the morning of 1 October, Ecomog troops pushed out of the freeport and began taking up positions within Prince Johnson's area of the divided city centre. The front line between the INPFL and the AFL troops still occupying the Executive Mansion, which had been reinstalled once the two sides' anti-Taylor pact had been followed by Doe's capture and killing, lay where it had always done, close to the Defence Ministry and along the road which ran through the city cemetery. Prince's troops fired barrages up the hill towards the AFL, just beyond the bright green Defence Ministry building. A blood trail off the street led to the back of a hut at a crossroads controlled by Prince's men, and the body of a man in civilian clothes lay in the mud, with the back of his head shot away.

By next day the same crossroads was silent. It was 7am. Ghanaian troops had gathered at the junction and convinced the INPFL troops to stop firing. Then, in the silence that followed, the Ghanaians walked out of the protection of the buildings, pushed aside a metal fence which lay across the road, and began walking up the hill to where the AFL troops were positioned. We walked with them, surrounded by white-helmeted soldiers. Nobody had any idea how the AFL troops would react. I had had no contact with them since crossing the line in August. Six weeks later – their president tortured to death, their politicians fled, their army run by the remaining sadists and murderers who knew that to leave would mean certain death – what had they become?

The AFL troops were all young, most out of uniform. There were some who looked more like college students than soldiers, with tortoise-shell spectacles and casual clothes. Nearly 1,000 AFL troops had immediately turned themselves over to Ecomog when Doe was captured; some had been herded into the freeport and some evacuated to Freetown. The estimated 1,000 who remained in the Executive Mansion were the die-hards, who had been burning shops and looting the city after Doe's death, yelling: 'No Doe, no Liberia', from the backs of the pick-ups in which they tore through the city, as Prince's men attempted once again to advance towards the mansion.

But that morning, the Ghanaians who confronted the AFL troops revealed the concern that at that time, inspired the motives of the soldiers who were sent to Liberia as the peacekeeping force. They talked and pleaded and promised these traumatised, hungry, haunted killers that Ecomog was there to help them. The brave Ghanaians had walked up the hill without knowing whether they would be shot at, and their motive was to help end the suffering, because if Liberia was suffering then it meant that everybody in the region was suffering. Only other African soldiers could have appealed to the AFL in that way, without malice or condemnation of what the AFL had done in the previous months. The aim was to end the slaughter.

'Leave the job to me, and wait for me to establish peace. I will help to see to your needs, but I demand that the centre of the city is ours,' the Ghanaian colonel in charge told the gathered AFL, who had been lined up in a ramshackle and barely containable guard of honour for the Ecomog troops, the first outsiders they had seen for months. But after three or four minutes the atmosphere suddenly changed. The AFL became agitated, and demanded to know who we reporters were. The Ghanaian colonel's eye caught mine and he signalled for us to leave immediately, and five of his men surrounded us and walked us back down the hill.

A week later, on 10 October, Dogonyaro, a close friend of Nigeria's then military leader General Babangida, and a member of the Nigerian junta's Armed Forces Ruling Council (AFRC), strode purposefully along the runway at Spriggs Payne airfield towards the sound of gunfire and the swamp at the end of the pock-marked runway.

White bones sprawled down the slope and across the mud into the mangrove swamp. Fingers gripped the lush grass. Legs lay entwined beneath crumbling ribs, skeletal puppets performing a medieval dance of death. Skulls lay in the cool shade of the undergrowth. Beyond the branches of the mangrove the swamp lay thick with bones, picked clean by insects.

Doe knew about this place, just as he knew about the Lutheran church. Did he die as he deserved? Who was I to say? Rumour has it that the AFL held trials at Spriggs Payne airfield during the summer, and that the accused were found guilty and taken to the end of the runway and either hacked to death or shot. I wondered about the man I had seen taken from the house beside my apartment in Mamba Point in August, whose family had been left screaming hysterically inside their tenement flat. I wondered if I was now looking at him. I wondered, briefly, what it must have been like to have been brought to this place, to see as we had just seen, the end of the runway, then the slope which slowly gave a view of the extent of the killing and what it must have been like, surrounded by the dead, to have been forced to the ground.

The tranquillity was broken by the sound of shooting.

Guinean troops were fighting Taylor just beyond Spriggs Payne, which they had captured the night before we went there.

General Dogonyaro, the unbuckled strap of his steel helmet swinging casually beneath his chin, strode back to his personnel carrier. The Nigerians we were with did not want us to see more. They wanted us to leave immediately, so we drove back to the airfield terminal building. The control tower was a burned shell and the bullet-riddled bodies of light aircraft lay scattered on the tarmac, where they had been dragged to prevent the runway being used during the fighting.

We drove back towards the city, through streets over which Ecomog had only tenuous control. AFL troops, who had regained their former territory in Sinkor, thanks to Ecomog having pushed Taylor back, occasionally appeared in jeeps or taxis. I could hardly look at them. I am not sure if it was from fear or disgust. The previous day General Nimley (the incumbent of the Executive Mansion who Prince Johnson had accused of ordering the execution of 200 children from Nimba county early in the war) had attempted to reassert the rights of a defeated tyranny by saying that 'this republic of Liberia is ours'.

Ecomog's recognition of the AFL's position, in the face of the continued fighting with Taylor, came swiftly. Whatever the AFL had done in the previous months, it reasserted itself as soon as Ecomog allowed it to do so. On 23 October the AFL's newly formed Interim National Defence Council issued a press release:

The National Interim Defence Council of the Armed Forces of Liberia has clarified that contrary to news reports on the BBC that only forces of the breakaway faction of Prince Johnson's rebels are fighting alongside Ecomog, government troops have been the main trained military force to co-operate and fight alongside with Ecomog against the recalcitrant Charles Taylor's rebel faction.

The peacekeepers' pact with the devil seemed to be complete. All that remained was for Amos Sawyer and his cabinet to arrive in Monrovia to find the Ecomog troops, who were there to protect them, fighting alongside the remains of the very same army which had tortured, harassed and forced many of them into exile under Doe. Eventually, in a bid to shed some of its atrocious image, the AFL on 6 November sacked Nimley as chairman of its ruling council, 'because of his strong desire to establish a military government in Liberia', and replaced him with the more moderate General Bowen.

As we drove back from Spriggs Payne airfield, Chris Otulana, the Nigerian major assigned to look after the press, told the driver of the personnel carrier we were travelling in, to stop.

On the left was a church.

Old clothes lay in the mud of the forecourt, which was surrounded by a wall and railings and an iron gate which stood open, one hinge broken. We walked into the forecourt, then up the steps and into the building, whose wooden door was open.

The floor of Saint Peter's rippled with maggots. Bodies had shrivelled, leaving only piles of rotting clothes on the floor. Contorted skeletons lay huddled beneath the pews. Others were piled up in a dark corner beside the alter. Up some narrow stairs, entangled bodies on the choir balcony testified to vain attempts to escape. Limbs dangled from the broken windows, killed while trying to flee the terror. In the classrooms next door, which had been used as dormitories, bodies were rotting into their mattresses and clothes clung to the skeletons of young children.

This was the monument to Samuel Doe, the leader and statesman who had drunk orange juice with the American ambassador, walked in the White House garden with Ronald Reagan, chatted with the Pope and nursed thoughts of going to Oxford for intellectual stimulation. There was nothing really to say, no conclusions to be drawn. The horror of Saint Peter's church was the reality.

Shooting broke out on the road outside the church. There stood Michael Tilly. I remembered him from the port, the day that I had walked there with Budu Kaisa. Tilly leapt down from his Korando jeep. He was followed by around 50 of his men, all well-armed, well-equipped, young, their heads wrapped in bandanas decorated with cowrie shells, charms dangling on rope around their necks.

'What are you white men doin'?' Tilly yelled at us. General Dogonyaro had driven on when we stopped at the church. Only Otulana and two other Nigerians were with us. 'You're just actors,' Tilly yelled, implying that we were pretending to be journalists when in fact we were spies. Tilly's men surrounded us and the Nigerian vehicle. They knew what we had seen, and there is no doubt that many of them had been at Saint Peter's church that night in July. Tilly himself was certainly there. But, like all the cowards of the AFL, whose experience of war was confined to killing unarmed civilians and preferably women and children, Tilly and his gang of murderers were frightened of real soldiers. Otulana calmed him with a few words, and told him that we were with Ecomog, and after a few minutes we simply drove away.

16 Feasting with the Grandees

According to the National Patriotic Reconstruction Assembly Data Command, the Nigerian government, in full co-operation with The Gambian government, have hired mercenaries to assassinate President Taylor.

NPFL radio, broadcast from Gbarnga, 19 October 1990.

Doe's death served as a lesson to all of us, that we must take it easy.

CHARLES TAYLOR, *Gbarnga, 22 October 1990.*

The Liberian problem is no longer a Liberian problem, it's a regional problem.

DR AMOS SAWYER, *Liberian interim president, Monrovia, November 1990.*

I want my name to be littered over the pages of history as being the man who started out the way it should be started out. If I had some chances I would really start some trouble in this region ... I want people to know that freedom is no threat to anybody.

CHARLES TAYLOR, *Gborplay, May 1990.*

IT WAS evening in late April 1991 when the soldiers appeared at the end of Kenema's muddy main street in central Sierra Leone. They stepped out of the forest and onto the road. The prisoner walked quickly in front of them, his tightly bound arms contorted behind his back. Blood coursed down his belly from a wound on his chest. More blood slid down his neck, because one of his ears had been cut off.

Outside the rosy-pink cinema, closed by the owner two weeks before to punish the staff who ran away when a band of troublemakers over-turned the tables on the terrace, the captive winced as the butt of an ageing rifle crunched into the back of his head. People watched from the balconies of the rain-soaked, pastel-painted houses. The captive was one of the few brought back from the battlefront by the Sierra Leoneans. Most were killed immediately. As the two soldiers beat and pushed him along the street, people watched, then followed. Policemen stood laughing in groups on the roadside. The crowd which gathered in the shade of the rain-forest trees began chanting. 'Rebel.' Slowly at first, then: 'Rebel, rebel, rebel.' as they followed him to the police station, where he was taken from view.

205

The sky above the forest turned dark grey. A priest drove me on to a mission station at Segbwema, deep within the darkness of the trees, along a mud track which wound through the gloom.

The mission was deserted. The priests had gone to Kenema and from there on to Freetown as Charles Taylor made good his threat to cause trouble in the region.

On 23 March 1991, a group of Liberians and Sierra Leoneans had crossed the border from NPFL territory in Liberia into Sierra Leone's eastern Kailahun district. Leading them was a disgruntled Sierra Leonean soldier, Corporal Foday Saybannah Sankoh, who had joined Taylor early in 1990. On 16 March Sankoh had telephoned the BBC to say that he was in the Sierra Leonean town of Makeni (though it is more likely that he was at Taylor's headquarters at Gbarnga) and demanding that the Sierra Leonean government of President Joseph Momoh either resign within 90 days or be overthrown. The rebel force then crossed the border.

'We were the first group to go into Sierra Leone, under Commanding Officer "Butterfly",' a former NPFL fighter, Foday Boaker, told me later in Liberia. 'Foday Sankoh used to talk all the time about the Sierra Leoneans, who he called: "the people I'm going to rule". But there was a problem from the start, because "Butterfly" told his men that if he wasn't going to be paid, then he would stop fighting in Sierra Leone. And he wasn't paid, and he and some others stopped fighting and deserted,' he said.

The 23 March attack saw a group of 60 invaders seize two border villages, Bomalu and Senge. Since the NPFL occupation of north-east Liberia, both villages had been used throughout the war by the NPFL as supply routes, whose fluidity depended until March 1991 on the ready corruptibility of the Sierra Leonean border guards. On 27 March three rebel groups, each 100-strong, attacked the town of Buedu, seized it, were reinforced by more NPFL troops the following day, and then took Koindu town and the road to Kailahun.

As the war stood poised to flood out of Liberia, attempts in Monrovia to broker peace failed to keep pace with the increasing vengefulness and ambition of the warring sides. The All-Liberia Conference, convened by the Catholic Bishop of Monrovia, Michael Francis, the Chief Imam, Sheikh Kafumba Konneh, and the Protestant Canon Burgess Carr, opened on 15 March, with representatives of all the factions meeting for the first time, at the hall in the western Monrovia suburb of Virginia in which President Tolbert had hosted the 1979 Organisation of African Unity conference, months before he was overthrown by Doe.

Charles Taylor stayed away, citing security concerns, but dispatched other NPFL officials. Whatever hopes the conference had generated were disappointed as soon as the NPFL incursion into Sierra Leone was reported on 23 March. On 27 March Tom Woweiyu led a walk-out of the NPFL and the discussions became largely meaningless, eventually grinding to a halt several weeks later, though only after Amos Sawyer's government had been officially mandated.

On 3 April the Sierra Leonean government responded to the rebel incursion by sending its troops across the Mano river into the Taylor-held Liberian county of Lofa. Fighting around Kailahun in eastern Sierra Leone left 19 NPFL soldiers dead, and the Sierra Leonean government openly announced that its objective was to 'occupy parts of Lofa county, so that our border can be protected'. On 27 March President Momoh declared that Sierra Leone's political opposition would be legalised, in a hurried effort to gain popular support in the face of the new threat.

Just as Taylor himself had done with Libya, Foday Sankoh denied any connection with his backer. But as the incursion developed, the Sierra Leonean army captured both Liberians and Sierra Leoneans under the Revolutionary United Front (RUF) banner. On 15 April the BBC interviewed a former NPFL fighter, William Burke, who said he had seen Sankoh in the Taylor-held port of Buchanan in January. Sankoh was in the town to collect military supplies, as well as to form the fighting force which became the RUF and numbered 400 soldiers three months before the first incursion. By 23 April the Sierra Leonean army had captured 83 insurgents, claiming that all but three were Liberians, and that those three had grown up in Liberia. By 1 May, 1,200 Nigerian and 300 Guinean troops were fighting alongside the Sierra Leonean army in the east of the country, in a regional bid to contain the conflict.

Thunder rolled through the darkness outside the wooden hut of the Segbwema mission. The smell of damp wood filled the air. A cool wind swept through the forest. Inside, a soothing warmth lulled me into a deep sleep as the thunder passed, until I was woken before six by strong morning sunlight.

We drove, the priest and I, to Daru. A long, straight mud road passed through thick forest, now doused in a dense mist. A herd of goats blocked the crossroads outside Daru village. Ahead we could hear gunfire. We drove towards an army barracks. A parade ground lay deserted. At its far side it dipped into the forest, which rose up the far bank of a river whose flow could not be seen for mist. A rocket sped across the parade ground and exploded in a ball of fire in the swirling haze from which the rain-forest trees soared. Machine-gun fire crackled in the forest. A second rocket roared across the morning dew of the parade-ground, rammed into the forest on the other side of the small valley and bloomed into flames.

Lieutenant-Colonel Conteh, the barracks commanding officer, rushed agitatedly from his office to the radio room. The corridors were dim and wet with boot prints. He called for his hat, and another officer handed him a steel helmet draped with thick foliage which dangled across his face so that only his eyes and moustache could be seen.

'I'm sorry,' he said politely. 'My men are in some trouble down there. I have no time to talk to you.'

A truck-load of troops sped towards Daru village on the other side of the valley, while a Morse-code machine muttered wildly in the radio room and Conteh disappeared into the mist, followed by a group of Guinean soldiers.

The radio officer disappeared. All the troops had faded into the mist. There was the soft silence of a winter morning, all sounds dulled by the mist. The chatter of the Morse-code machine stopped; only the military radio crackled and hissed occasionally, but there were no voices to be heard. We sat on the damp stone parapet of the deserted headquarter's veranda. There was movement in the mist, fleeting dark shadows, briefly glimpsed then fading, then the air was pierced by the clap-clap-clap of machine-gun fire and the hiss of a bullet passing overhead. No army could stop the invaders. Just as I had seen in Liberia, government troops lacked all will. They had neither the skill nor the resources to oppose. Daru would fall soon, I thought.

After an hour the priest and I drove back towards Segbwema. As we passed through the forest outside Daru I stared hard into the thick foliage along the roadside. And there, just for a second, I saw a white-painted face staring silently at us, motionless as we passed, and I realised that Daru had already, in effect, fallen. It was surrounded, and the nervous soldiers would die in the mist unless they fled. I said nothing to the priest, and we drove on. I looked back, but I did not see anybody crossing the road.

To confront the invasion, Momoh's troops began organising a fighting force from among the 250,000 Liberian refugees in Sierra Leone. In early May the existence of the Krahn-dominated Liberian United Defence

Force (LUDF), under the leadership of Arma Youlu, became known. Their base was outside Kenema and their role was to fight the RUF incursion alongside the Nigerian, Guinean and Sierra Leonean forces. In addition, by 29 May, a former head of the Liberian Broadcasting Corporation, Alhaji Kromah, had gathered support from his fellow Mandingo Muslims and Krahn refugees in Freetown. On 11 June his spokesman announced the creation of the United Liberation Movement of Liberia for Democracy (ULIMO) under the military leadership of Raleigh Seekie. The spokesman gave Taylor 15 days to disarm or face armed action from ULIMO. The third phase of the war was launched.

Crocodiles basked in the steaming heat of the moat which ran the length of one wall of President Felix Houphouet-Boigny's palace at Yamoussoukro. Their keeper, in a long, torn robe, appeared from nowhere at 5pm every afternoon to feed them. The presidential guards ambled out of their sentry boxes to watch the spectacle. The keeper descended some steps to the flat, concrete bank where the mud-caked beasts' black eyes flickered open momentarily as they perused the slabs of red meat the keeper began throwing towards them. Ranks of teeth were bared, and with sudden rapid movements the crocodiles shifted their great bulks towards the dripping flesh where it lay on the parched concrete, snapping it up, using their armoured snouts to ward off rival claimants as six-inch teeth gnawed and tore at the meat, and with a few backward jerks of the head ground it to pulp. Then the jaws lay still, the eyelids open a slit, as the keeper reached into the bottom of the bucket in which he had carried the meat and pulled out a live chicken, bound by its feet, which he threw into the midst of the savage gathering. Within seconds only a few feathers lay on the bloody concrete, and the crocodiles lay still.

From Houphouet-Boigny's palace the crocodiles were just visible. The multi-storey building was deceptively plain from the outside. A top-floor balcony gave a view of the moat on one side. On the other, sweeping upwards from a sea of palm trees, was the basilica of Our Lady of Peace, the edifice whose gleaming white dome rises into a cloudy haze of smoke from fires in the courtyards of the hovels which surround it.

Within the palace, behind its five miles of wall, as the Liberian war plunged into its second year, Houphouet-Boigny fell into a Nigerian-laid trap and decided to stake his reputation as a peacemaker on finding a solution to the Liberian crisis. The Nigerians flattered the Ivorian president into believing that only his influence could save the sub-region from more bloodshed. At four separate two and three-day meetings between 30 June and 31 October 1991, Yamoussoukro became the scene of fabulous banquets and triumphal walks through the tapestried halls of the palace. The setting was designed to impress the region, which had never before been hosted in such splendid fashion. It is uncertain whether Houphouet-Boigny realised that the peace process had been handed to him, not out of respect but in the hope that he would be forced to stop supporting Taylor and would steer him towards a negotiated solution. He had also been pressured to take the initiative by the United States, which has a close bilateral relationship with the Ivory Coast. The Nigerians also wanted to force the Ivory Coast's closest allies, the French, to show their hand in Liberia.

By October 1991, Houphouet-Boigny had overseen the signing of two accords, by which all sides would agree to a ceasefire and disarm to Ecomog, which would then police Liberia's borders. A few days after the fourth summit, the Ivorians even agreed with Amos Sawyer's interim government on measures to end arms supplies to Taylor being trans-ported through the Ivory Coast. At the same time, the US convinced Senegal to join Ecomog, and offered $25 million in cash, equipment, uniforms and transport to allow 2,500 Senegalese troops to provide a significant element of Francophone troops to the force. This was in order to undermine Taylor's claim that Ecomog was dominated by Nigeria and the English-speaking states of the region.

As the sun set behind the basilica of Yamoussoukro on 30 October, it seemed the only thing in the world of importance to me was that the war should end. And there, on the top-floor banqueting hall of his palace, sat Houphouet-Boigny, flanked by Nigeria's Babangida, The Gambian president Sir Dawda Jawara, Charles Taylor and the other players in this awful drama. Beneath the twinkling chandeliers, sitting at tables placed on the sea-like floor of marble, we journalists had been invited to a banquet comprising the national dishes of all the countries of the region, the most sumptuous meal I have ever had. The fruits of the African earth. But to have believed it would bring an end to the war would have been to deny the validity of what I had witnessed during the previous eighteen months. Could all that horror be washed away, signed away with a pen? I had no faith in the people before me, none of them. I had seen too much to believe that the wave could be halted at the shore.

The next day, 31 October, Taylor and the Liberian interim president, Amos Sawyer, signed the Yamoussoukro accord. Taylor did so only after the Nigerian vice-president, Augustus Aikhomu, took him aside and told him that if he did not sign within five minutes everything would become very unpleasant for him, though he did not say how. It was predictable therefore that Taylor would rubbish the accord within hours of signing it and find a new ploy to ensure the peace failed.

I stood at the entrance to the palace after the document had been signed, between the two life-size, gold-plated rams – 'boigny' in Houphouet-Boigny's native Baoule – which flanked the entrance. A figure stood beside me.

'Well, now, Mark. You've really been writing some things about me. I don't know where you get that information from.'

Charles Taylor looked little different from the first time I had seen him. We had not talked for a year, though I had seen him from some distance at the previous Yamoussoukro meetings. He did not like the newspaper reports I had written. Sometimes I felt as if I had let him down. He had been content with what I had written about him after that first meeting in Liberia, when he had portrayed his leadership of the civilian uprising as a national need rather than a personal ambition. Then the war had driven a wedge between us, and I had found myself increasingly hostile to all the protagonists, as their motives appeared to disintegrate into a bloody mire of greed.

'Well, perhaps we should talk about it,' I said, rather lamely. But he walked away.

At a press conference in one of the elegant guest-houses within the Yamoussoukro presidential compound, Taylor declared that for him there was no chance of disarmament unless the ULIMO force, which was not party to any of the accords signed at Yamoussoukro, and was at that moment two miles from the NPFL-controlled town of Tubmanburg, was first dealt with.

Taylor went back to his headquarters at Gbarnga as if there had been no discussions. Amos Sawyer went back to Monrovia, hoping that Taylor could be forced to comply with the accord. On 21 December the interim government imposed an economic blockade on NPFL territory, barring fuel, cigarettes, beer, and consumer and luxury goods from passing between Monrovia and Taylor's area. It followed up the blockade with the introduction of a new five-dollar note, aimed at undermining Taylor's wealth-generating enterprises by deeming the old 'J. J. Roberts' invalid. But by the end of 1991 Taylor was entrenched in his territory, charging thousands of US dollars in down payments to allow foreign companies to move in and exploit the natural resources over which he had asserted his authority, and from which he used the proceeds to rearm himself.

In early December 1991 the Nigerians confirmed that Taylor had visited the Burkina Faso capital Ouagadougou and was developing plans to train mercenaries at the Po military base south of the city. The force included nationals from Liberia, Burkina Faso, Ivory Coast and Guinea, and was being trained as new weapons were transported across Ivory Coast into Liberia, in apparent defiance of Houphouet-Boigny's promise to Sawyer that the supplies would be stopped. US intelligence reports at the same time claimed that arms were not only being brought in overland but were arriving by air at Abidjan airport from Burkina Faso on Air Burkina flights, and were then taken overland to the far eastern Liberian town of Harper and on to Buchanan. Meanwhile, French engineers were seen in NPFL territory installing a powerful radio transmitter with which to broadcast propaganda.

In February 1992, Amos Sawyer led a delegation to Tripoli in an effort to explain to Colonel Gadaffi the damage he was doing by supporting Taylor.

'Gadaffi told me [that he] made a mistake in supporting Charles Taylor, because he [was] now a tool of French imperialism, to whom he had stopped supplying weapons in December 1991,' Sawyer told me later.

Determined to continue with the albeit limited momentum of the Yamoussoukro meetings, Nigeria encouraged Houphouet-Boigny to make a further attempt to bring the sides together and to retrieve some of his own lost dignity by summoning the factions and regional leaders to his residence in Geneva, where he was on an extended holiday. On 8 April 1992, Taylor and Sawyer agreed to abide by the accord they had signed at Yamoussoukro the previous October. A few days earlier, President Mitterrand's son and adviser on African affairs, Jean-Christophe, and the French foreign minister Roland Dumas met Babangida to stake a French claim in the negotiations. Babangida told them bluntly that, if they insisted on playing a role, they would have to be prepared to see Ecomog action against Taylor if the Geneva talks failed. Babangida's pessimism proved accurate. Within hours of signing the Geneva accord Taylor again claimed he had done so only under pressure.

Pressure to stop the war from spreading further intensified on 29 April, when Captain Valentine Strasser and a group of middle-ranking officers in Sierra Leone overthrew the Momoh government, citing among other reasons their discontent at the government's failure to provide adequate facilities with which to fight the NPFL-backed insurgents in eastern Sierra Leone.

Charles Taylor's stockpiling of weapons bore fruit on 15 October 1992, when he launched 'Operation Octopus'.

'Taylor had planned a strategy over the last two years that had meant to deceive the sub-region and allow him to amass a military force, and that at a given moment he would overrun the city of Monrovia. Then he would negotiate on his terms. I think that's what he tried to do the other day,' said Amos Sawyer, as we sat in Doe's old office in the Executive Mansion on 4 November 1992, the date which all sides had agreed in Yamoussoukro would mark the beginning of an election campaign. 'Taylor is using his military capability, and obviously has more in store,' he said, as rain beat at the salt-coated windows on the seaward side of the cavernous and dilapidated building.

On 5 November Monrovia's packed Catholic cathedral throbbed with the damp heat of the congregation after the early morning rain. A cold breeze swept through the open windows from the blackened, scarred streets of the crumbling, haunting city. The congregation filled every seat, aisle and inch of floor-space to listen to Archbishop Michael Francis. In the bright pinks and yellows of their Sunday best, in their dark suits and polished shoes, in the matching clothes of brothers and sisters, they mourned and wailed in helpless despair, faces drawn and thin, eyes sunk into their sockets, their hands wrinkled, young faces aged by two years of sorrow and anxiety.

Archbishop Francis used a large straw-fan to cool himself. He had wiped away the sweat. Then he wiped away the tears.

'We are prisoners,' he yelled. 'They are destroyers, not builders. They have done nothing for their country. We prayed for these wicked people – liars, who kill us and murdered the sisters.'

Operation Octopus had hit the city two weeks earlier.

The NPFL denied it was planning an attack, saying its manoeuvres were intended to reinforce its control in the north-west of the country. Then it laid siege to Monrovia by pushing in from all sides. Prince Johnson's base at Caldwell was overrun, and Prince was rescued by Ecomog troops when he paddled across Stockton Creek after radioing the UN office in Monrovia to save him. Glad to have him in their hands at last, the Nigerians whisked him off to Lagos, where he now lives in a government villa and continually updates versions of his memoirs, entitled: 'The Guns That Liberate Should Not Rule'.

Monrovia cowered beneath the full force of Taylor's military capabilities. So close did the NPFL get to defeating Ecomog and seizing the city, that even the Ecomog chief of staff, Brigadier General Victor Malu, was at one point shooting with his pistol at NPFL fighters as they advanced towards the Ecomog headquarters. Nigeria poured in more troops from its contingent in Sierra Leone, increasing the size of Ecomog to 12,000, and bombed NPFL targets and Taylor's capital at Gbarnga using Alpha Jets. The NPFL barrage sent mortars and rockets deep into the heart of the city, leaving 3,000 dead and 8,000 wounded by the time Ecomog demanded a ceasefire on 7 November.

Among the dead were five American nuns. Archbishop Francis's condemnation of their murder by NPFL fighters in the Monrovia suburb of Gardnersville filled the cathedral with anger and fear and a tearful fatigue which could be seen on the faces of the congregation, who I had last seen gathered there in such numbers two years before, in June 1990, when the city was turning into hell and the churches started to close. There was the same fear. I walked out into the clammy air numbed by his words.

I drove out towards Gardnersville on 6 November, across the Johnson Street Bridge, before the ceasefire had been declared. Fighting was still raging in Douala and the other suburbs, but I felt strangely free. In previous years my fear had been of the AFL, whose troops now wandered unarmed, in ragged uniforms, along the city streets, civilians in uniform – which is what they had only ever really been – having handed control to the peacekeepers. Long queues of traffic gathered at Ecomog checkpoints close to the city centre, but further out towards the freeport there were fewer people. Beyond, the long road through Viatown and Claratown was deserted. I turned up UN Drive, the by-pass which loops around the city from Bushrod Island to the suburbs in the east. Ahead, a plume of black smoke belched hundreds of feet into the grey sky. A sheen of rain coated the tarmac, strewn with the debris of the clashes. Spent bullets, the breeze-blocks and car wheels of now-abandoned barricades, rocks, twisted metal, oil drums punctured with bullet holes. And over it all the smoke rising in the distance, into the darkening sky.

At a derelict petrol-station a group of Nigerian troops ordered me to stop. We talked beside the road. They were agitated and aggressive and did not want me and the two other journalists I was with to remain. We lingered. The commanding officer had hidden his men behind a long wall which stretched away from the road and into grassland. There were several hundred troops, lying quietly, their weapons trained on the empty road ahead.

'We're trying to bring them out onto the road,' the Nigerian commander then began to explain. It was rare that Ecomog troops explained anything to foreign journalists. We pressed him with questions. He said

Taylor's fighters were hidden less than half a mile along the road, and he wanted to encourage them to approach so that he could talk to them and ask them to end their assault. For more than an hour he and his senior officers stood in the centre of the road, calling out to the NPFL, telling them it was safe and that they could come forward.

I watched. The NPFL had no reason to know about the Nigerians hiding behind the wall. Was it a trap? The officers called out through what had become driving rain, and suddenly three figures appeared on the road ahead. They circled in the road, ran from side to side, darted into the undergrowth, reappeared, turned circles again, disappeared, reappeared, but slowly moved forward towards the Nigerians.

'If you foreign journalists could stand in the middle of the road, while we stand here on the side, then that would give them some confidence to approach us,' the commander said. 'Then they can see that there will be witnesses, you foreigners, outsiders. They can be given some confidence that way.'

So we stood, there, in the middle of the rain-swept road, waiting for the fighters who moved steadily closer. After ten minutes we could see their faces, then they were a few yards ahead of us, the front-line troops, perhaps the same fighters who had killed the nuns, shirtless, sweating, sprinkled with rain drops, rasping, frantic, whistling, circling in the road, weapons on their backs, headscarves bound tightly, all of them young, carrying their mascot – a huge brown teddy bear.

I heard a Nigerian soldier murmur that the NPFL approach may be a trap, just to see where Ecomog had its front-line position, and that they had no intention of real dialogue. The Nigerian commander brought them cigarettes. The NPFL posed for photographs, all the time agitated, jabbering wildly, drawing heavily on marijuana which filled the air. They took cigarettes from the Nigerians, then gathered in a group around the teddy bear and chanted and ran in circles then posed some more.

The suddenly the atmosphere changed.

The oldest-looking of the group became serious. He muttered loudly and the fighters began edging away, back towards the distant plume of smoke. They circled away from us. The NPFL commander's gaze darted from side to side. He yelled at the fighter carrying the teddy bear:

'Teddy-bear man. Go back now. You go back now teddy-bear man,' he ordered him, and the teenager dragged his Kalashnikov and his teddy bear back along the wet road towards the smoke and the swamps. The Nigerians shook their heads with pity as they watched them go – the boys of Liberia, playing with their lives among the swamps of the suburbs where the dead nuns still lay. A few days later Taylor ordered his guns to be silent.

Summer came to Monrovia in 1993 just as it had done that first year.

The NPFL fell back after the failure of Operation Octopus. The winter of 1992 was spent licking their wounds, while the regional states sought new avenues for discussion. The United Nations, for the first time since the start of the war, decided that Liberia was worth taking a direct interest in and imposed an arms embargo in November. By the dawn of 1993 disillusionment with diplomacy had reached the most senior levels. Benin's President Nicephore Soglo assumed the rotating chairmanship of Ecowas; he was unsympathetic to the view that the region had a responsibility to find a solution, despite the obvious inability of Liberians to find that solution for themselves. His tenure as head of the regional body consequently saw political initiatives falter, while a military build-up by Nigeria reflected the exasperation felt by Ecomog's main financier. Ecomog retained its troop strength at 11,000 after Operation Octopus, and amassed tanks, artillery and troops in Monrovia to force Taylor to abandon hopes of military victory and abide by the accords signed in Yamoussoukro and Geneva.

The strategy was never likely to work. Not only did Taylor have sufficient funds with which to strengthen his armoury, he also had sound arguments with which to counter calls for disarmament. The Krahn and Mandingo-dominated ULIMO force had, by the summer of 1993, scored military successes over Taylor which had secured it control over the north-west of the country, with its headquarters at Tubmanburg, an hour's drive north-west of Monrovia. As ULIMO was not party to the Yamoussoukro accords, it was not under pressure to disarm and was undoubtedly viewed by Ecomog as a welcome source of pressure against Taylor and the NPFL. Cornered as he was, albeit in the 80 per cent of the country over which he asserted himself, Taylor had good reason to refuse disarmament.

On a hot quiet morning in May, ULIMO's representative in Monrovia, appointed to liaise with Ecomog and able to pass freely from Ecomog to ULIMO-controlled territory, led a small convoy out of the city and onto the Bomi Hills highway. I had not made the journey for three years, when the road had been packed with refugees streaming out of the city towards Sierra Leone as the NPFL drew closer. Clay checkpoint, where the AFL had then turned us back, was now the limit of Ecomog control. Beyond it, ULIMO was in charge. We drove for an hour, then pulled off the road, which rose up a hill to some huts, where we stopped and were told to wait.

A young woman sat on a stool beneath an iron-roofed lean-to. A man wearing military trousers and a dark vest sat beside here. They were preparing lunch. Slowly, methodically, they prepared their meal. In that quiet place, the dryness of the earth beneath the lean-to seemed somehow protected. The war for a moment appeared not to have disturbed them. The man (still a teenager) gathered the stems of the potato leaves tightly, lining up their ends perfectly. He held them with both hands, with perhaps half an inch of the deep green shoots protruding from where his hands gripped them. With a small knife the woman carefully cut away at the stems, a neat pile of the cut leaves gradually forming in a wide pan lying on the earth between them. It was slow, calm. They talked in low murmurs, not in Liberian English but a vernacular which I could not follow. They were gentle with each other, working together on a daily task, making the lunch at the beginning of the morning, well in advance, for the people who would eat it sometime in the afternoon.

I watched them for perhaps as long as two hours. They did not speak with me or the armed teenagers who had brought me there. They slowly worked their way through a large heap of leaves, until they had shredded them all, and then we were summoned to the trucks in which we had arrived, and left them together.

We drove along an overgrown track which emerged between the walls of empty huts on the edge of Tubmanburg, and then followed the winding mud road among the huts, until we reached a gateway opening onto a flat track lined by trees. The track ended at a school yard, where we sat on a concrete terrace and talked with Alhaji Kromah for an hour or more. He denied he was being assisted by Ecomog in his fight against Taylor, but predicted that he would lay siege imminently to Taylor's headquarters at Gbarnga. He posed outside for photographs, and then repeated that we would see him next in Gbarnga. He disappeared into the headmaster's office, from where he ran his campaign, and our convoy returned to Monrovia.

A few weeks later he did indeed lay siege to Gbarnga, and Taylor withdrew, first to Ganta and then further north to Saniquellie. In the build-up to the ULIMO siege, Ecomog also began its most concerted effort to annihilate Taylor.

After talking with Alhaji Kromah we arrived back in Monrovia at midday. The Nigerians took us out along UN Drive towards Gardners-ville. We passed the point where the previous October they had used us as guinea-pigs to try to lure out Taylor's troops. Now the NPFL were gone. As we passed a unit of Ecomog soldiers the sky exploded overhead. From a stretch of wasteground beside the road a line of cannon launched a barrage of missiles which screeched about twenty feet above us. We drove on. UN Drive had been won back by Ecomog, and we arrived at the Paynesville Red Light junction, sped through checkpoints back towards the city, then turned onto the coast road and followed it east towards Camp Scheffelin.

The Nigerians wanted to show that they had had some successes. Their two-week-long offensive meant the NPFL was on the run. I wondered how they had achieved this, as we sped along the tarmac road past Scheffelin. After an hour it became clear. We stopped close to a side road which leads to Robertsfield airport. The engine of our military personnel carrier throbbed. A heavy rain began to fall. The Nigerian major accompanying us talked with a group of Ecomog soldiers on the road. With them were other armed men. I approached them. There was the smell again. The smell of death.

'Wanna see?' I was asked. The boy smiled as he asked me. His shiny face was puffy, his eyes only open a slit. A green bandanna decorated with cowrie shells was bound tightly round his head. On it he had pinned a sergeant's three-stripes. 'I' the commander o' these men.' He wore a charm bound with cloth around his bare neck, and a vest which exposed scars on his arms and chest. He and his men were responsible for Ecomog's success.

I asked him which force he was part of, knowing already what he would say:

'AFL,' he said. I knew then that the war would go on and on. Doe's defeated army had found another way to come back. The Nigerians had enlisted them to the front line, where we were now standing. What they had done in the past did not seem to matter. Ecomog's desperation had forced them into a pact with the very army whose brutality had done more than anything else to encourage popular support for the NPFL when it had first crossed into Liberia almost four years previously.

'We got our mascot,' the AFL soldier said. He called a boy over to him. The boy held something in his hand covered by a cloth, then he pulled the cloth away and balanced a white skull in the palm of his hand.

'He' the man,' said the boy. He nodded to the ditch beside the road. In it lay a naked body already decomposing. A body with no head. The boy chuckled. The rain pounded heavily on the canvas roof of the army truck. I climbed into the back and looked down at them gathered around the decapitated body. Then we drove away, and I left Liberia, not knowing if I would ever return.

Epilogue

Budu Kaisa called me from Monrovia in May 1996. I was living in Morocco, and had not been to Liberia for some time. Taylor's fighters had allied themselves with Alhaji Kromah and tried to arrest Roosevelt Johnson, the leader of another faction which had based itself in the Barclay Training Centre. Johnson had been accused of murder by the other faction leaders. Their troops fought for nearly a month in the centre of the city. Severed heads were kicked like footballs along streets where teenagers fought to the death with knives, and the terror of those first years of the civil war returned. Budu telephoned me to see if I could help him escape. Eventually he flew to Senegal on a US helicopter. Sometime in the autumn he reached America, and since then I have not heard from him.

Charles Taylor became president of Liberia on 21 July 1997, voted in by a large majority. The prize was his, at last. He had achieved the victory he could perhaps have won at the polls five or six years previously, but which he never dared seek in case he lost. I saw his inauguration on television. His hair had turned grey, and his face was lined. He smiled rather meekly at his success. Liberians were wise to vote for him. If he had lost, there would have been another war. So they voted for him to bring a little peace to their lives, after the horror.

The war, in the end, had lasted almost as long as Samuel Doe's rule, give or take a year or two. Perhaps as many as 160,000 people died. What did they die for? What was achieved? Was the country cleansed of evil by the war? Did it rid the land of darkness? Did it, as Taylor had said, when we stood talking at our first meeting beneath the rain forest trees of Gborplay in April 1990, end 'the shame Liberians feel at the Doe government?' Does anybody remember Samuel Doe – what he did, and what it was about him that turned Liberia into what it is today?

The answer to so many of these questions is: no. Now, only Charles Taylor is left. Prince Johnson has faded into obscurity in Nigeria. President Felix Houphouet-Boigny of the Ivory Coast died in 1993. He was buried in a gold-lined mausoleum in the grounds of the palace in Yamoussoukro, where I had banqueted with the grand old men of West

Africa when they had tried to bring peace to Liberia. Ibrahim Babangida, the Nigerian military leader whose yearning for regional power led to the creation of the peacekeeping force Ecomog, lives in luxury in the Middle Belt of his violent, corrupt country. Sir Dawda Jawara of The Gambia was overthrown in a military coup and lives in London. Joseph Momoh of Sierra Leone nurses his wounds in Guinea, having watched his ouster, Valentine Strasser, also be overthrown in what has become an horrendous conflict now racking Liberia's neighbour. I believe that Samuel Dokie, who eventually fell out with Taylor and, along with Tom Woweiyu, publicly denounced him, is to be found in Monrovia, probably forgiven by his new president and old comrade-in-arms.

Since those hot January days in 1990 I have travelled throughout most of Africa. I have seen it moving, crawling, standing still and spiralling out of control. When I want to remind myself of why I am here, I think of my editor telling me in April 1990, over a crackling telephone line to Monrovia, that it appeared my aim was just to go looking for wars, to play 'the war correspondent'. The accusation still stings. When I left England, in the hope of seeing the world so I could make sense of myself, there were no wars in West Africa. There was the desert, the forest and the grey sky, looming over steaming cities thronging with people. There was the ocean, the red earth roads curling through the savannah. There were villages and plumes of smoke rising from the charcoal cooking in the yards where children played. There were trucks and buses roaring along roads of melting tarmac, as if towards the scorching sun. There was a world of people to hear and see and feel, in a way that I had never previously experienced.

But there were no wars in West Africa and I did not go looking for war. I went looking for experience, though its value in the end is only to oneself. When I think back over more than seven years of my experience of Liberia, and of the people I know there, I wonder what I would say to Budu Kaisa? I would certainly have more questions than answers. Does he know how much I wish for peace in Liberia? If there was peace in the country that offered me a journey into the unknown and then delivered me up on the other side it would bring me peace of mind. With Taylor's election victory, I wonder if it is over. I want it to be over. I want it to be over, because Liberia's experience can offer nothing but the proof that humanity is living in terror of itself, hostage to nightmares played out in the light of day.

Now, as I sit here and watch the sun setting over another new home, all I know is that Liberia as it once was has gone forever. In this book

I have tried to tell its story as it unfolded before me. In a continent driven by a dynamic that the outsider takes time both to sense and to understand, the truth lies in the story from the moment it starts to unfold, not halfway along the track, and not just in the aftermath.

Truth in the telling of a story lies in knowing what happens long before the news edges its way into the media. The story of Liberia is one which started long before the first shot was fired, and which, despite its implications for West Africa, went largely unnoticed across the world. It is the story of a country which lost its way.

Cairo, November 1997

Index